AS YOU WERE

Timothy Redmond

NEW HAVEN PUBLISHING LTD

Published 2018
NEW HAVEN PUBLISHING LTD
www.newhavenpublishingltd.com
newhavenpublishing@gmail.com

All names in this story, other than the author's, have been changed.

Cover design © Pete Cunliffe
pcunliffe@blueyonder.co.uk

newhaven
publishing

THIS BOOK IS DEDICATED TO:

Ryan Matthew Redmond, in whom I am well
pleased.

And to the United States Army,
Particularly, the men of the Special Forces
De Opresso Liber!

Plead my cause, oh Lord, with those who strive
against me
War upon those who war upon me.

Psalm 35:1

Content

THE EXTREME COLD WEATHER TRAINING FACILITY

"TEN MINUTES!" the jumpmaster cried over the roar of the C-130 aircraft.

"Ten minutes, ten minutes, ten minutes," we all hollered back in response.

I looked across the fuselage at "Little Mike," the new guy I was supposed to mentor. He was just a buck sergeant, looked to be about 23. He was new to the team, and new to the Special Forces. Fresh out of the "Q Course," the Qualification Course, he was my A-Team's junior demolition sergeant. I was the senior demolition sergeant, so it was my duty to show him the ropes.

I'd made more than forty parachute jumps, so it wasn't exactly 'fear' I was feeling. More, it was *acute attentiveness*. Airborne operations were inherently dangerous, but the training was strictly by the numbers. All you had to do to get yourself out of an aircraft moving at 123 knots at an altitude of 1200 feet onto the ground uninjured was to perform the many minor tasks you were trained to do. But because the price of forgetfulness was so dear, it had the tendency to really, really focus your mind.

"GET READY!" came the command.

"Get ready," came our response.

"You ready?" I asked Mike.

"I got 25 jumps under my belt," he replied. "I got this."

"You've never jumped with the Green Berets," I said. "And when that door opens it's gonna be wicked cold."

"I got this," he replied curtly. I was glad to hear Mike had it down already. The jumpmaster opened the door of the aircraft, and the dark, cavernous fuselage exploded with blinding white light, and a vicious gust of frozen air slapped us in the face. All you could see out the open door was blazing white, and all you could smell was that smell that isn't a smell at all, but the fury of winter driving through your nose and mouth, overrunning all scents, all tastes, all small and nuanced distinctions.

"OUTBOARD PERSONNEL, STAND UP!" called the jumpmaster.

"Outboard personnel, stand up," came the chanted response. The company of soldiers struggled to its feet, encumbered by heavy rucksacks resting on our knees, rifles in carrying cases, and the bulky parachutes attached to our backs. We were wearing over-whites, the bleached white garments you pull over your uniform for camouflage in a snow-covered environment. Strapped to our rucksacks were our snow shoes.

"HOOK UP!" we were commanded.

"Hook up," we chanted in response. I hooked the steel snap link of my static line to the anchor line that ran down the length of the aircraft. The bright yellow static line, fifteen feet long and capable of holding 6,000 pounds, connected my parachute deployment bag—"D bag"—to the aircraft, so that when I exited the aircraft, the bag would come off and the parachute would open. I double-checked the snap link's connection to the anchor line. It was important to me that my parachute opened. It was something I really, really wanted to happen.

"CHECK STATIC LINES!" we were ordered.

"Check static lines," we shouted in response, and we all traced the yellow line of the man to our front, making sure there were no snags, tears or misroutings. We also each traced our own line from the point where it came over our shoulders and into our hands.

"CHECK EQUIPMENT!" came the command.

"Check equipment," we shouted back. I traced my helmet's chin strap from left to right, then traced the parachutists' retaining straps, which strapped the back of my helmet to the chin strap holding the front in place. I then inspected both of my leg straps' quick-releases and my chest strap quick release, making sure they were not open—I really, really didn't want them to be open. I had checked them at least 100 times already, but I was doing it again because I was commanded to. Sometimes taking orders can be comforting.

"SOUND OFF FOR EQUIPMENT CHECK!" barked the jumpmaster, placing his hands behind his ears.

"Sound off for equipment check!" we barked in response. Coming from my rear and growing louder, I could hear each jumper smacking the lower back of the jumper in front of him, shouting, "Okay!"

"Okay!"

"Okay!" It sounded like a wave rolling toward that open door. All I could think about was the open door. When I felt a smack and heard the man behind me shout, I continued the chain, "Okay!" This wave carried through to Sergeant "Panama Jack" Perez, my A-Team's medical sergeant, who was the first jumper in the door.

As first jumper his duty was to shout to the jumpmaster, "All okay, jumpmaster!" This task was to be performed in a very unusual, almost vaudevillian manner. In order to be heard and understood above the roar of the aircraft, the first jumper was required to step forward and stomp his foot on the deck while at the same time throwing his hand forward with his open palm facing up. It looked like the finish to a tap dance routine, but it allowed the jumper (usually a lower enlisted) the chance to get in a dig on his superior. "All okay, drunk bastard!" was the usual report. Panama Jack did not disappoint.

The jumpmaster waited for word from the pilot on his headset, while all of us kept our eyes glued on the glowing red light in the open doorway.

"ONE MINUTE!" the jumpmaster shouted.

"One minute! One minute! One minute!" we sang to each other, the index fingers of our free hands shooting up, imitating the jumpmaster.

The jumpmaster turned to the open door, grabbed the handles on either side of it, and leaned way outside the plane into the roaring white abyss. This act of studied bravado was probably the greatest re-enlistment tool in the Army's arsenal. Ostensibly, the jumpmaster was looking for potential hazards and obstructions. In fact, he was just showing off. It would be impossible to over-estimate the power this scene had on young paratroopers, watching a man, maybe three years their senior, as he hung out the side of an airplane careening through the sky at break-neck speed. The Army should have left re-enlistment contracts sitting on the drop zone.

The jumpmaster re-entered the aircraft. "THIRTY SECONDS!" he shouted to us.

"Thirty seconds! Thirty seconds! Thirty seconds!" we shouted back. It was too late now to cancel the jump. This thing was going to happen.

"STAND BY!" he commanded. This command was not repeated. Panama Jack handed off his static line to the jumpmaster and pivoted to face the door. The rest of us shuffled forward a half step. The engines were screaming, but above their roar I could hear my heart pounding with excitement.

"GO!" the jumpmaster shouted, as the light changed from red to green. Panama Jack wrapped his hands around his reserve parachute and stepped out the door. There was no hesitation, but we all began shuffling relentlessly forward. As I shuffled, my eyes were locked on the jumpmaster, my mind glued on the next thing to do—*think of only the hand-off, think of only the hand-off*, I kept repeating in my head. I

9

handed him my static line, pivoted toward the door, and took a bounding step into the vast, vacant void. With my elbows tucked into my side and my chin on my chest, I concentrated on counting, "One-one-thousand, two-one-thousand . . . ." I felt the angry rush of the piercing wind, then the tremendous heat of the engine exhaust, "three-one-thousand," then—WHUMP—the violent shock of the parachute opening. I began to laugh maniacally. I don't know why, but I always did that when the parachute opened.

Then came the stillness. The incredible silence of floating through the air. And with it, the feeling of knowing I was a part of that profound calm. I checked my descent, checked to see where the others were, checked that my canopy was fully open, then gave myself exactly 20 seconds to just . . . be happy.

I could see the chute turn-in point, and I was not at all in danger of colliding with anyone. I could see Donnelly Dome to my left, the small isolated mountaintop that sat on the western boundary of Donnelly Drop Zone. To my right was the tiny town of Delta Junction, Alaska, sitting along the frozen Tanana River. And all around me was an endless sea of snow. *It is a good thing*, I thought, *to be a paratrooper. It is a good thing to drift through the air on a March day, and to be convinced—at least for a moment—that I have not a care in the world.*

I hit the ground in a quiet crunch of soft snow, and lay there in place for a good minute—the longest I determined I could do that without someone noticing. I then grabbed my rucksack and pulled off the snow shoes. Landing in snow is great. Trying to collect up your parachute, and carry it to the collection point, is anything but.

I dumped my parachute and reserve off at the turn-in point, then made a spot for myself in the snow-covered drop zone, faced out and pulled security for the others, who came in and did the same. Once the entire company had arrived at the collection point, and a good headcount had been taken, the company commander shouted, "Rally! Rally! Rally! Come on in boys, we're goin' admin for the rest of the day."

'Going admin' meant that we were not in a training scenario. That wasn't going to mean we wouldn't have to pull guard duty overnight. The woods were teaming with wolves and bear, who would love nothing more than to make a meal out of a Green Beret bundled up in his sleeping bag. It only meant that we could talk and give our opinions about the training scenario up to that point, which is something only an idiot would do anyway.

In a regular infantry company, the company commander would be a captain, the first sergeant would be a master sergeant, and the platoon leaders would all be lieutenants. But in the Special Forces the company commander was a major, the company first sergeant, a sergeant major, and the A-Team leaders were captains.

The company formed a ragged circle around the major, each A-Team forming up around its team leader, as each team leader positioned himself around the major, so that we looked like a little solar system—separate planets revolving around a common sun.

Major Thorton was tall and athletic looking. With his face covered by his frost and frozen-saliva encrusted balaclava, he looked to be in his twenties, every bit the look of a Special Forces company commander. But when he pulled off the balaclava, the leathered skin and wrinkled brow gave away his age. Like all of us, he was wearing trigger-finger mittens, thick, fur-lined mittens with individual digits for both the thumb and the trigger finger. You could keep them on and still fire your weapon. Like the rest of us, he also wore his load-bearing equipment—the belt and suspenders with pouches for ammo, grenades, first-aid kit, and whatever—over his over-whites. On his feet he wore VB boots—vapor barrier boots—enormous white, rubber, Mickey Mouse-looking boots that surrounded the foot with a sealed membrane filled with methane gas. He smiled at us and let out an involuntary whup: "Hell, yeah!" he shouted. "Airborne drop, practically on the Arctic Circle. Let's see the Russians do that!"

We cheered. It felt good to know that leadership shared our excitement.

"How's the weather?" he asked, not really caring to hear our dramatic groans. "Well, there's a chance—a small chance—that things are going to get a lot worse." We groaned again, mostly out of habit, but the major continued. "We're getting reports that there is an 'arctic blast' building up just north of us. If it hits, temps will drop into the negative 50s, and with it will come high winds and—of course—the usual 'blinding snow.'"

I looked over at Donnelly Dome. It looked just like Sugarloaf Mountain in Maryland, where I grew up—a lone bump on the terrain. I stared up at the sky. It was clear and bright. It was 20 below now, but it was March. We were getting maybe 15 minutes more sunlight each day than we'd gotten the day before. I wasn't worried at all about the weather report: winter was in full retreat.

Major Thorton looked around at us all, doing a deft 360 degree turn in his snow shoes. He would be leaving in a month. This would be his last field exercise with us. Soon, he would go to some staff college and then onto a slot at the Pentagon or at the Special Operations Command or some other elephants' graveyard, where once-revered field officers lived out the rest of their days. It felt like he was trying to glean great meaning out of this last field exercise—it felt awkward.

His eyes rested on Little Mike, the new guy. "How 'bout that, Mike?" he said. "Ever do anything like that back in the 82nd?"

Mike was quick at the repartee. "No, sir," he said. "In my entire life I have never jumped out of an aircraft, 20 below zero, into two feet of snow, in *March!*"

The entire company laughed. Major Thorton looked at me. "Keep an eye on this one, Jet Set," he said. "He's either gonna be your boss someday, or he's gonna die trying." I slapped Little Mike on the shoulder. He was in. That was all it took in a Special Forces company. You just had to be good at your job, committed to the unit, and quietly cocky about yourself.

It was the first thing they taught us back in "the Q." On the very first day of the Qualification Course, this short, hard-looking sergeant with black, slicked-back hair and a widow's peak—we called him Eddie Munster—stepped onto the stage in the lecture hall at Camp Mackall and stared at us, saying, "There are three rules in the Green Berets. Number one: always look cool; number two: always know where you are; number three: if you don't know where you are, for Christ sake, at least *look cool.*"

The session with the major over, the A-Teams made camp at the various ends of the drop zone, which stretched over a mile long and a quarter mile wide. We made our radio checks to be in communication with the headquarters element, then busted out our MREs (meals ready to eat) and had chow. Little Mike sat down next to me. "Why do they call you 'Jet Set'?" he asked, clearly looking for some entertainment.

"Oh," I said, "the sergeant major gave me that name two years ago when I came back from vacation."

"But why?"

"Well, I had 30 days' leave that I hadn't used up," I said, "and it was like a use-it or lose-it deal. Company had to let me go, and I had to take the full 30."

"So whatcha do?"

"I had a buddy in the 25th ID in Hawaii who also had some leave. I hopped a 'Space Available' flight to Scofield Barracks and we hung out on Waikiki for about five days. But then I was like, 'Okay, I get it, let's do something else.'" I shifted in my seat, moving my sleeping bag under my cold ass. "So he and I took a Space A flight to Korea, where we had another buddy."

"So now you're in Korea."

"Right. But after a few more days those guys had to get back. But I'm still sitting around with over 20 days' leave. *And* I had a pocket full of cash—so I bought a ticket to India."

"You went to India on a whim?"

"Well, first I went to Singapore. That place is booming. Singapore is goin' to be the future."

"Then to India?"

"Yeah. Flew into Mumbai and took the train up through Gujarat, across Rajasthan and into the Punjab. Then I took another train to Delhi."

"So then what happened?"

"Stupidly, I called my mom," I said, "And, of course, she was all like (I dropped into a Marge Simpson voice), 'You've got 30 days of leave and you won't see your mother? HMMMM...' So then I felt bad, and I knew I had to see my folks. But—you know—not right away. So I got a ticket for Dubai, and I hung out there for a few days. Then, 'fuck it,' I said, 'I'm going to Israel', and I flew off to Tel Aviv."

"Wait," said Little Mike. "You went from Dubai to Israel? I'm callin' bullshit. Arabs and Israelis don't mix."

"Well," I said, "you'd think that, wouldn't you? But if you've got money in your pocket and you move with a sense of purpose, people, the whole world over, will open the door for you, no matter where it leads."

"No shit?" said Mike.

"No shit," I replied.

Mike paused for a minute to think about that. "So anyway," he finally said.

"So anyway, I still have to see my parents on the east coast. So I booked a ticket to Rome, checked out the Vatican, did the tourist thing at Saint Peter's, got a good confession, then attended Mass. After that, I drove to Paris, took a train to London and hung out there for a few days. Then I flew to New York, where I set up for a couple days at the Soldiers, Sailors and Airmen's Club on Lexington Avenue, got bored and took the Chinatown bus down to DC."

"The Chinatown bus?"

"You never been on the Chinatown bus?" I said. "It's insane."

"What are they?"

"These buses go from Chinatown New York to Chinatown DC in four hours for $25.00—the train is like $120.00, and it takes forever. You go down to East Broadway and there are these three crappy buses sitting out under the bridge, and next to each bus is an old Chinese lady banging on pots and pans, yelling, 'Get on bus! Get on bus! Get on bus!' You get on the bus, and everybody sits up front because they don't clean the toilet and it's frickin' disgusting toward the rear. The buses all take off together, and they race each other to DC, because they all want that first parking spot so they can get the most customers coming back."

"No shit?"

"Oh, it's crazy. The first time I took the Chinatown bus, my driver got arrested by the New Jersey State Troopers."

"That's awesome."

"Not if you're on the bus. But, anyway, this time my driver is racing this other driver, and the whole time, I kid you not, he's talking away on his cell phone."

"No shit?"

"No shit." I looked down at my crackers and crumbled them into my pouch of stew. "Anyway, I saw my parents, hung out for a few days, then flew out to San Francisco—most beautiful city in the world—then back to Anchorage. When I got back, sergeant major said, 'Whatcha do on vacation?' When I told him, he didn't believe me. 'Let me see your passport?' he said. I showed him my passport, and he looks at me and says, 'You're a regular Jet Setter, ain't ya, Redmond?'"

"And ever since?" said Little Mike.

"Ever since, I've been Jet Set."

I took the first and last guard shifts, taking an extra hour of duty, but getting four hours of uninterrupted sleep, and woke the others up just before dawn for Stand-To. As the gray dawn arose, I saw the top of Donnelly Dome shrouded in clouds, and I felt the cold whip of an Arctic blast strike my half-exposed face.

"Me no likee," I said to the captain, as the wind intensified.

"Yeah," he replied. "*No es bueno.*" The captain radioed in to the B-Team. "Sir," he said, "looks like that blast is coming in."

"Yeah," the major said. "We might have to shelter in place. But I'm getting mixed messages from weather. Some are saying it's coming our way, and some are saying it's not."

"Your call," replied the captain.

"Out," said the major: his way of telling the captain he was getting above himself.

"Roger," replied the captain: his way of letting the major know he was keeping notes.

By breakfast the weather had improved remarkably. It was almost ten below when we ate our chow, and the wind had died to nothing. "Begin link-up operations," came the command from the sergeant major over the radio. One of the other team leaders got on the radio and asked for the weather status.

"What are we talking about?" replied the sergeant major. "Movements of less than 500 meters?"

We all laughed when we heard that. The whole idea of the link-up was to *not know* until the last minute how far you would have to traverse, and here the sergeant major was telling us the maximum distance we would have to go.

"500 meters?" said Panama Jack. "You could phone that in."

"Easy as sin," Little Mike agreed.

Mike and I rucked up, prepping for the '500 meter' march to our link-up. And as we did, we were hit with another Arctic blast, this one surprisingly severe. I almost fell backward into the snow.

"Shit," I said, "this is getting serious."

"It's half a klick," said Little Mike. "We'll be back here in the hooch within two hours." I said nothing.

We field-checked ourselves, both of us kneeling down to check the other's snow shoes and other gear. And then we marched off, Mike taking the lead, his map in his hand and his compass strung through his over-whites, dangling around his stomach. You don't want your compass too close to your body when you read it; all the steel and hardware will move the needle. Little Mike had it just right.

"What azimuth are we on?" I asked.

"173 degrees," replied Mike. I picked up my compass and shot the azimuth and looked at my map. He was dead on, so I let go of my compass, pulled in behind him and just followed along.

As we came to the top of a slight incline about 70 meters from the team, I gave a quick look back. The team was in a tight 360 degree formation, weapons pointed out in each direction, as they lay semi-concealed within a hastily constructed hooch they'd carved out of a snow bank. I figured they were lying on their sleeping bags, and

15

shaking quietly with the relentless, but not-quite-severe cold that passes for normal up here. They had hung a marking panel from a tree limb over the hooch for recognition. *Shouldn't be that hard to see coming back,* I thought.

Mike and I trudged along, the snow softly crunching under our show shoes. We came to a frozen creek about 150 meters out, and as we climbed across, a furious blast slammed into us. Immediately behind it came the snow, driving sideways.

"Holy crap!" said Mike.

"What the hell!" I replied.

We both adjusted our balaclavas, and tightened the hoods on our Gore-Tex jackets, but the wind was whipping, and the snow was battering our eyes and faces.

"Want to turn back?" I said.

"Can't," said Little Mike. He looked at his compass again, and said, "My first field exercise with the company. If we turn back and everybody else makes their link-up, I'll be the biggest pussy in the unit. I ain't gonna be no pussy."

Mike was right. The worst thing in the world was to be a pussy.

We pushed on, and the Arctic blast did too. The temperature dropped at least another 15 degrees, and the wind did not subside. We leaned into the wind, and walked with steps that were nothing near our regular pace count. Soon, things became ridiculous.

"What's your pace count?" I said, after about 10 minutes.

"I got us right about 500 meters out," said Little Mike. "But my pace has got to be way off because of the . . . blizzard." I hadn't thought of it as a blizzard, but that was exactly what it was. I kept thinking it would just be a short burst, but it wasn't letting up.

"Well," I shouted through the wind. "The link-up is notional anyway. Shoot your back-azimuth and let's go back." I looked at Mike and was surprised to see that his lips were blue, and he was shaking fiercely. He opened and closed his eyes a couple of times as if unclear where he was. "What azimuth are we on?" I asked.

"178 degrees," he replied.

"I thought we were on a 173?" I replied, doubting myself.

"No," Little Mike replied, now looking more focused. "178."

I should have written it down, I thought. *Why hadn't I written it down?*

"So," I said, thinking this was still a teaching moment, "what's the back azimuth to 178?"

"358 degrees," he said, rousing himself.

"Shoot it," I said, "and we'll be warm and dry within the hour."

Mike pulled out his compass, and I could see he had a large hole in his trigger finger mittens.

"Mike," I said, "you shouldn't have come out here with those. You should have DX-ed them back at Fort Richardson." Mike was clearly freezing. He could barely pull his compass out, and when he did, he kept it very close to his body. We turned around. I looked at our trail. Ten feet beyond where we had come was completely covered with snow. I pretended I didn't notice this, and allowed Mike to start us back to base.

We now had the wind at our back. But it was a wicked wind just the same. There was no trail at all, and the snow kept piling up.

"What azimuth are you shooting?" I asked after about 100 meters. Little Mike pulled out his compass—again right against his body—and said, "358."

We began to climb a small hill that I had not remembered us coming down. "Mike," I said, but before I could finish, he turned around, his eyes filled with anxiety.

"We didn't cross this hill, did we?" he said.

I took out my arctic mittens, much thicker than the trigger-finger mittens, and gave them to Little Mike. "Put these on," I said.

"But what about you?" he replied.

"Put them on, Mike," I said. "That's an order." He put the mittens on. "We'll go to the top of this hill and send off our signal flares," I said.

"But that's failure!" he replied.

"It's my failure," I said. "I'm the senior here, and I'm the one who failed."

When we came to the top of the bluff, I saw that the downward slope dropped almost straight down. I slid over and leaned against a tree. "Watch yourself," I shouted behind me without turning. "It drops right off."

I didn't see Little Mike, who was trudging directly behind me, oblivious to everything around him now that I was taking the lead. His head was down as he just stared at the ground directly in front of him.

"Mike, no!" I shouted, as I grabbed at his Gore-Tex hood, my fingers just missing the lip of the hood encircling his head. I could feel my fingers scratching against the slick surface of his outer jacket even as he fell away from me.

17

"Mike!"

He tumbled down, his snow shoes splaying his legs first this way then that, his torso hitting an exposed outcrop of rock. Then reeling over, he lay, one leg jutting out sideways at an impossible angle.

I fired off two flares, then, taking off my snow shoes, and holding them in my hands, I jumped down the incline, sliding my way to Mike. He was unconscious, his young face collecting snowflakes that landed on his lips and eyes. I took off his snow shoes, and pulled out my thermal blanket, spreading it out next to him, hoping to roll him onto it. But when I tried to move him, he let out a violent moan. Instead, I scooped out the snow from underneath him and slid the thermal blanket under his body, then wrapped it around him, pulling it tightly around his chest, leaving just a small opening for his mouth and nose.

I then fired off three more flares—I had only three left. I cut down two long branches to make a skid. I took out my poncho, laid it out on the ground and tied off the poncho to the two branches with some parachute cord I kept in my cargo pocket. It didn't look all that secure, but it was the only thing I had.

I checked on Little Mike. He was shivering—the beginning of shock. I didn't know which direction to go, but I felt I had to get him moving. I fired another flare, then loaded up another one and pointed it into the air.

"Jet Set!" I heard a voice shout. "We're here!" I looked to my front and saw Panama Jack racing toward me, his medic bag slung over one shoulder. Behind Jack were the captain and the team sergeant. Panama Jack ran up to Mike, threw down his medical bag and began immediate first aid. He then began barking orders and observations, "Clavicle dislocated, severe numbness in the left arm. Significant disarticulation in the right knee and right ankle. Severe loss of circulation in the lower right leg."

The captain had a radio and began calling for an extraction—which was not sure it could make it in this weather.

"You *will* arrive at my designated coordinates!" the captain shouted into the radio. "You have an extraction litter, and you *will* use it!"

The helicopter arrived within 25 minutes, and Mike was lifted up within the half-hour.

That was the last time I ever saw Little Mike.

They assigned the Line of Duty Investigation to a full bird colonel—which right away told us that they were gunning for the major. The

18

colonel was a fleshy, double-chinned man with no marks of distinction on his uniform, just a name tag and 'U.S. Army' to show for his life in the service. I wanted to tell him the things I could have done to prevent the accident, but he didn't seem particularly interested. Most of his questions revolved around the major's orders to continue to train "in the face of clear and present danger," the colonel repeatedly said. And also to the sergeant major's "dismissive" comments of a land navigation exercise that was "only 500 meters."

I was interviewed by the colonel three times, and it wasn't until the third time that I learned about what had happened to Little Mike. "Oh," said the colonel, shaking his head in a manner that told me it was bad, but that he didn't particularly care. "He lost his left arm at the shoulder and his right leg just below the knee."

As he walked out the door, I stumbled over to the waste basket and vomited.

The major got a letter of reprimand—which is a career killer for an officer—and the sergeant major got removed. But nothing happened to me at all. Even the guys in the unit didn't place any of the blame on me. Little Mike was a buck sergeant, I was a staff sergeant. He was qualified, I was qualified. It was his mission. I was just riding in the passenger seat. But that wasn't how I felt. Mike had never been in Alaska before. He'd never been to the Extreme Cold Weather Training Center before. *Geez,* I thought, remembering the drive up through downtown Fairbanks. *When we pulled up to that light in the center of town, and a damn Snow Cat pulled up alongside of us, Mike's eyes almost popped out. When we drove past the 'time and temperature' display at the credit union, he thought the thermometer was broken, laughing that it read '40 degrees.' And when I explained that it was reading 'negative 40' his face went blank.*

I couldn't stop thinking about Little Mike. *I should have done more. I hadn't even properly checked his equipment the day we went out. I hadn't even checked his trigger-finger mittens.* I couldn't tell anybody about how I was feeling—my God, they might agree with me. I owed him a duty, and I failed in my duty. *What the hell was I doing in the Army?* I kept thinking. *What the hell was I doing in the Special Forces?* My enlistment was scheduled to expire on January 13, 1998, and I had two weeks of terminal leave. I decided that I'd get out of the Army by the end of the year.

The new sergeant major sat me down when he heard I wanted out. We reviewed my file together, and he looked at me, and said, "I've got a note here from my predecessor saying that your goal is to be the Group Sergeant Major." He stared at me hard. "What happened, Jet Set?"

I didn't say a thing to him.

"I can get you Ranger School," he said.

I didn't reply.

"What happened out there last March?" he finally said.

"I failed," is all I said in response. "I had a duty, and I failed in my duty. I have no business being in the Special Forces."

The sergeant major picked up the phone, said a few words, then the new major came in. "How's it hangin', Jet Set?" he said, trying to be colloquial. I didn't dislike the new major, he was gung-ho, squared away, and all that. Major Thorton had been removed, and a slot had opened, so he took it, simple as that. "The Army has a lot invested in you," he said.

"I did my tour," I replied.

"No one's sayin' you're shortin' the Army," he said. "But we thought—you know—that we were married."

"I thought so, too," I said. "But maybe I don't deserve to be married to the Army."

The major looked at me. "This is about Little Mike, isn't it?"

"No, sir," I said. "It's about me."

The major, the sergeant major and I bantered around a bit, like family members talking about, but never actually mentioning, the exact issues that were driving us apart. But at a certain point things turned, and it became clear that I was leaving and there was nothing to be done about it. At that point the major excused himself because of a 'prior commitment,' and it was just the sergeant major and me.

"I've got a friend," the sergeant major said in a conspiratorial whisper. "We went through the 'Q' together and were on the same A-Team in 10th Group. But he got out—wife was getting sick of him being gone all the time. Anyway, he stayed in the National Guard—20th Group. You're from Virginia, right?"

"Maryland, sergeant major," I said, "but right over the river."

"Whatever," said the sergeant major, waving his hand at me. "These guys drill every month down at Fort A.P. Hill, about 2 hours from DC. It's a very high-speed unit for the National Guard." The sergeant major raised his eyebrows. "What do you have now, five, six years in the Army? You could do 15 years sitting on your hands in the National Guard and still get a retirement." He passed me a slip of paper with his buddy's phone number on it. "You'll need a recommendation to get in

. . . but I've already sent it."

We both stood up, and the sergeant major shook my hand. "Just because a guy screws up," he said, "or *thinks* he screwed up, doesn't mean there's no place for him in the Army." The sergeant major laughed. "My God, look at me. I can't find my own ass with both hands in my back pocket, and they made me a sergeant major."

We drove along the Alaskan Highway, my brother Robert and I. It was 3:00 p.m., but already dark. He had flown up from Richmond, Virginia just to drive back home with me. He was a partner in a prestigious law firm, had a wife and six children, but when he learned I was getting out of the Army at the end of December, and driving back home, he blocked off his schedule, shrugged off his wife's enormous—and very legitimate—concerns, and booked a one-way ticket to Anchorage to ride back with me. One last adventure, like we were kids again going down to the creek to catch crayfish.

We had just finished five decades of the rosary—that was Rob's one requirement, that we pray the rosary every day. Sometimes if we were bored, we'd pray a second and sometimes a third rosary, but always we prayed the five decades of the rosary. That was his only rule.

It was the last day of the year, December 31, and we were pulling into Beaver Creek, Yukon Territory. "So," Rob said with a casual air, but with obvious underpinnings to it, "Mom says you want to go to law school."

"Yeah," I said. "I think so. I got the GI Bill. I'm stayin' in the guard, so I'll have enough to survive on for a couple three years. Why not?"

Robert slowly nodded his head, thinking about everything, putting it all into place. He pointed out the window toward the bleak, barren whiteness encompassing my little car. "What happened last March?" he asked.

I froze. "What are you talking about?" I said, maybe a little too defensively.

"Well," continued Rob, "last Christmas all you could talk about was the Special Forces. You went on about how you were trying to get a slot in Ranger School, then maybe dive school, and that one day you would be Group Sergeant Major." Robert shifted a little in his seat. "Next thing I hear is Mom sayin' some guy on your team lost his arm and leg, and now you're getting out of the Army." Robert looked at me. "And talkin' about going to law school—sort of hard not to notice the change."

I grimaced. "I don't know," I said. "I guess I just don't see the point anymore."

For the longest time Robert said nothing, but just looked out the window at the endless expanse of snow. "So, what happened?" he asked.

The way he said it—it was so direct, so uninterested in my prepackaged answers. "I failed," was all I could say. "I had a duty, and I didn't do it. I owed a man, and I failed him. And now that man is going through life with an arm and a leg missing—because of me!" I shouted this last sentence into the windshield.

Robert remained silent. But at last he said, "Is that what happened, or is that what you've convinced yourself is what happened?"

"What's the difference?" I said.

Robert didn't reply for the longest time. But after a while, he reached up and took the rosary off of the rearview mirror, crossed himself and said, "You're going to have to find out. Eventually, you're going to have to find out."

BALTIMORE

I didn't exactly *wow 'em* in law school. Mediocrity had been my academic aspiration, yet even that proved beyond my grasp.

Joe Hurska, Ali Begum and I were standing out on Joe's balcony, overlooking a small park and the partially renovated law school on the other side. We were smoking cigars and sipping on scotch prior to the Super Bowl, talking about everything, but mostly about school. Looking out at the half-renovated law school, I started thinking about the three years I'd spent studying there. "You know," I said, "I was the very last one accepted into our class."

"Bullshit," said Joe. "How would you know that?" said Ali.

"The Dean told me," I replied, "the night before school started."

"The Dean told you that you were the last one accepted the night before class started?" Ali replied. "Doubt it."

"Why would he even do that?" said Joe.

"Because that was the night I *was* accepted," I replied.

"Wait, what?"

"I wasn't in," I said, "until that night. I was just on the wait list. Then—the night before classes started—I got a call from the Dean, and he told me there was a single spot available, and did I want it?"

"What'd you say?"

"Well," I replied, "I had already enrolled in the University of Baltimore, at the night school. I had a job with some computer company, and I had planned on going to school at night. So I asked the Dean if I could—you know—get into the night program."

"And what'd he say?"

"He said 'nah.' Just like that. Not, 'no,' not 'I'll see what I can do.' Just 'nah.'"

"So what'd you say?"

"I asked him if I could have some time to think about it."

"And what'd he say?"

"He said 'nah,' exactly the same way. Just 'nah.'" I looked down at my cigar. "And what I remember most about that phone call," I said, "is that I could hear the sound of the TV playing in the background. I will never forget it. It was the 7th inning, and the Orioles were up by two."

We stared again at the construction across the avenue, the unfinished school, half-demolished, half-restored. The old building had been a nondescript structure, like some amped-up high school built in the 1950s—red brick, grey concrete flourishes and rows upon rows of steel framed windows that opened skyward. The emerging new building was much more grand and scholastic looking, but the windows didn't open, and the main entrance didn't spill you directly onto the street the way the old entrance did—the way a proper Baltimore doorway does, right onto the sidewalk, studded with the gleaming white marble steps of a once charming city.

Joe took a tug on his scotch, and leaned against the rail. Like me, Joe had worked at a few jobs before attending law school. We were politely referred to as "nontraditional students." In other words we were old. Joe had been a naval officer on a submarine before law school. His shoulders were broad and his arms were large from many hours spent in the gym. And, like me, Joe had struggled through law school.

"Did you guys go to the Christmas party in December?" he asked.

"Yeah," I said. "It was great—one of those all-is-forgiven affairs, with an open bar and instructors saying nice things about you."

"Well, I brought my brother along," continued Joe, "and, of course, he was half-in-the-bag, so he goes ahead and throws his arm over my favorite professor, and he asks him, 'So, how was Joey as a law student?'"

"What'd the professor say?"

"Oh, he froze up like a snowman," Joe continued. "He was all like, 'Ummm, ahhhh.' Then, he gets this big grin on his face and he says, 'Actually, as a law student, your brother had *terrific upper-body strength.*'"

For guys like Joe and me, law school was a cascading series of slights and humiliations. Still, I loved it, every embarrassing minute of it. It beat the hell out of the Army. I was in my thirties when I went to law school, much older than most other students, and yet I can honestly say it was like a Paris Island of the brain, a place where they hammer your reasoning into shape. A lot of attorneys roll their eyes about the difficulty of law school, but for me it was every bit as hard as they make out in the movies—one big *Paper Chase*.

I had always been a "smart guy" in school, witty and conversant, telling "Dave's not here" jokes from the back of the room, never reading a book and getting a B. But I didn't know how to study, how to put thoughts together, how to even sit down and *think* for more than two minutes—that first semester of law school I didn't know whether to shit or go blind.

But slowly I learned, or learned how to learn. And eventually I fell in love with the Law. The Law is an intricate thing, an enduring thing, and a constantly astonishing thing. A thing that exists unto itself—as old as humankind and yet every day it springs forward brand new. It is the communion between the human and the divine, and those who study the Law will always bear a responsibility equally as profound as it is generally ignored.

So, there we were, the three of us, staring blankly at the unfinished building across the expanse. I pushed off from the rail, breaking free from the hypnotic vision. "Whatever it was," I said, "it's all but over now. And it's not about school anymore. It's about getting a job." I turned to Ali, "Obviously, you've got it sewn up."

Ali smiled sheepishly. He had done well in school. He was focused, funny and well-liked across campus. He was an editor of the *Maryland Law Review*, and would be clerking for a federal judge in the fall. Beyond that, he had already accepted an offer with a firm in what is known in attorney circles as 'Big Law'—one of the 100 or so law firms that seem to run the whole country. He was set.

Ali also broke free from the rail, and Joe looked at him quizzically. "Ali," he said, "I know how you and I started hanging out—we shared a wall locker. But how did you and Timmy become friends? I mean, Ali Begum and Timmy Redmond?" Joe shook his head. "You're an up-and-coming legal eagle, a man with a future. But Timmy over there, he walks around campus like a duck hit in the head."

"Thanks, Joe," I said. "Coming from you that means a lot."

"True," replied Ali, with a smile. "But Timmy and I worked at the gym together." This was true as far as it went. People were always surprised by the friendship Ali and I had. He was a deft and brilliant scholar and a (not very devout) Muslim, and I was a perpetually-struggling veteran sergeant on the GI Bill, and a (not very devout) Catholic. But Ali and I were both on work-study, and we were the two people who opened up the university gym in the morning.

The University of Maryland, Baltimore gym was on the top floor of a parking deck. We would meet each other at the door every morning at exactly 6:00 a.m., then one of us would open the office and the other would make coffee. As the few early-risers signed in, we would throw down our books and begin to study. For three solid hours every morning we would sit at the front desk studying. Although older, I became Ali's apprentice, and he would patiently answer whatever questions I had. He had an unobtrusive, calming manner, and a way of pointing out glaring mistakes in a face-saving way. I appreciated his patience with me, and I think he appreciated my willingness to accept his instruction. It was Ali who taught me to give a text a close reading, and to think like a lawyer. I truly liked Ali, he was not a man who *hoped* to do something, or *set goals* to be accomplished. He just did it. If Ali said something would happen, it would happen.

"Yes," said Ali, to no one in particular. "I have my position established, but what about you two, what will you be doing in a year?"

In the last year of law school, you begin the interview process for your first attorney position. It is the cumulative event of law school. It is the point of law school. Joe turned to me. "What happened to you, Timmy? Seems like I remember you had an interview with one of the bigger law firms over in Bethesda. What happened with that?"

I rolled my eyes. "That was a disaster," I said. "Let's be honest, I was completely unqualified for the job." I raised my glass to my lips thinking about that interview, then put it back down again. "My grades were well below anything this firm would normally consider, but I knew some people, and I figured I could play up my security clearance. I was wrong."

Law firms like this one typically hold a series of interviews for their prospective attorney-hires. The initial interview is done by a mid-level associate who understands the firm, but whose time is not of infinite value. My initial interviewer was Julianne. Julianne was thirty-something, tall, sexy and smart. We were both divorced, both physically fit and both "fun." Julianne and I clicked. We WAY clicked—it wasn't an interview, it was a lap dance.

Julianne felt I was a good fit for the firm (she even had me convinced), and she scheduled a follow-up interview for Thursday afternoon one week later. Then she winked and mentioned that she wanted to schedule it for Thursday, because they were "having a happy hour that night," and I should "come by after the interview." She said it would be "worth my while."

For attorney-hires at prestigious law firms, the second interview is the real interview. This is where you meet the parents. There will be no lap dance.

"Things did not go well," I said. "Let me set the stage: a dark, forbidding office, where a senior partner sits in his overstuffed chair as a well-dressed but nervous younger man stares at him from across a vast mahogany desk. The older man has a look of both anger and confusion on his face as he examines the younger man, then examines the younger man's transcripts. He looks back up at the man, then down at his grades, up again at the man, down again at the grades. The senior partner does not understand why the man is sitting before him. It is to him as if the landscaper has entered his office looking for his leaf blower."

Joe laughed. "That sounds like me with the IRS," he said, stepping away from us and pacing up and down, clearly uncomfortable with telling his story. "Even though I'm a dumbass," he said, "I had actually done well in tax law, which, I think, is the most difficult law to master. And for a time I dreamed of becoming a tax attorney." Joe raised his hands up in self-deprecating mockery. "Yeah, I know all the jokes about tax attorneys: 'What does a tax attorney use for birth control?' 'His personality.' 'What do you call a tax attorney having lunch with a friend?' 'Popular.'" Joe looked at us sheepishly.

"But I like tax law. Tax law is what sits at the crossroads of power, wealth and politics. Tax law," Joe continued, with reverence, "is where great forces battle one another. To be a tax attorney is to be at the helm of a ship, navigating it through the treacherous waters and dangerous shoals of commerce, money and the state."

Joe turned toward us, his eyes alight with a distant vision. "A tax attorney fights in the biggest arena of them all."

Ali looked bemused. "So you were going to be the 'Battlin' Tax Attorney'? What could go wrong?"

"Oh, I had big plans," said Joe. "I was gonna become *That Guy.* That Guy, who rides the Red Line into DC every day with a *Washington Post* under one arm and a *Wall Street Journal* under the other. That guy who scours the classifieds for "fixer-uppers" and slowly accumulates real estate wealth. I would leverage my VA loan, and at first live close to the margin. But slowly my sources of income would multiply, and my wealth would replicate itself again and again." Joe was beaming. "I would be a real estate baron," he continued, stepping closer to us with growing excitement. "Then, maybe, a middling politician. I would own a sky suite at Redskin Stadium and stable a horse in Potomac. A seat in the General Assembly would be dangled before me, and—who knows—maybe even a congressional district. I would marry well, but not above my station, and my children would go to school with the children of the powerful."

Joe spoke with passion, but both Ali and I also knew that he did not have an offer from the IRS. "So what happened?" Ali asked.

"What happened?" replied Joe with slight hostility. "What happened is I ran into my past." He paused as if wondering whether to go on.

"I had a strong interview with an IRS division that monitors municipal bonds. Cities and counties don't have to pay federal taxes on bonds for the bridges and firehouses they *plan* on constructing. So, of course, they *plan* for nothing but bridges and firehouses that never get built. And they use the money for conferences in Hawaii and meetings at the Ritz Carlton."

"So it's a federal hand-out," I said, "that then needs to be federally regulated."

"Exactly."

"Making for more federal jobs."

"Nothin' escapes you, does it, Redmond?" Joe said. "Anyway, I slam-dunked the interview, so the Divisional Director escorted me around the office to meet the people I'd be working with." Joe picked up his drink and took a big swig. "While we were meeting my future co-workers, I ran into a girl who I had seriously wronged years before."

Ali and I laughed. "Uh-oh," said Ali, "a woman scorned?"

"The fact is I stabbed her in the back." Joe looked down at his hands ashamedly. "Do you know what it's like when a person hates you because they *should* hate you? Because you've *earned* their hatred? They hate you because they once loved you, they once trusted you, and you pissed it away. When a person hates you because you deserve their hatred, that's something you have to carry for the rest of your life."

Ali and I fell silent, and for the longest time no words were spoken as we each examined our own unclean consciences.

Finally, Joe said, "That was the last I heard of the IRS."

"So where are you now?" I asked.

Joe shrugged, and said, "I'm going to be working for a guy up in Bel Air. He runs a full-service shop, I should get a few tax defense cases. It's exciting work."

Ali cleared his throat. "So, finish your story, Timmy," he said. "We know about the job you didn't get, what else have you been up to?"

"I got an offer from the Brooklyn DA's Office," I said.

"Congratulations!" they both exclaimed.

"Yeah," I said, "I just had my second interview, and it was with the

District Attorney himself. But, I don't know, I'd have to take the New York Bar, and it's hard trying to manage New York City on an ADA's salary."

"Yeah," said Joe, "but still . . ."

"But still!" I said as a smile came to my face. "I'd still be an Assistant District Attorney in New York City—and that ain't nothing!"

"As I remember," said Ali thoughtfully, "it's not actually *called* the Brooklyn DA..."

"No," I said, "it's Kings County District Attorney's Office. The Boroughs of New York assume their roles as counties for jurisdictional purposes." The words rolled off my lips like the ready answer to an interview question, and for the first time, I actually thought about moving to New York and taking the job. Until that moment, it seemed like a crazy thing to do. I had been playing with the idea for the last month, constantly weighing the pros and cons of the job. On the one hand the salary was terrible, and I didn't know many people in New York, so if it didn't work out, I'd have to take another bar. But on the other hand, the people I would be working with would be incredible. I would be practicing law at the cutting edge—arguing in open court every day, dueling with some of the fiercest defense attorneys in the country. Still, it seemed like a stretch.

"The game comes on in half an hour," Ali said, looking down at his watch. Joe turned around and looked back through the glass doors into his apartment.

"We better get back inside," he said, "we've got a Super Bowl party to prepare for, and if the Ravens win, this city is going to go berserk."

Within ten minutes, the apartment was filled with people, all wearing purple and black, all excited about the upcoming game. It was a good mix of people: just about all the "non-traditional" law students where there, many of the girls from the Dental School and Medical School, with a smattering of Pharmacy School people as well.

In deference to the women, we tried to stay on our best behavior— keeping the yelling, screaming and cussing down to a minimum during the first half of the game. But it was the Super Bowl, and Baltimore hadn't seen a Super Bowl since the Colts over 30 years before, so soon our best behavior deteriorated into shouting out the window onto Paca Street, slamming punches into each other's arms, and generally causing a nuisance.

But the night was enormous for Baltimore; Ray Lewis rampaged up and down the field like a loosed bull, Jamal Mohammad ran a kick-off back for a touchdown, and Trent Dilfer couldn't miss. Joe and I shouted our loud, frantic banter at the TV, as we gave out our own play-by-play of the game. Ali—uncounted single-malts under his belt—sounded off like a Mexican soccer announcer every time the Ravens scored—"GGGGGOOOOOOOOOOOOOOOOOOOOAAAALLLLLL!"

There were apparently other parties going on in the apartment complex, and at halftime everybody flooded into the hallway until the entire floor became one big party. Someone had ordered pizzas hours earlier, and the pizza delivery guy was still at the party: his hat was on backward and he was talking to a nursing school graduate. Nerf balls were being hurled through the air, and a girl was going around showing everybody her purple and black Ravens bra.

As the clock ticked away in the fourth quarter, someone shouted, "Let's start a bonfire!" and all eyes fell upon Joe's dining room set. Joe was not in favor of this idea, and hastily suggested that we all head down to the Inner Harbor—and away from his furniture—where we could celebrate victory with the whole city. The crowd shouted out in agreement and we poured ourselves into the street.

Pratt Street was a parking lot. It seemed all of Maryland was converging on the Inner Harbor. People were dancing, honking horns and high-fiving each other. Helicopters were hovering overhead, and news crews were everywhere. It was beautiful, and it went on for hours. No violence, no posturing, no acrimony, just exuberance, joy and mutual delight.

To understand what that victory meant to the City of Baltimore, you have to understand Baltimore—a squalid, deadly, beautiful disaster. Baltimore was like that stray dog from your neighborhood when you were a kid; the one that didn't belong to anybody, but was always around when the great events of your childhood occurred.

This was the dog with only three legs, and a missing eye from a fight he lost. This was the dog you couldn't pet without clumps of hair falling out; that had sores, mange, ticks, fleas, worms, and chiggers. But this was the dog that always came running up, wagging his tail, when you called out for "Lucky."

Later on, exhausted from the night, Ali and I walked back to our apartments. And as we began to walk home, graduation looming only months ahead, we began to discuss our future plans. "I'm going to buy a house in the county, and I'm going to try to help my brother get into school over here," said Ali. We grew silent again, contemplating the steps necessary to do that. "What about you?" he asked. "What are you going to do?"

"I'm really not sure," I said. "I'm not as squared-away as you are, Ali. I've got a lot of losses on my scorecard. I'm divorced, my grades aren't that good, I've never really had much success outside the Army, and the success I've had in the Army is just from showing up at the right place, at the right time, in the right uniform."

"What, are you kidding me?" replied Ali. "You're a Green Beret. How many people can say that? You enlisted, what, eight years ago? And what's your rank now?"

"Staff sergeant."

"Yeah, and when did you make your staff sergeant?"

"After five years."

"I don't know much about the Army, but I know soldiers don't routinely make staff sergeant in five years."

"Yeah, the Army's been good to me."

"Hell, you've been good to the Army," said Ali. "Dude, you're a reservist in the Special Forces, *and* you'll soon be an attorney. You've got the world on a string!"

"You're right," I said. "Things are pretty good. The problems I have other people would kill for."

"Damn right. Dude, we're on the brink. Soooooo, what are you going to do?"

I realized it at once. I knew exactly what I was going to do. "I'm going to New York," I said. "I'm going to take that job with the Brooklyn DA's Office, and I'm going to do what people do when they go to New York. I'm going to become the person I want to be, not just the person I happen to turn out as."

IN THE COUNTY OF KINGS

SEPTEMBER 4, 2001

"HELLLLLLLOOOOO EVERYBODY!" The tiny, middle-aged woman standing on the stage laughed out loud as she spoke into the microphone. "I'm Deputy Assistant District Attorney Edelstein, and I want to be the first to welcome you to Brooklyn . . . And if you're *from* Brooklyn, then I just want to say, fuhgetaboutit!" With that, Deputy ADA Edelstein laughed again.

Mrs. Edelstein was a plump woman with jet black hair, brilliant blue eyes and an infectious laugh. She stood in front of us, the incoming class of more than eighty Assistant District Attorneys, and held us spellbound—instantly, she became all our mothers. "Yes," she said, "that's right, *Mrs.* Edelstein. My husband, Morty—also an attorney—says 'No Trespassing' signs must be posted. So you're all on notice!" Again with the laugh.

"Okay," she continued, "so before we get started, who knows any Brooklyn jokes? That *don't* have the F-word in them? Nobody! That does not speak well for our borough. But, that's okay, I speak well for our borough. And I want to tell you a little about it so that you better appreciate your important role in the life of this wonderful city and this, its most extraordinary borough." Mrs. Edelstein opened her arms like she was opening a book.

"But let me start by asking, when each of you took this job did you understand that Kings County meant Brooklyn, New York?" Everyone said yes. "Good. That's very good, because it sure would have been awkward to have to tell you that now."

The guy beside me whispered, "What kind of a dipshit wouldn't know that?" I looked over at him and rolled my eyes, as if to say, "Yeah, what the hell?" But I was thinking, *I didn't know until my second interview.*

Mrs. Edelstein brushed away some invisible crumbs from her skirt. "The thing you need to know about Brooklyn, the thing that is never appreciated about Brooklyn, is that it is . . . *just* . . . *so* . . . *big!*" And with that Mrs. Edelstein's eyes grew wide, and she stretched out her arms, just like teacher did back in second grade. "In fact, if Brooklyn were still a city unto itself, it would be the fourth largest city in the U.S.—right behind New York, Los Angeles, and Chicago. There are 2,300,000 people living in Brooklyn. It is by far the largest borough of the five boroughs making up the great City of New York." Mrs. Edelstein paused, as if to let us know that now was the time for a history lesson.

"Up until 1897 Brooklyn was a city unto itself. We didn't need any 'New York' back then. The world's most famous bridge isn't called the 'New York Bridge' is it? How many of you took the subway in to work today?" Almost every hand shot up. "And how many got off at 'Borough Hall'?"

This was uncanny. I looked over at the guy next to me and he was looking back at me, and we both had our hands in the air. "What is this woman, a psychic?" he said in a thick Long Island accent. I looked over at the guy. He was wearing a well-cut, charcoal gray suit, a crisp white shirt and a solid red tie. He was lean and athletic-looking, young—maybe 27—but already going bald. He looked every inch the tough, Jewish prosecutor you didn't want to mess with.

I introduced myself in a hushed whisper, and he said his name was Joel "from Longah Eye-landah." We shook hands under the desks. "I'm licensed already," he continued. "I've been waiting for this day six months."

We both turned our eyes back to Mrs. Edelstein. "Well, that station was originally 'Brooklyn Hall,' and it sits right below the old City Hall building of Brooklyn."

Joel looked at me as if sizing me up. "Where you from?" he asked.

"Maryland," I said. "Went to law school at University of Maryland."

"Brooklyn, you should know," Mrs. Edelstein continued, "is unique in that fully one quarter of all families in America can trace their ancestral history to having at one point lived in Brooklyn. Since this country became a country, Brooklyn has been the first home for new Americans—and it still is today. You will find Brooklyn about the most diverse place you have ever lived in."

Joel jerked up his head as if to say, 'figures.' Then he said, "Went to school on Longah Eye-landah." I didn't ask where, I had a feeling the place wasn't exactly covered in ivy.

"But even before this country was a country, there was a Brooklyn. Back then it was called *Breukelen*." Mrs. Edelstein wrote the word on a dry erase board. "*Breukelen* was then a forgotten settlement across the East River from the Dutch town of New Amsterdam, in the Dutch colony of New Netherlands. The Dutch had been halfhearted colonists in America—nothing like the British or the French. But eventually, the Dutch did something about this sad state of affairs, they commissioned the great Peter Stuyvesant to take command of the colony." Mrs. Edelstein paused for a moment to give proper solemnity to the name. "If you're from New York, then you know who Peter Stuyvesant was, but if you're not, then you should learn about this fearless soldier, statesman and patriot—well, of course he was a patriot for *the Dutch*!" There was that laugh again.

"My dad was a deputy assistant here for twenty years," Joel said proudly. "And my brother was here for five years." I said nothing, but nodded my head. Here was a guy who could be a big help—a good friend or a terrible enemy. I took note.

"In 1682, the mighty British Empire came to *Breukelen*. They wanted Peter Stuyvesant to surrender the colony of New Netherlands, and they sent very generous terms of surrender to him. But Peter laughed at them. He took their letter of terms and tore it up into little pieces. He was a fighter, and he would rather go down in a blaze of glory than surrender to an enemy of his King!" Mrs. Edelstein had captured the house, all of us rooting for Peter Stuyvesant.

"But the people of New Amsterdam were not made of such stern stuff," she continued, her voice dropping mournfully. "They collected the little pieces Peter had tossed at the British officer and pasted them back together. They read the terms of surrender and thought they were pretty good. So the next morning a delegation of the leading members of the colony arrived at Peter's door and delivered to him a letter demanding that he surrender. More than 90 of the town's most prominent citizens signed that letter, but do you think Mr. Stuyvesant gave a whit what those weaklings wanted? He would fight!"

I looked over at Joel, and he looked back at me, both of us smiling and cheering on the Dutch Governor. "But at the bottom of that letter," continued Mrs. Edelstein, "the very last signature was the one that broke Peter Stuyvesant's heart. For there at the bottom of the page, Peter Stuyvesant saw the name of . . . his . . . very . . . own . . . son."

The room went still. All of us were outraged. How could he do such a thing? How could Peter Stuyvesant's son break Mrs. Edelstein's heart? Mrs. Edelstein lowered her head, and took a minute to collect herself. Eventually, she raised her head. Mrs. Edelstein was a strong woman, and she would not be broken by the slings and arrows of outrageous fortune. "So, anyway," she finally managed to say, "you are in a terrific place, you have a wonderful boss, and the people of Brooklyn have placed an important trust in you. Do the very best you can every day, and I know you will make me proud, and you'll make Brooklyn proud as well." Mrs. Edelstein left the stage to a standing ovation, and as soon as she stepped down from the podium, she picked up her files and proceeded briskly to work.

Then, the senior leadership of the DA's Office stepped onto the stage. Each officer was introduced and gave a short greeting. You could see that they were all sincerely glad to have us with them. There was no pretense, they were happy to bring us on board. Still, it was very formal. They were not our buddies by any stretch of the imagination. I was reminded of the speech given to me and the other new soldiers by the company first sergeant when we arrived at our unit after basic training. He huddled us all together in his office and said, "I'm glad each and every one of you is here, and I hope you all like your new unit as much as I do." Then he paused and said, "But if I have to see any one of you *individually* in my office, then you are wrong, and I will break you like a dry stick."

As we were being introduced to the key leaders, the District Attorney, Ted Hughes, waited at the edge of the stage. Joel leaned over to me and out of the side of his mouth said, "There's the old man."

"Yeah, Ted Hughes," I responded.

"Guy's a freakin' legend in New Yawk."

"His reputation goes beyond the city," I said.

"Let me tell ya a little somethin' about Ted Hughes," replied Joel, ignoring me. "Guy's classic Paddy—right out of the old school—but somehow he manages to keep swimmin' in the waters of modern Brooklyn, and he ain't been hooked yet."

Oh, I thought, *you're gonna school me on Ted Hughes?* "He's played his cards well," I said. "His personal life is spotless, married to the same woman he met in law school, has a brood of kids, all of whom have kept their noses clean. Good work."

Joel was not to be outdone. "He started out as the Commissioner of the Fire Department—head of the FDNY."

"Oh yeah, he did that," I responded, letting Joel know I could take it up a notch, too. "He also ran for Governor—did pretty well."

"I thought he got robbed in his run for Attorney General." Joel responded with just a hint of challenge in his voice.

I smiled. "It's no secret that if things cut the right way, he'd be ready to make a run at the premier municipal office in the country."

"A run for Mayor of New York?" said Joel. "I'm sure he wouldn't turn it down, but he's a little long in the tooth for that, don't you think?"

"Meh," I said with a shrug.

"You know he was a Marine," said Joel.

No, you didn't, I thought to myself. *Don't tell me you fell for that bit of malarkey Hughes sometimes tosses around.* "No, he wasn't," I said. "He sometimes peddles that bullshit, but he was no Marine." Mr. Hughes always has a personal interview with whomever he hires. Mine was in his office, and as I looked around his "Love Me" wall, I noticed a plaque from the Marines. I asked him if he had been a Marine, and he said yes. Being interested, I asked what unit he was in, and he coughed out something about getting asthma in the Officer Basic School. I wasn't trying to dime him out, but it got kind of awkward, because we both realized he was just pumping up his resume. "He likes to tell people he was," I said, "but he wasn't. He got asthma or some shit, and fell out of Officer Basic at Quantico."

"Well, he was in, wasn't he?"

"That's not a Marine," I said firmly. "You're not a Marine until you *graduate*. Anybody can fail out of Basic. Dan Rather failed basic."

"Are you a Marine?" Joel replied, stunned by my sudden seriousness.

"No," I said, "I was . . . uh, in the paratrooper in the Army. But I worked regularly with the Marines—and the DA ain't one." For a moment I was embarrassed that I had brought the subject up, but then I remembered that I had not, Joel had. All I had done was set the record straight. Still, I felt like I had done something wrong.

"Well," said Joel, after a difficult silence, "he's our boss, so you better keep that stuff cool."

"Hey, man, we never had this conversation," I said. "I like the guy. He gave me a job."

When Mr. Hughes walked to the podium, we all took to our feet. Waving us down with his hands, the District Attorney began, "As newly minted Assistant DAs, you will be given misdemeanor cases—many, many misdemeanor cases." A low groan echoed through the room, as we glory-hungry attorneys contemplated the road to stardom. "After a time, you will move to the grand jury and begin indicting felonies. The cases you indict in grand jury will stay with you. You will follow them through to trial." The DA looked to one of the deputies and smiled. "The contract you each signed when you agreed to work for the

Brooklyn DA's Office is a three year contract, and there is no reason to think that you will not have a number of felony trials under your belts by the time that contract has expired." The District Attorney continued, "You may want to remain with us after the contract expires—many, many do—or you may move on. But either way, you will be well-versed and highly skilled in criminal litigation when the time for that decision comes." The District Attorney paused, clearly finished with his overview. "Tomorrow," he reminded us, "The NYPD commanders of Brooklyn North and Brooklyn South will brief you. I would pay close attention. The NYPD has gone through a revolution in the last ten years, a revolution that has captured the attention of the world. Crime in this city has fallen exponentially. The Mayor loves to take credit for this, but I'd like to think the District Attorney of the city's largest borough might have had something to do with that decline, as well." We clapped, and the DA smiled.

District Attorney Hughes gripped the podium with both hands. "I selected you all personally," he said. "I picked you for your qualities as attorneys, as public servants and as fair-minded and unbiased human beings. If I was wrong . . . well, then we will sort that out. But looking at you all right now, I feel very good about this class, very good indeed."

Mr. Hughes exited the stage, and we rose to our feet clapping loudly. Immediately upon his exit, a short, red-faced deputy came to the podium, lowered the mic and said, "Your mentor-Deputy District Attorneys will now come up. If they call out your name, then you are in their section. They will take you to whichever zone has been selected for your training. You will take all orders from him or her until your training is complete; the day your bar results are posted."

After 15 minutes of deputies shouting out names, there were only a few of us still sitting, but neither Joel nor I had been called. Then an attractive woman with long hair and a short skirt stepped forward to the mic, popped her chewing gum, and in a thick Long Island accent said, "My name is Tracy Silverstein, and I'm the deputy in charge of the Grey Zone. If you hear me call your name, move your tail down to me with a sense of urgency. You want to lollygag your way down, I'll put your ass in a sling." Joel was called, and then I heard my name called as well. I immediately double-timed it down to Tracy. I didn't want my ass in a sling.

Once Tracy collected her brood of six new ADAs, she began firing off directives: "You will be here every day by 7:55. You will have your New York Criminal Law and Criminal Code books on you at all times. You will dress as professionals at all times. You will be at every place you are told to be five minutes early. You will treat senior ADAs as your superiors—because *they are* your superiors. You will treat each other with respect, and you will never forget and forever be glad that you had Tracy Silverstein as your instructor."

Tracy brought us back to the conference room of the Grey Zone on the 13th floor of the DA's Office, and we filled out forms and questionnaires, but mostly we got to know each other. Since we were all in the exact same boat, and since we all were afraid of screwing up, we bonded immediately. We talked about ourselves, we went to lunch and talked about ourselves some more. Then we came back and Tracy let us have an hour of free time in which we talked about ourselves. We went to Superior Court to watch a murder trial. Then we went to Criminal Court and watched other ADAs arraign defendants on charges varying in severity from open container violations to armed robbery—and the entire time we talked about ourselves. After all that talking about ourselves and hanging out with one another, Tracy brought us back to the conference room and asked us to tell the group about ourselves. Somehow we still had more to say.

There were six of us. First there was Claude from Nigeria. Claude was about my age, and was, he claimed, a scion of an important Nigerian banking family (aren't they all?). He had a terrific sense of humor, and a broad, infectious laugh. He had been recently divorced from an American citizen in a manner that gave off the strong whiff of marriage fraud—but, whatever, I liked him.

Next there was Patrick, a few years younger than I was, of Irish descent and part of that whole Red-Sox/Patriots/Celtics loving Irish mafia that makes New England so impossible to like.

Then there was Jose, a Brooklyn born *"Nuevo Rican."* Jose was quick-minded and had an eye for style. He wore a bespoke navy blue pinstripe suit with a white shirt and light blue tie and matching kerchief in his jacket pocket. He was lean and smooth—the picture of *suavemente*. Although Jose was only 25 years old, he was already well-connected to the Democratic Party, and was clearly going to make a name for himself in the city. He was very personable, you couldn't help but like him. When we broke for lunch, I watched him getting up from his chair, elegant and polished, and I said, "You're going to be the Mayor of New York City, someday." Jose blushed and feigned indifference, but as he was walking away, he checked himself in the mirror and thrust out his jaw proudly.

The last of the guys was Joel, whom I'd met at the introduction. Intense and sharp, Joel didn't like to joke around. He was the son of a Brooklyn ADA and the brother of another Brooklyn ADA. He was a man one had to admire. He had a knowledge of criminal procedure and case law that I knew I would never attain, and from the start I envied him. Joel took himself very seriously, but with a sincerity that was touching. It was obvious he was going to go far in life.

The only woman in our section was Nancy. She was an organized, intelligent, warm and personable black woman in her mid-twenties. She came to New York from South Carolina, and always carried herself with the amused smile of a woman who found humor in the ridiculousness of life. She was smarter than all of us, and she knew it, but to her that fact only seemed comical.

We were released around 5:30. I got on the subway at the height of rush hour and squeezed myself in with the army of evening commuters. I took the subway to the World Trade Center and headed toward the PATH train terminal to pick up my train to Jersey City, where I had a temporary apartment. But once I was inside the WTC, I got the urge to look around and check things out. The train station was swelteringly hot, but the mall was cool and invigorating. There were so many people running around—people just like me, burrowing along, tired and bored and worn-out from the work day. It was like something you'd see in one of those smart-guy films that are supposed to make you think. Where you're supposed to feel overwhelmed and dejected by the furious anonymity of the 'faceless city,' or the 'heartless corporation,' or the 'stifling sameness'—or whatever. But I wasn't depressed at all. I was elated.

I sat down on a bench and watched the wave upon wave of people hurriedly pass by, and an incredible sense of peace came over me. I was an assistant district attorney for the greatest city in the world. I was a drone—just another guy—busying myself with my tiny task. But I was also a part of all of . . . *this!* This splendid, astonishing thing that is New York City, in all its greatness, all its depravity, all its hostile indifference. I was in the heart of a free people performing the tasks they had freely chosen to do. It felt at once both extraordinary and completely unremarkable.

THE PROUD TOWERS

**From a proud tower in the town
Death looks gigantically down.**

Edgar Allen Poe

I got up at 6:15 a.m. (three hits on the snooze button past wake-up), showered, shaved, and threw on a suit. Before walking out the door, I looked at myself in the mirror, just to make sure the same steel-eyed, barrel-chested defender of justice was heading into work that had left the night before. I then proceeded briskly, purposefully and with a manly stride to the Pavonia PATH station, and stepped on board the WTC train at exactly 7:20. While on board, I said my prayers and repeated my Tony Robbins affirmations—"Visualize success, realize success."

By then we were pulling into the World Trade Center, where I stepped off the train with the above-mentioned purposeful stride, and boldly made my way onto the Brooklyn-bound subway. Disembarking at Borough Hall, I walked to the DA's office, bought a large coffee and "everything" bagel from the Pakistani gentleman in the kiosk on Jay Street, and arrived at my desk five minutes before eight.

At exactly 7:55, I sat down at my desk, and silently congratulated myself for being the first—and therefore smartest—person in the office. The warm glow of self-satisfaction brightened my morning for exactly one minute, at which time I realized why no one was there. We had been instructed to report across the street at the Brooklyn Law School for our 8:00 a.m. training lecture. I raced across Adams Street to the BLS, caught a lucky break on the elevator and slid into the lecture hall just as the door was closing—managing to be "noticeably" late, but not "actually" late.

Returning to the DA's building after the lecture, I got on the elevator with this guy who (I swear) had a 1960s-style transistor radio against his ear, and what were clearly hair plugs in his head. As the elevator arrived on the 13th floor, the guy shrugged his shoulders and said, "They're sayin' a plane crashed into one of the towers of the World Trade Center—what are the odds?"

That seemed peculiar. Maybe it was a Piper Cub flying around the downtown area doing a traffic report, but even that didn't make sense. You can't fly anywhere around those towers in any kind of plane. Still, my office had a great view of lower Manhattan and the East River, and I wanted to check it out. I walked toward my office and as I got closer, I could see that there were already a number of people huddled around other office windows, their eyes affixed across the river. Exactly at the moment that I stepped across the threshold of my office, the second plane slammed into the second tower, and I saw a tremendous fireball erupt from the point of impact.

"Oh God!" a woman yelled. "Another one!" Simultaneously, we all realized that this was terrorism—this was what is meant by terror.

"Get in here, Grey Zone!" Tracy shouted, almost maniacally. "Get in here where I can count you!" Gone was the iron-willed, no-nonsense prosecutor. In her place was the efficient, concerned protector. Tracy picked up the phone and saw that we could not call out, so she had each of us write down the names of three people whom we needed to contact. By now the entire office was in crisis mode.

"Bonita's got her aunt on her cell!" someone shouted. Bonita was a receptionist with an aunt in the South Bronx with whom she hadn't spoken to in years. Bonita collected ten names of people who needed to be contacted, and she forwarded them to her aunt. Most of the land lines were down, but Lavronda, another receptionist across the hallway in the Red Zone, got hold of her half-sister, Tina, and she gave Tina a list of ten more names of people to call. Tina got hold of seven of the ten, and came back with reports of those seven's knowledge of people who either were or were not accounted for. For the next two hours Lavronda and Bonita shuttled information and whereabouts for everybody on the 13th floor, and if I were mayor, I'd give them both the key to the city.

We all sat in Tracy's office staring at the horrific scene transpiring across the East River and listening to the radio. Soon we began hearing the first reports of the larger attack. We heard a report that the Pentagon had been "flattened," then a report that the Capital dome had collapsed, the gates of the White House had been breached, and the State Department had been hit. At first I believed the news reports. It sounded like an incredible take-down. A part of me was frankly impressed. Then an "unconfirmed report" came over the radio that a car bomb had exploded in front of the Supreme Court building. Some woman cried out, and other people gasped, but I jumped up in the air at the news, actually delighted. "Bullshit!" I exclaimed. "They didn't hit the Supreme Court."

"What are you talking about, Tim?" Pat said. "They just reported that they did."

"Are you kidding me?" I said. "These fuckin' guys don't know what the Supreme Court *is!*"

"But we don't know who did this," Pat said, almost like he believed it.

"Oh, put it back in the deck, Pat," I said. "Of course we know who did this. What do you think, it was the KKK? Everybody knows who did this, and we're all just pretending we don't."

"We haven't been told yet," said some girl.

"You have to be *told*?" I said. "And you call yourself an attorney?" I threw my hands in the air. "Radical Muslims did this," I said. "And they *didn't* set off a car bomb at the Supreme Court building. They can't wrap their minds around such a thing. These are people who want to chop off hands for shoplifting. How are *they* going to understand a court of appeals?"

"Anyway," continued Pat, "the Supreme Court has been hit."

"No it hasn't," I said. "And probably a lot of this other stuff didn't happen either." The room became heavy with awkwardness. I felt like the boy who noticed that the emperor had no clothes. Sometime after that, the order came down to evacuate the building, because—you know—after the World Trade Center and the Pentagon, the Kings County District Attorney's Office was the obvious next target.

Once outside, there wasn't too much to do. Someone suggested that we give blood, so about 70 of us went to the Red Cross. But the sole nurse there had already barricaded the door—apparently, the Red Cross wasn't sitting around prepped and ready for the wave of New Yorkers to suddenly get a conscience. Jose suggested we go down to the Brooklyn Heights Promenade, and about twenty of us headed down Montague Street toward the river. The Promenade was crowded with thousands of people by the time we got there, all watching in hushed horror. A few minutes after we arrived, the first tower fell. Even as I watched, I couldn't believe I was actually seeing it. The upper floors just began to slide, and from it a large plume of smoke and dust covered the view. The midsection of the building was enveloped in smoke, and then I saw the upper section just collapse on itself. All along the Promenade, screams and cries went up. I kept thinking only a part of it had fallen, like a part of a glacier that slides away. But I was wrong.

The entire building went down of a piece. I kept thinking the rest of the tower was hidden away in the smoke and dust, but then the smoke cleared away and nothing remained, just a big hole in the sky.

Then, after the second tower fell, there was an uneasy feeling among everyone that the worst was yet to come. We waited and watched, thinking this was just a preliminary action, but nothing happened. After a while we started to feel ridiculous. I huddled up with Claude, Pat, Jose and Joel, and said, "Listen, this is the biggest thing that's ever happened to this city in its history. Whatever we do, we've got to get into Manhattan." I wish I could say we were serious and determined to help our fellow citizens, but it wasn't like that at all. We were more like twelve year olds, and just wanted action and adventure. We walked to the Brooklyn Bridge, and as we drew closer, we began to see the first of the wave of refugees streaming silently across the bridge from Manhattan. The police were guarding the bridge and wouldn't let anyone into Manhattan. They looked dazed and overworked. I walked up to one police officer and flashed him my District Attorney Badge, making like I was on official business.

"What the hell's this?" he said wearily.

"We're with the DA's Office. We got to get in there."

The cop stared at the badge, like he was trying to make sense of it. I could see his mind flipping through possibilities and none of them registering. "Nobody's getting into the City," he finally said, and tossed the badge back at me.

Dejected, we walked over by the barricades and watched the people walking by. They came in hordes, thousands of them. And that childish yearning for adventure was replaced by horror. They were like zombies, shell shocked, their eyes confused and pleading. They were completely covered in a fine, delicate ash and looked like exquisitely crafted works of art—living, moving statues, intricately depicting human beings. The ash was so fine it seemed to touch even into people's thoughts, revealing things about them you would not usually notice. I saw the pattern of the leather on a woman's shoe and realized how conscientiously she had dressed herself that morning. The herringbone of a man's suit emerged from the fine ash, and I imaged how proud he was when he bought that suit. Whatever feeling of historic witness I had was gone, and all that remained was a sinking feeling of dread.

Pat was visibly shaken, and said, "Man, I've gotta have a cigarette." He pulled out his pack and asked around. I almost wanted a cigarette as well, and I didn't even smoke. A stunningly beautiful girl broke away from the refugees, came over to us and asked Pat for a cigarette. She was wearing a pleated skirt, and each pleat was perfectly covered in gray ash. She had a Louis Vuitton purse, and through the ash I could see each "LV" embossed on the material. Pat gave her a cigarette and the lighter, but her hands were shaking so much she couldn't get it lit. "Here," said Pat, helpfully, as he grabbed the lighter. But his hands were shaking as well. Finally, he held the one hand with the other, and lit the cigarette.

We stood in a circle—Pat and the girl smoking—none of us speaking, only staring out across the river, sickened by it all. Just then small, gray flakes began falling on us. I was wearing a navy blue suit, and I noticed these flakes collecting on my lapel and shoulders. "What is this?" I said to no one in particular. I brushed the flakes off, but more fell on. "It's *ash*," I said with disgust. "The ashes are falling on us." It was revolting, like the hands of those murderers were reaching out and caressing me, mocking me, covering me in their filth. It made me sick just thinking about it. I took off my jacket and beat it against a tree. The others were looking at me like I'd lost my mind.

"Get it off!" I shouted. "Get this filth off of me!" It was like the filth of an animal covering me. I could see their eyes, their murderous eyes laughing at me, at us, at the nation, and it made me sick. Suddenly, I couldn't breathe and I began to hyperventilate. I couldn't get air, but I couldn't stop breathing. I fell to the ground trying to get air, trying to stop breathing. I felt disgraced and humiliated, as I gasped for air. I had to get their filth off of me. I couldn't stand to think of it touching me. I felt like their dead hands were pawing me. But the flakes kept falling, and each flake sickened me worse than the one before. They were mocking me, and I couldn't stand the thought of being mocked by such filthy people. Every fleck, every bit of their debris disgusted me, enraged me. It was in my hair now, and on my pants and even on my shoes. The girl came to me and gave me a bag to breathe into. It slowed my breathing. I began to recover. "I won't take it," I yelled. "I won't take their filth!" But I had already taken it. Their filth, their mark was already on me.

The others all gathered around me. "Are you going to be okay?" The girl asked. "Do you want anything?"

Spittle was hanging from my mouth, and my voice was hoarse, but I looked up at her and I said, "Yeah, I want something. I want war. Give me war."

THE GIRL ON THE COVER OF THE NEW YORK POST

September 14, 2001

You know how when there's a catastrophe somewhere—like a train wreck or a shooting rampage—and there is always someone in the office whose second cousin or niece's babysitter or whatever "was almost on that train," or "went to high school with that shooter-guy?" At the DA's office, you *wish* it were that attenuated. You don't hear "second cousin" or "niece's babysitter." You hear, "My brother is missing." You hear, "Bridget's husband was a firefighter. . . Bridget won't be in today."

I read a quote in the *Times* yesterday from some guy who'd gotten out of the first tower: "We were all running down the stairs as fast as we could, and they [the firemen] kept running up the stairs as fast as they could. They kept coming—hundreds of them—and they were all so young."

The commute to work is now a nightmare; what had taken 25 minutes now takes well over an hour. The trains run infrequently, and there are constant delays for security purposes. Although the cars are packed, everybody's helpful, friendly and cooperative. No one complains. There is a definite "us" versus "them" feeling in the city right now—and "us" is feeling pretty sure of victory.

The courts were closed for regular business, and there was nothing much to do, but it seemed important to get to work anyway. Jose, Joel, Pat and I went to the Criminal Court and helped out at arraignments—that being the only part of court that must stay open. At lunch, we grabbed a couple of slices of pizza on Court Street, and when we came out of the store, there was a Humvee sitting across the street with a squad of National Guardsmen from the 42nd Infantry Division setting up a "check point" (although they didn't actually *check* anybody that I noticed). The other guys were impressed, but I was sort of embarrassed. The soldier in the cupola was pimping an M-60 machine gun, but he didn't have any bullets. The other two guys had M-16s, but they didn't have magazines in them either. I did a quick little recon of the scene and didn't see any evidence that they had the ability to defend themselves, much less anyone else. I'm not a big fan of giving soldiers weapons without bullets. They did that when Hurricane Andrew came into Miami in the 1990s, and a bunch of soldiers from the 82nd either had their weapons stolen, or just said they did. Either way it was bad for the Army.

Before returning to court, Pat wanted to buy a newspaper, so we stepped into a bodega and on the front page of the *New York Post* was a picture that crushed me. There on the cover of the paper was a picture of a woman searching for her fiancé. The woman was a stunner— blonde, stylishly dressed, and with a large but tasteful diamond on her ring finger. It just hurt to look at that picture, because I knew the type so well. This was the woman who'd been busting my balls all my life. She was the complete package and she knew it, confident, cold and beautiful—to the manner born. Jay McInerney described her best in *Bright Lights, Big City*, "She had cheekbones to break your heart, and you knew she was the real thing when she steadfastly refused to acknowledge your presence. She possessed secrets—about islands, about horses, about French pronunciations—that you would never know."

This was the woman who had rolled her eyes at me all my life. The woman I longed for, and who disdained me. She was my unattainable woman, and here she was, on the cover of *The New York Post*, broken and crying—a woman of iron will and unlimited privilege utterly shattered by the savagery of a brutal band of men. I would have liked to have felt some low pleasure in her tragedy, but instead it buckled me. For this was *my* untouchable woman. This was *my* perfect jewel—and here she was laid to waste.

GRAND JURY

On the first Monday of October, we ADA trainees from the Grey Zone were herded into the grand jury office in the Supreme Court on Adams Street. We were excited because we'd be spending the entire week in Grand Jury, where they indict felonies.

At exactly 8:00 a.m. ADA Vivian Tomasi stepped in front of the podium. Vivian was very well put together. She was attractive, smartly dressed and she wore a rather large engagement ring on her left ring finger. "Hello, and good morning" she said, the fingers on her left hand fidgeting happily. "My name is Vivian Tomasi and I am the deputy ADA for the Grey Zone, Grand Jury." Then she added with a beaming smile, "I'm not sure who's going to take over for me when Brad and I are away on our honeymoon—which is 23 days away—but I'm it for now." Subtle, she was not.

"To say that things have gotten back to normal," Vivian continued, "is a bit of a stretch, but life goes on, the courts are open, and New Yorkers are back to committing crimes. We're on the rebound!"

I looked around the room. It was wall to wall with files. You couldn't open the door without moving a chair, and the only window hadn't seen a wash since the Nixon administration. "You will note that our offices here are cramped, and they open onto a large waiting room where the arresting officers, the investigating officers, and the various witnesses wait for their turn to testify. Although some of the people in the waiting room are civilians, at least 90% of them are cops, and most of the cops are men, so it's like a locker room over there—you'll hear it all."

Right then, as if on cue, a cop yelled over to his co-worker, "Well, if it isn't Mick O'Shea? Jee-zus, look at you, Mickey, you've put on some weight! Hey, somebody frisk this guy, he looks like he's tryin' to shoplift a VW!"

"Is that you, Di Palma?" replied O'Shea. "Well, it warms my heart to see an I-talian up before noon—must feel lonely."

Vivian waited this out, then began in earnest, "As you know, grand juries are constituted to determine whether there is enough evidence to try someone for a felony. The burden of proof for a criminal indictment is 'reasonable suspicion'." Vivian tapped the flat of her left hand on the podium when she said 'reasonable suspicion,' causing her engagement ring to clack against the wood. Vivian smiled. "Think of reasonable suspicion as a 25% chance the guy did it. If the grand jury decides there is reasonable suspicion, they will vote the indictment a 'True Bill', and the defendant will stand trial. If the grand jury decides that there is not a reasonable suspicion, it will vote, 'No True Bill'." I found myself tapping the flat of my left hand on the table. I wasn't sure why. "Because the standard for indictment (reasonable suspicion)," Vivian continued, "is so much lower than the standard for conviction (beyond a reasonable doubt), it has often been said that a good prosecutor can indict a ham sandwich. In some jurisdictions this may be the case," Vivian touched her ring nervously, "but in Brooklyn, grand juries can derail very quickly. So I stress to you, in no uncertain terms, realize that grand juries are delicate things, and that they must be treated with the greatest respect. Jurors do nutty stuff. They fall asleep, they get drunk, they write you pornographic notes. But they decide if you get an indictment, so you best treat them with the utmost respect."

Vivian tugged at her ring for reassurance. "The grand jury system is the greatest system of justice in the world; where else do the citizens among whom the defendant actually lives determine whether or not the state can haul him before a court of law and make him answer criminal charges?"

So that was Monday, and all week long all we heard in the office was how Vivian was God's gift to the grand jury. Vivian was brilliant, Vivian was top of her class—it was all Vivian all the time. Frankly, I wasn't seeing it. The only thing I saw was Vivian consumed with her wedding plans.

That week, I thought Vivian was just an ADA who was skating along doing the bare minimum to get by. I wasn't learning anything about the grand jury from her. What I was learning about was Vivian's bridesmaids' gowns, the color of the seat cushions for Vivian's reception, and the seating arrangements (Uncle Dominic, don't even *think* about sitting next to Aunt Rita). While not impressed with her performance as an ADA, I was impressed with her ability to make caterers jump through hoops, to pick tasteful floral arrangements, and to scold bridesmaids for not getting the shoes Vivian specifically selected.

Do I think Vivian just pulled those shoes from her back pocket? No, I do not. Why would Vivian go through the trouble—and yes it was a lot of trouble—of picking out shoes, if Vivian didn't care whether Sheila wore them to Vivian's, yes, Vivian's wedding? When Sheila gets married (fat chance of that happening), Sheila can pick out the shoes, but last Vivian checked, this was Vivian's wedding, not Sheila's, so Sheila better pony-up and buy the shoes Vivian choose for her! Did Vivian make herself clear? Yes, Vivian made herself very clear.

One day, detectives from the Eight-Four Precinct came in with evidence from a raid on a house that was selling guns, and they brought with them a box of evidence collected at the scene. At the bottom of the box of evidence was a packet of photographs that they found in the house.

The photographs couldn't be used at trial, but they were interesting nonetheless. The pictures were a whole series of shots of this very attractive Latina girl—no more than 17 years old—posing with the guns for sale. The girl wore tight jeans and a cute pink hoodie. In the first picture, she was smiling wickedly at the camera, with a pair of .45 caliber semi-automatic pistols tucked into her waist band. In the next picture, she wore that same smile and was now pointing loaded revolvers at the camera. The pictures got progressively better. She had taken off the hoodie, and wore only a clingy white T-shirt. She was laughing now, and had the revolvers to her lips, pretending to blow the smoke from their barrels. It was picture after picture of this beautiful young girl cavorting around with the very guns that would likely one day kill her. The whole time we were going through the box of evidence, Vivian was on the cell phone prattling on to her mother about who was and was not invited to the wedding. When she got off the phone, she took one look at the pictures, twisted her engagement ring sternly around her finger, and said, "Well, I can tell you right now, *she's* not invited."

Unsurprisingly, I had not taken Vivian quite as seriously as many others had. That was until one particular morning. Around 9:00 a.m. Police Officer Jim Dolan came into the grand jury office announcing himself with great fanfare, and looking for ADA Vivian Tomasi. It was immediately apparent Officer Dolan was not your average, smokin' and jokin' flatfoot. This dude was wired tight. He had that lean, muscular look of a real shit-kicker. "I'm with the Street Crimes Unit," he said (like we hadn't guessed), "and I want to make sure my gun arrest gets an indictment."

I told him Vivian was in the grand jury on another matter, but I asked what I could do. He just repeated to me that he was here to make sure his gun case got an indictment. I pulled the file and read the report. Officer Dolan and his partner, Officer Scales, had received credible information that a group of men were hanging out in the park after dark waiting for a drug dealer, whom they believed had cheated them. Officer Dolan had been informed that at least one of these men had brandished a handgun. This same man had composed a rap song about executing the drug dealer, which he was singing continually (as is the fashion).

Upon receipt of this intelligence, Officers Dolan and Scales moved aggressively to the park where the men were reported to be waiting, and found a group of five men hanging around in exactly the place they were told they would be. Seeing the two plain-clothed officers approaching, one of the men broke away from the group and walked over to a trashcan and put something in it. Dolan went immediately to the trashcan and found a loaded 9mm semi-automatic sitting on top of the trash. He arrested the suspect and ran his name. He found that the suspect was a convicted felon out on parole. Caught with a loaded weapon, the suspect would be looking at a very long sentence upstate.

It looked like a pretty good bust, but it had one very major flaw. According to the report filed by Officer Dolan, he did not actually see the suspect with the weapon. What Dolan saw was a man walk suspiciously toward a trashcan, place something inside the trash can, and then, upon inspection, Dolan saw a loaded 9mm on top of the trash. It was enough for an indictment, but not enough for a conviction.

As prosecuting ADA, Vivian *could* bring this before the grand jury, and *possibly* get a True Bill, but then what? Even if Vivian got an indictment, the best she could hope for would be for the defendant to cop a plea. But why would he do that when he knows that he would never get convicted at trial? The entire process would be one big waste of judicial resources.

When Vivian returned from the grand jury, Jim Dolan was waiting for her. He pulled her aside, and in a quiet, professional voice, explained that he was the arresting officer in her gun case and asked if she was going to push for an indictment. Vivian, sensing what was coming, became formal and polite—and then she crisply told him, "No."

Officer Dolan went bonkers. "Are you kidding me?" he yelled. "You cowardly little woman! You couldn't prosecute your way out of a paper bag!"

Vivian remained calm. She did not lose her composure, but coolly explained her reasoning to the officer: "Technically, Officer Dolan, the grand jury *could* indict the defendant. Is there reasonable suspicion that the defendant was in possession of that gun? Yes. However, based on the facts as *you know them,* is it not beyond a reasonable doubt that he was in possession of that gun? No. Based on the evidence that I could bring to trial—*your testimony of what you saw*—I would never get a conviction." Vivian paused for a moment to let Officer Dolan process all that.

"I don't think I have to remind you, Officer Dolan," she continued, "that this is Brooklyn. People don't necessarily *like* the police. Many people *want* to believe bad things about the police." Vivian looked hard into Officer Dolan's eyes. "People believe these things because it's what they want to believe. And now *you* are asking me to affirm their beliefs. You work in the streets, and I respect what you do, and when I'm in your office, I defer to your expertise. But you don't show me that same respect. You come into my grand jury, and you yell at me, and expect me to genuflect before you just because you really, really, super-really want your gun indictment. But that's the point isn't it, this is *my* grand jury. And here *I'm* the expert, and you need to show me the respect I've earned."

The other cops out in the waiting room grew quiet and began edging closer, listening intently to Vivian. I thought she was finished, but she was just getting started. "I've got 25 cases to bring before this grand jury," she said. "25 indictments I've got to persuade them to bring down. And right now, I've got my people eating out of my hand. Right now, I am the Queen of Sheba, the Belle of the Ball and the Blessed Mother all rolled up into one." Vivian flashed her ring in front of the officer. "I go in there and tell them about my up-coming wedding, and about the flower arrangements, and the shoes the bridesmaids are wearing, and we have a bond. Right now our minds are united, because I have been decent and honest and respectful to them. But if they even suspected that I'm trying to lead them by the nose, they will blow every case I have right out of the water. They will literally become a body intent on thwarting the judicial process. It's happened to other ADAs. I won't let it happen to me!"

Dolan knew she was right, but he wasn't ready to hear it. "That son of a bitch was carrying a loaded 9mm on a playground," he said. "I know that guy, he's a killer with at least two bodies on him. If you indict him, he'll definitely violate his parole, and we can get him off the streets." Dolan was going to make his case, one way or the other. "I'm out in the hood every day. Everybody knows me and they know my unit. They don't screw with us, because they know what we are capable of doing—that's fear, and it's the only thing I've got. Everybody down there wants to kill me. The only thing stopping them is that they know what retaliation will look like. If they see that I don't have the juice to send an armed felon back upstate, then I lose respect. And if I don't have respect, I'm just a punk—and bad things happen to punks."

"Well, I'm sorry," responded Vivian. "But that is the exact situation I am in with my grand jury. I need their respect, the same way you do out on the street. If I don't get that respect, they blow out my indictments. Your situations are out on the street, and my situations are in the grand jury. But the issue is no longer in the street, it is now in *my* grand jury. The issue has been taken out of your control and placed into mine. That's our system. It was also our system when you swore an oath to uphold it, and I will not circumvent the system nor jeopardize my grand jury just so you can keep your street cred." Officer Dolan realized he had lost, and he stormed out of the office, as Vivian stared him down coldly, her right hand spinning her engagement ring around and around her left ring finger.

For the longest time the waiting room remained quiet. Then, from the back, some crusty, old cop said loudly, "A cop's arrest is like his baby. He loves it, he frets over it, he stays up nights thinking about it. You tell a cop he's got a bad arrest, it's like telling him he's got an ugly baby."

CONEY ISLAND BABY

Don't ever leave me, don't ever go
You're my Coney Island Baby
I love you so.
The Excellents

Like everyone new to New York, I wanted to live in Manhattan, and like everyone new to New York, I simply could not believe the prices people were asking for a Manhattan apartment. And the idea that I couldn't even get one of these ridiculously priced apartments without paying a broker left me incredulous.

To be honest, I had no idea how the broker-thing worked until I started looking at places. One Saturday in late September, I saw a listing for something I could afford. I called the guy I thought was the owner, and made an appointment to see the place. It was in Morningside Heights, so I took the train in. When I knocked on the door, this very well-dressed, young Asian man with fluttering hands and dramatic mannerisms opened up, and identified himself as "Anthony." We were about 10 minutes into our conversation when Anthony got this *the-bumpkin-doesn't-get-it* look on his face, and he said, "Oh, no, sweetie, I'm not the owner, I'm the broker—ohmigawd, I wouldn't be caught dead with this property in my portfolio."

I sensed he was being condescending, so I put on my most paternalistic tone and said, "I don't think you understand—Anthony, is it?—I'm not here to *buy* the place. I'm here to *rent* the place."

My tone did not go unnoticed by Anthony, and he dropped any pretense altogether. "I think somebody just fell off the turnip truck," he said.

At that moment we both stopped and looked at each other. And for a second, I thought about slapping him in the face. He knew what I was thinking, but he just stood there giving me his raised-eyebrows stare— he was a defiant little prick, I'd have to give him that. Then, at exactly the same time, we both started laughing.

"The *turnip truck*?" I said. "Who even says that anymore?"

"Hey, girlfriend," replied Anthony, "I'm working without a net,

53

here."

"Yeah, but, geez, that was pretty bush league. Good delivery, though."

"Yes, well, it's a gift."

"Alright, Gift-Boy," I said, "as you've noticed, I'm not from around here. If you're going to be my broker, you have to get me up to speed."

"Oh, so now I'm your broker? A minute ago you were going to beat my little gaysian ass, and now you want me to be your broker?"

"You don't know what I was thinking."

"Oh, honey, I knew. Gaydar doesn't just detect *friendlies*, you know."

"What about you, with your snarky comments? Geez, talk about perpetuating a stereotype."

"And don't you forget it sister. . . This kitten's got claws."

"So, are you going to be my broker or not?"

"Sweetie, of course I'll be your broker. If nothing else it will be fabulous fun."

We shook hands (because that's what men do), and I asked, "So what's the deal with my needing a broker? How come I can't rent my own apartment?"

"Well," said Anthony, returning to the subject he cared most about in life—New York real estate, "look at the transaction from the owner's point of view. The owner only wants tenants who have J-O-Bs. He needs to know that he's going to get his rent check and not get jammed up in Landlord-Tenant Court, which is death to a landlord. In order to find good tenants and weed out the bad ones, owners use brokers like me to vet the prospective tenants."

"And how exactly do you vet the prospective tenants?"

"I charge them my broker's fee."

"Your fee for what?"

"For vetting them."

"But what do you do to vet them?"

"I charge them my fee."

"Let me get this straight," I said. "Your job is to make sure the renter is good for the rent. And your test for the renter's ability to pay the rent is to charge him a fee. If he pays the fee, he's a good tenant, and if he doesn't pay the fee, he's not a good tenant."

"Exactly."

"You—by being you—prove the necessity of your you-ness."

"That's it in a nutshell."

"Brilliant."

I didn't get that apartment where Anthony and I first met or the next one, which was on West 14th Street, over-top a Chinese massage parlor. But I was learning a lot from him. We both actually liked the apartment on West 14th. It was tiny, and it had a micro bathroom where you had to stand in the shower when you wanted to use the sink, and stand on the toilet when you wanted to lather up in the shower. The "kitchen" was a two-burner stove and an oven that could fit a TV dinner (sideways).

Over the stove was a hooded fan with a little cabinet. I mentioned to Anthony that the fan was a nice extra, but he just rolled his eyes. "Sweetie, I *should* be agreeing with you," he said dramatically, "I mean, I'm supposed to be *selling you* on the place, but, honestly, I get so tired of these tacky little tricks. They've all just been *so done* already. This trick's a common one. The stove's got a fan and—look—the fan even works, right?" Anthony then opened up the cabinet and let me see that the fan didn't lead anywhere; it just spun around over the stove.

"Here," he said, "let me show you another cheap landlord trick." With that Anthony whipped out a night light. "You see all these outlets in this place?" I counted five. Anthony went around plugging in his night light to see if they had power—only two of the outlets worked. "See what this cheap bastard did? He cut holes in the drywall and slapped in outlet covers, but they're not wired up. They're just like that fan—display items only."

"That's low," I agreed.

"It's such a cheap trick, but none of you bumpkins ever check. You're from the suburbs where everything works. It never occurs to you people to check things like this."

"Yeah," I said, "but you can always complain."

Anthony looked at me like I was from Mars. "Of course," he said, "after you sign the lease and move in, you'll start plugging in your appliances and nothing will work. You'll call the owner and say, 'Gee whiz, Mr. Niceman, for some reason the outlets aren't working.' And of course, he'll act all shocked and concerned, and he'll tell you he'll get someone over there right away to fix the problem. But, of course, no one ever shows up. You call again, and now he's 'shocked,' *shocked* he tells you. He can't believe 'his guy' didn't come over. He's gonna take care of it himself."

"And he'll never come over, huh?" I said.

"Sweetie, you've just been welcomed to New York."

55

"So you think this is a bad apartment?"

"No, actually, this is a really good deal. If I were you, I'd take it."

"But what about all the tricks?"

"Welcome to New York, Sweetie," Anthony said with a triumphant smile.

We tried to rent that apartment, but it rented to someone else before we could even get our bid in. It was amazing how fast the market moved.

Since that first meeting, Anthony and I had crisscrossed the city a couple times a week looking at apartments. I think Anthony just liked exploring the city. He knew so much about New York—every block, every building, had a story, and Anthony had an encyclopedic mind. It wasn't until we'd seen maybe three apartments, before Anthony and I sat down for a drink and spoke about ourselves.

I told him about growing up in Maryland and about my time in the Army. Anthony then told me about his life, about his seven brothers and sisters, his devout Filipino parents, and about how they moved from Quezon City to Daly City, California when he was 13.

"Eight kids," I said, "wow, your parents sure are devout. . . ."

Anthony picked up on what was not being asked. "It's a common story," he said. "My parents pretend they don't know I'm gay, and I pretend to be looking for a *Pinay* girl to marry. Every Christmas I promise to move back home, and they promise to come visit me in New York. The whole thing is Kabuki Theater, but it's important to keep up appearances."

"Why don't you just come out?" I asked.

"I don't believe in that," he said, "it would be disrespectful."

"So you hide your life?"

"How much am I really hiding?" Anthony replied. "Most of these queens with their big 'coming out' stories just embarrass themselves—news flash, Sally, everyone knows. I mean, how many eleven year old boys make their own curtains?"

We went to see a studio in Little Italy that really wasn't too bad—by New York standards—except that the bathroom was on the other side of the hall, which, for the longest time, I could not wrap my head around.

"Wait," I began, "you're saying this is exclusively my bathroom?"

"Exclusively."

"But it's across the hallway from my apartment."

"Convenient, huh?"

"But it's not in my apartment."

"But it belongs to the apartment."

"But it's over there."

"But it's yours."

"But it's across the hall."

Anthony just sighed. "Look, Edison," he said, dragging me into the hallway and placing my hand on the apartment door. "This is the continental United States." He then stamped on the floor of the hallway. "This is Canada. And this," Anthony put my other hand on the bathroom door, "is Alaska. Alaska doesn't belong to Canada does it? No, it belongs to the United States. It's not touching the United States, but it is the United States. Do. You. Get. It?"

"Ahhhhh," I said, as the light finally came on. "The apartment is sovereign, but non-contiguous."

"Yes," replied Anthony with delight. "Sovereign, but not contiguous."

The landlord wanted $1,200 a month. I didn't even reject the place, I just thought about it too long. I waited two days before I called Anthony and told him I'd take it, but by then someone had already snatched it up. And so our search continued, but it was becoming clear that I wasn't going to be able to afford to live in Manhattan. We started looking in Brooklyn. Anthony and I looked at a place in Park Slope, which is about the best neighborhood in Brooklyn. This apartment was *in* Park Slope in about the same way that Staten Island is *in* New York City—on a clear day you can see Battery Park.

I'd been getting a little tired of our city-wide sojourns, and I knew Anthony was too, but then he called me up and told me that he had an "AMAZZZIIINNG find" on Coney Island. He came by the office around 5:00 p.m. and we split a cab out to the shore.

"The rent is a steal," Anthony explained. "And the place is spacious beyond words." But Anthony saved the best for last: "And—are you ready for this—it's got an *ocean view.*"

"You're bullshittin' me," I said.

"Is that my job?" said Anthony, "is it my job to bullshit you?"

"I just don't see how it can be," I said.

"Let's just check it out," he said. "But this is the real thing."

"Well, what's the catch? I know there's a catch."

"Not really. It's just that the tenant has . . . expired."

"Expired?"

"Yes, Julia Sandston, she died in the second tower. The *New York*

Times did a whole piece on her—24 years old, from the Midwest, went to Northwestern. One of these Wall Street super-achievers." It was sad to hear—and I felt sorry for the girl—but, really, what was it to me? A bargain is a bargain. As we drove out on the Belt Parkway, I noted every exit, every point of interest, certain that I would soon be moving in.

When we arrived at the building, I was blown away by the splendor of the place. It was one of those pre-war buildings with a beautiful and inspiring lobby. It had a Hart-Benton-type mural on the wall and ceiling. This was probably the best address in Coney Island. I was already seeing myself jogging up and down Mermaid Avenue.

Anthony and I rode the elevator to the seventh floor, and I had the apartment number in hand, 727. As we walked down the hallway toward the apartment, I noticed that at the very end of the hall a door was left open. Light was streaming through the open doorway into the darkened hall, and I could hear the murmur of voices. I didn't know why, but I just didn't want that open door to be the door to my new apartment. As we passed each door, I looked at the numbers, hoping to see 727, but the closer we got, the more sure I was that this open door was the door to the apartment I wanted.

We came upon the open door, and, naturally, it was to apartment 727. Anthony and I both looked inside, and what we saw was an elderly couple in an almost completely empty room boxing up odds and ends, and commenting to each other as they did.

"Oh, look. This is that dolphin she wanted so much the summer we vacationed in Florida."

"Oh, yes, I remember. Wasn't it crystal?"

"No, just blown glass."

"What was she, thirteen?"

"Thirteen or fourteen... No she was thirteen, because you remember the summer when she was fourteen, she went to French camp. There was that boy that year. What was his name?"

"Wesley."

"Yes, Wesley. Sort of a drip. Wrote that horrible poem—dodged a bullet there, didn't we?"

"Hello," Anthony said, tentatively.

This broke up the couple's remembrance, and the man responded, "Why, hello. Can we help you?"

"Well, yes," said Anthony, "but can we help you with that packing?"

"No," the man said distractedly. "We'll manage."

"We're here to look at the apartment," Anthony said, the words hitting the couple like a body blow.

"It still belongs to Julie through the month," the woman said with a hint of defiance.

"And besides," said the man, "these are Julie's things, and they must be returned to us."

"We can come back some other time," I said, not knowing what to say. But they carried on as if I hadn't said a word at all, methodically placing things into boxes.

"This was her first apartment," said the woman.

The man laughed, and they both shared a look of pride. "That's right," he continued, "her first apartment. She used to remind us of that all the time. A 24 year old girl with an oceanfront view in New York City—have you ever heard such a thing?" The man paused for a moment, then returned to wrapping a porcelain figurine in newspaper.

Anthony and I introduced ourselves and expressed our condolences. The woman, Jeanne, offered to make us tea. We both declined. The man, Arnold, asked us to sit, but we said we preferred to stand. We spoke of random things for a few minutes, then Anthony asked if there was anything we could do for them.

"No," said Arnold. "Everything is finished." He did not seem to be talking about the packing.

Despite our objections, Jeanne made us tea, and we all sat down on the bare floor to drink it. Julie was their only child, Arnold explained, and that she came late in life, they were both in their late 30s when she was born. "She was our miracle, and we cherished her so," said Arnold wistfully.

"We've been staying here since September 13th," Jeanne said. "Julie was our only child—oh, Arn just told you that."

"At first we thought surely she'll be found alive," said Arnold. "Then we thought, well, at least they'll find her body."

"We wanted to give our little girl a proper burial," Jeanne said, her eyes welling up.

"But they're not going to find her," Arnold said. "She won't even have that."

"She was just a girl," Jeanne said, "our little girl—and they took her from us." Jeanne's eyes flashed with anger. "They took her away from us!" Arnold reached over and put his arm around his wife, and she began to cry. "What is the world?" Jeanne said, rocking back and forth in Arnold's arms, a look of utter perplexity on her face. "What is this place where such things happen? I keep thinking I'm losing my mind, that I'm crazy, and that this didn't happen. But then I realize I'm not crazy, that it did happen. And all I do is wish I was crazy, I wish it was me who was crazy." Jeanne let out a deep groan, astonishing me with its plaintive sorrow, and Arnold tightened his grip around her. "I wish I was crazy," Jeanne said through her tears, "but I'm not. The world is crazy, but I have to be sane. I have to be the one who is sane. Why can't I be the one, why can't I be crazy instead of the world?"

We finished our tea, and Anthony and I said our goodbyes. I loved that place, but I knew I could not live there. It was haunted, and will forever be haunted. Not by the ghost of Julie Sandston, but by the eyes of her ageing parents—depleted, exhausted and tortured by the memory of their only child, who was erased from the earth without pity or remorse.

FROM HERE TO ETERNITY

Finally, I thought, *drill weekend.* I couldn't wait. It was the first drill weekend since the terrorist attacks. Everyone was wired to finally get back to the range and get behind a rifle. Since September 11th, the fact that I was in the Special Forces had trumped all other thoughts. Everybody in the unit had been emailing and phoning each other. The whole company was abuzz with rumor and anticipation. We wanted the call-up. We wanted to go to war.

I had been trying to settle-in as a lawyer, settle-in as a civilian, but now all I wanted was to be in uniform and to have a rifle in my hand. Maybe all those dead bodies from the World Trade Center had spoiled civilian life for me. The apartment search had turned sour, and my visions of life as an attorney had become tainted with the ashes that fell on my suit, my hair and my life. The ghost of Little Mike had been crowded out by the ghosts of New York. I could feel them touching me as I walked the streets of Brooklyn. It felt as if they were pushing me, hurling me forward, back to the Army, back to the Special Forces, back to the life I was familiar with. At least with the Army there would only be one ghost following me.

My unit, Bravo Company, 3rd Battalion, 20th Special Forces Group, was a National Guard unit, but it was like a pack of wolves. There were always guys either coming in from or moving out to active duty Special Forces Groups, and the core of the unit was made up of guys culled from the most selective law enforcement agencies in the country—FBI, DEA, Secret Service, U.S. Marshals and the ATF. These were men who made up the security infrastructure of Washington. They were the bricks in the invisible wall surrounding the city. They took the terrorist attacks personally, and they wanted payback to be personal, too.

Along with them were the cops—almost all of them SWAT team guys and other hard asses, and they came from all over the east coast to be in Bravo Company. We had cops from as far north as Newark, and as far south as Atlanta. It was a mark of pride to be a part of our unit, a pride you felt as you drove through the concertina wire into the compound, which stood in the most remote corner of Fort A.P. Hill, Bowling Green, Virginia.

When I came into our team hooch Friday night, Richie "Boy Band" Gennaro, the A-Team weapons sergeant (and a City of Richmond police officer) was in the middle of a story about his vacation to Chicago: ". . . had the whole fam in the minivan—you know—and it's like an eight hour drive or whatever. But I'm so jacked to see South Chicago that I can't even get to my sister's house before checking out the Cabrini-Green Housing Project, right?" Boy Band was hopping around and bobbing his head in his usual excited fashion as he spoke. "I mean, these are supposed to be the meanest, most crime-ridden housing projects in the country, right? So naturally, I've got to cruise'em."

"Like a moth to the flame," Clinton "Crunk" Stitch said, laughing softly. Crunk was Boy Band's best friend. The two did everything together when we were drilling.

"I know, right?" said Boy Band. "I'm cruising Cabrini-Green in the minivan and Diane's screaming at me, the kids are crying. But I don't give a shit. I got my Glock in my waist band, and I've come all the way to Chicago. Ain't no way I'm missin' the action in the 'hood of all hoods'."

Crunk, our communications sergeant, was a famously hard-ass Baltimore cop. He shook his head in bewildered agreement. "I know, man," he said, "I love workin' the hood. It's like playing football. . . . *But with guns.*"

Boy Band and Crunk were extremely close friends—goin' for brothers, as they say. Boy Band was white, with a wide-streak of white pride; and Crunk was black, and he loved to say how much he hated 'whitie'. But the two were inseparable.

It was hard not to like Boy Band, with his wide Dennis the Menace smile and goofy, aw-shucks mannerisms. He was all frantic energy, jabbing the air and bobbing his head when he spoke. Although thin and wiry, he had played tailback in high school, and had gained some local fame. The other thing about Boy Band was that he loved to fight. It was nothing personal with him, he just loved the action. Cruelty was an element of his charm. "You know how there's always that guy?" Boy Band said, looking at Crunk and me. "Whenever you go to a bar, there's always that *one* guy you know you're going to get into a fight with."

"No, Boy Band," I said, "I don't know that guy. *You* know that guy, because you *are* that guy."

Boy Band continued, "As I was sayin', there's always that one guy you know you're going to be throwin' down with before the night is over. Anyway, last week I was down on Cary Street, right? And I'm gettin' my drink on, and here comes That Guy." Boy Band jabbed the air as he told the story. "Dude's lookin' at me all hard and shit, so, of course, I put in my mouthpiece—"

"Wait. What?"

"I put in my mouthpiece, so—"

"You bring a mouthpiece with you when you go to a bar?"

"Do you not?"

Boy Band was handsome, and slightly vain about it. He pushed the regulation on hair length and liked to keep a few locks sweeping across his forehead—thus the nickname, "Boy Band." The other thing about Boy Band was that he loved kids—not just his own, but any kid. As mean as he was and as ruthless as he was to adults, he was a push-over to children. He coached little league and was a scout master. I always got the feeling that he'd had a rough childhood and didn't want that for anybody else.

Crunk was his opposite in many ways. Taller and more stout, Crunk looked like the linebacker he had been. Of dark complexion, Crunk kept his head shaved. He was married to a devoutly Christian woman and had two daughters, whom he constantly worried about. During his first enlistment, Crunk had been a member of the Old Guard, a Tomb Guard of the U.S. Army Honor Guard. Although Crunk claimed to hate white people, he had made his career and his reputation in west Baltimore, beating the shit out of blacks. He got the name Crunk because, as he liked to say, "I drinks a bit."

The drill weekend didn't really start until Saturday morning, but a lot of the guys liked to get there the night before to get things ready and to hang out. Friday nights were when we usually trained with Crunk's or Boy Band's hand-to-hand weapons—the saps, nunchucks, asps, night sticks, leaded gloves and various other non-lethal weapons they carried when working their precincts—"Better-Be-Cool-Tools," Crunk called them.

Boy Band laid his weapons on the cot, and we worked for a time with the sap. If you've never been hit with a sap, believe me it's traumatic. With just a forward flick of the wrist, a lead ball encased in leather will hurl toward your head, and the last thing you'll remember before the lights go out is how sissy Boy Band looked, flicking his wrist that way.

Boy Band and Crunk were tough, but they were hardly the anomaly in Bravo Company. The entire unit was infected by an exquisite recklessness. My first jump with the unit was out of a helicopter. The company sergeant major was the jumpmaster, and for some reason he made a big production about making sure the officers jumped with the first stick. "It's a tradition we have in the SF," he told our team leader.

"That's bullshit, sergeant major," said the team leader. "I've got 55 jumps since I got the long tab, and I've never heard of that tradition."

"Is that right, sir?" said the sergeant major. "Well, here's another tradition for ya, we have a tradition in this unit of losing young officers' promotional paperwork when we think they're not being accommodating enough to the sergeant major. That sounds traditional enough for ya, sir?"

"Roger that, sergeant major," said the team leader. "Officers out in the first stick."

The pilot brought the aircraft up to 1,200 feet, which is the typical elevation for a parachute jump, and the sergeant major released all the officers. As the last officer exited the aircraft, the sergeant major turned to the pilot and gave him the thumbs-up, and the pilot banked into a steep climb. The sergeant major turned to us with a grin and I could just hear him over the prop blast saying, "Had to get them off the bird so we could pull some shit. Pilot's gonna take us up to 2,000 feet. Any of you pussies says anything I'll have your ass." The pilot took us up and we exited the aircraft at 2,000 feet elevation. Once aloft, we all steered our parachutes around each other, circling like boxers, shouting insults and challenges to one another. None of us was anymore young, most in our 30s, some into their 40s. Everybody had families, entrenched careers and mortgages to account for, but that only made it all the more exciting. We could die in combat—hell, we could die right there—but so what? We could go out stupidly, we could go out randomly or we could go out courageously. But, outside the unit, it wasn't anybody's business how we died. We were "the unit" and nothing else mattered, nothing else existed. We were Green Berets, who the fuck were you?

Saturday morning my team was tasked to run the Medium Machinegun Range for some transportation company from the 29th Infantry Division, and instruct them on the use and maintenance of the M-240 Bravo and the M-249 Squad Automatic Weapon (aka, the SAW)—the two machine guns found in every platoon in the Army.

We took a trunk down to the range, set up our instructional area, gave the safety briefing, and then Jason "Jiggy" Molineux—my closest friend in the unit—began the familiarization briefing. "My name is

Sergeant Molineux," he began, clearly enjoying his role as center of attention, "and I will be instructing you on how to lay-in, fire and maintain these two weapons systems." Jason picked up the 240 Bravo, his hands working the cocking handle assembly with ease and confidence, lifting and lowering the cover assembly with equal dexterity. "This is the 240 Bravo, it is the replacement weapon for the M-60. Who can tell me the nickname for the M-60? Anyone? . . . Anyone at all? Guess you kids are too young to remember, but the M-60 used to be called—what was it called, Staff Sergeant Redmond?"

"The Pig!" I shouted back to Jiggy.

"The Pig—exactly, and it was the heart and soul of an infantry platoon." Jiggy swung the weapon around, making sure not to blade anyone with the muzzle. "Do any of you know the nickname for the 240 Bravo? No one? Good. It was a trick question. The 240 Bravo doesn't have a nickname, yet." Jiggy walked over by the ammunition, and stood in front of the ammo crates, making sure to block the boxes from the eyes of the soldiers. "Now," he said, "can anyone tell me what bullet the 240 Bravo fires?" A young private raised his hand. "You there."

"The seven-six-two."

"The seven-six-two. That is correct. You are a winner."

"What do I win, sergeant?" the soldier said with a look of bewildered delight.

"You win the right to make Sergeant Molineux a sandwich at lunchtime. That's non-transferable, so you can't sell your right to another soldier." Jiggy picked out another soldier in the audience.

"You there, if the 240 Bravo fires the seven-six-two round, what does the SAW fire?"

Jason had caught the soldier off guard. "Um," he said, " . . . bullets?"

"That is right," Jason replied. "The SAW fires bullets . . . but can we be a little more specific on the *type* of bullet it fires?"

The PFC recovered. "The five-five-six."

"Outstanding, soldier! You get to give me your apple at lunch!—Can't wait."

Later in the day, while the soldiers were field stripping the weapons, Jiggy came over for a break.

"You should be a school teacher," I said.

"I wish," he replied, "pays better than police work."

"What if you made detective?"

"Fayetteville is a cheap, cheap town," Jiggy said, "and that farm I bought out in Laurinburg is costing me a fortune. I got the bank breathing down my neck every day." The firing line was ready to go live. Boy Band was waving us forward, so Jiggy and I moved back to our duty stations.

"You are about to fire the M-240 Bravo, medium machine gun," Jiggy said, addressing the soldiers through a megaphone. "You have with you the best instructors in the world, and you have the proper left and right limits on your weapons. It is highly unlikely that any of you will be shot on the range today." Jiggy paused for effect. "Having said that, the fact is that you are privates, *and privates will do anything.*" We all shouted in unison. "Therefore, I give you one last piece of advice before we begin firing. If you find that you have been shot by one of your fellow soldiers, and you see a warm, inviting white light in front of you, and you see your dead grandmother beckoning you to come hither . . . DO NOT GO TOWARD THE LIGHT! I repeat, DO NOT GO TOWARD THE LIGHT!" I looked over at Boy Band and we both mouthed the words, "do not go toward that light," even as Jiggy said them. It was the oldest joke in the Army, but it always got a laugh.

One of the better things about drill weekend was catching up with the guys on the team. Most of us in our civilian careers were basically outsiders, we just didn't fit in. It was nobody's fault, it was just a fact. "The guy's busting my balls," Boy Band said to me as we walked the firing line.

"What's the problem?"

"Commissioner says I'm not 'reflecting the cultural values of the community.' Says I make too many arrests."

"Wait, you're a cop, right?"

"Exactly," said Boy Band. "Let the preachers and the politicians 'reflect the cultural values of the community.' I just keep the community safe for them to do so."

"But this is the community *you* chose to work in," I said, clarifying the issue.

"Damn right," Boy Band said, "I want to bring some order there."

"But the people who live there, and who have elected your supervisors, don't want you to," I said, stating the obvious.

"No, they hate me," Boy Band replied.

"But you chose to work there."

"Yeah," said Boy Band, "to clean up the town."

"But they don't want to be cleaned up."

"But I'm helping them."

66

"But they don't want your help."

"Dude, you're an asshole."

"But I'm trying to help."

"I don't want your help."

"So it comes full circle."

"Dude, you're an asshole."

At lunch, the team intelligence sergeant, Martin "Spooky" Schmidt, brought us out a box of MREs. Spooky was an enigma to the rest of us. He was one of us, but he scared us. Spooky had been a captain and an A-Team leader in the first Gulf War, and something had gone wrong after his team had been inserted behind enemy lines. He got his entire team away safely, but he lost his commission in the process. No one was ever clear about what had happened, but Spooky was drummed out of the 5th Special Forces Group. Thirty days later he showed up in our company as a buck sergeant.

Trained as a sniper, Spooky was gifted with a rifle, and even better as an interrogator—a skill he wasn't supposed to use, or even have. Spooky seemed to know about people, and what he knew about people seemed to put everyone else on edge.

In his civilian career, Spooky was a Special Investigator for the Immigration Customs Enforcement Agency—ICE. He would routinely make observational statements that would seem completely racist, but were, in fact, just obvious truisms that polite people were supposed to ignore. "Noticing patterns of behavior," he liked to say, "is a thought crime. And articulating the patterns of behavior everyone sees, is a felony." He would say these things, but at the same time he would express his deep admiration of those people. It was all very confusing. For over a year, Spooky had been dating a Muslim woman from Iran— "Persia", as he constantly called the place. When they were together they spoke mostly in Farsi.

"Frickin Fariba," he said, dropping off the box of MREs, "she called me four times today, just to tell me she feels we're not communicating."

"Awww, that sweet," Boy Band said mockingly.

Spooky continued, "She feels we're not connecting on a higher level."

"Not surprised," Boy Band said. "Pretty much all you care about is connecting on a lower level, don't you think?"

"Shut up, Boy Band. Seriously, she calls me and says she wants to talk. I say, 'Okay, let's talk' and she sits there and gives me the silent treatment. It just aggravates the crap out of me—and next week I'm going to propose to her."

"What could go wrong?" said Jiggy.

The training was a two-day operation, so Jiggy and I volunteered to sleep out on the range to guard the ammunition and weapons. Our team sergeant, Master Sergeant Frank "Dragline" Lawton, drove out in the evening to take one of us into town to pick up some dinner and beer (hey, it's still the National Guard). He told us with raised eyebrows that the battalion commander was flying in from Florida to give the company a briefing Sunday. And he mentioned with a smile that the officers in the "head-shed" had been unusually active all day.

It was a beautiful night—warm, but without a moon. Jiggy and I sat in our sleeping bags surrounded by absolute darkness, me sipping cool beer (Jiggy was some sort of Baptist, and didn't drink).   "You think we'll get called up?" Jiggy asked.

"I don't know," I said. "You've been in the Army as long as I have. You know how these things happen—baseless rumor, baseless rumor, baseless rumor. Then one day it's all asses and elbows, you're flying out the door as fast as you can."

"Hope we go," Jiggy said.

"Why, want to be a hero?"

"Been there, done that," said Jiggy. "I just need the money. We get over there, we'll have combat pay and hazardous duty pay and . . . I need to get promoted to sergeant first class. That would be huge."

I grunted my agreement.

"What about you, Jet Set, don't you want to go?"

"Definitely."

"Why?"

I didn't know what to say. *Why* I thought. *Because I want to be on the other side of it, and to know I did it right.* "We took the oath," I said. "We take the money, we have to do our duty. Besides, it'll be cool."

"Cool?" Jiggy said. "It's anything but cool."

Jiggy never liked to mention his past, but he left the deep impression that he was in the shit more than once.

"In Somalia," he said, his bodiless voice clear in the darkness, "it was mostly a lot of nothing. But one day I was sitting out by the landing pad, and here comes this UH-60 limping onto the landing zone. This thing had smoke pouring out of the rear and bullet holes all over it. The pilot's windshield was caved in from machinegun fire, and as it turned to position for landing, I saw that there was a guy hanging out the side of the chopper. He looked to be just dangling in mid-air, his arms outstretched, his head hanging limp. And as the chopper turned, I saw another guy with his arms wrapped around the guy's legs, just straining every muscle to keep him from falling out of the chopper." Jiggy paused, and in that pause, I wondered if I could hold on to Jiggy if he was hanging out of a helicopter door. "You need a better reason than that for going to war," Jiggy said. "It's gonna suck over there—they don't call it 'The Suck' for nothin."

When we got back to the company area Sunday afternoon, there was a lot of buzz going around the headquarters building, and at 4:00 p.m. we had a formation in one of the old Quonset huts. Everybody was curious and excited and hoping that we'd hear the words we wanted to hear. The battalion commander brought us to attention and started to tell us that we were the best company in his command—the usual stuff that battalion commanders say. He then told us that the Pentagon had given him a decision to make, and that he had made it. He paused for what seemed like eternity, then let out a breath, and said, "Boys, I'm putting you in the SHIT!"

The room exploded. A shout went out from behind me, then another and another. Everybody was high-fiving and laughing all at once. It was delirium—we were going to war. It was the most magnificent feeling I've ever had.

I know that these days it is the fashion to put on a facade of angst-ridden regret when sending soldiers off to war. You're supposed to wring your hands and make a great display of brooding sorrow. Fuck that. There is nothing more liberating or invigorating than going off to war. Cheering men aren't having delusional dreams of glory when they dance at news of war. They laugh and dance because all at once, in the blink of an eye, all their burdens, all their responsibilities, all their trivial worries are brushed aside. They laugh because the world has become instantly wide open to them. The boss, the girlfriend, the creditors, they can't say shit. You're fighting for your country, you're throwing the dice on something others are afraid to even think about.

The world is full of bankers, bosses and pain-in-the-ass girlfriends. But fighting men come dear, and when the balloon goes up, you celebrate. When you are called to defend your country, you delight in it. The future? Fuck the future. The future is always a tragedy, but to be a man is to laugh in the face of that tragedy.

LAST EXIT TO BROOKLYN

The mobilization orders came Monday. On Tuesday, I handed Tracy Silverstein my orders, thinking she'd be pissed. Instead she threw a party.

Thursday, after we finished work, Tracy marched us all down to the Brazen Head on Atlantic Boulevard, and more or less ordered us to have a blast. The party was a good time and I appreciated what Tracy did, but this going-off-to-war thing could turn out to be the biggest embarrassment of my life. I mean, what was I going to tell these people if I spent the next year down at Fort Bragg picking cigarette butts off the parade field? Still, it was great. I couldn't buy a drink, which is why I showed up for work the next morning 20 minutes late and looking like an unmade bed. Naturally, I slunk into the conference room, where everybody was already seated and busy, and immediately all eyes were on me. I apologized, tried to look sheepish, took my seat and then sort of stared at my notebook for a minute. When I finally looked up, everybody was still staring at me like I had horns growing out of my head. "Well," Tracy finally asked, exasperated, "did you pass?"

I looked around the room for some clue as to what she was talking about. "Pass what?" I asked.

Sitting next to me was Joel, serious and confident. He coughed up a laugh, "Oh, listen to this! He's pretending he doesn't know what you're talking about. You got some balls, Redmond!"

I looked back around the room, and everybody was smiling like they were all in on some big joke, but I wasn't getting it. So I asked again, "What are you talking about?"

Now Joel could see that I really didn't understand the question, and he got pissed. "Omigawd, he's serious!" Joel said. "He's frickin' serious! Hey, dumb ass, they posted the bar exam results last night! You remember the bar exam, don't ya? It was that ulcer-inducing two day exam you took in July? Sort of a milestone in an attorney's life."

"Oh, that's right!" I said, jumping out of my seat, "I've got to see if I passed." I ran out into the hallway and headed toward my desk. But from the conference room I heard Joel yell out, "Fuhgetaboutit numb-nuts—ya passed. I checked on your ass last night ten minutes after

70

midnight. In fact, everybody checked on the website ten minutes after midnight—everybody but you. The site took so many hits it crashed. In the entire State of New York you are the only member of the legal community who 'forgot' that the bar results were posted last night. You're gonna make one hell of an ADA, Redmond—a real John-John Kennedy."

And that—I shit you not—was the true story of how I learned that I had passed the New York State Bar Examination.

So that morning was a time of departure, not just for me, but for all the ADAs in my class. The people who passed the bar were getting their assignments to their respective zones and divisions, being given their caseload and sent to work. The people who did not pass—what would happen to them was not entirely clear. Tracy gave us her last instructions as our mentor, "Those of you who passed are to go to the Criminal Court to receive your assignments. Those who—um—did not pass, are to go to the District Attorney's Office on the 19th floor. He has some words for you."

My section spilled out into the elevator lobby—some excited, others subdued—and waited for the elevator. Once out in the lobby, we ran into people from other sections who had been given the same orders. The first elevator to arrive was going up, and as it stopped on our floor we all held our breath and stared at the floor, curious, but not wanting to know, who we would see inside, and which of us would walk toward the opening doors. The doors opened, and the elevator was packed—and I knew every face. Many of the people in the lobby walked toward the elevator, but none of them could get on and had to step back and wait along with us for the next elevator. I felt so bad for them, having to stand there knowing, and knowing that we knew, that they had failed the bar exam. When the next elevator arrived, it too was completely packed. In it also we saw the faces of those in our class who had to take that long ride up to see the District Attorney. Before a third elevator could arrive, I made a dash to the stairway. Standing there in the lobby felt like I was salting a wound.

At the Criminal Court we were given our assignments. Even I was given a zone assignment—Domestic Violence—although it was known throughout the DA's Office that I was leaving that very day. By 3:00 p.m. all those who had passed the bar were settling into their new offices, so I said my goodbyes, got into my car, and headed down Flatbush Avenue toward the Belt Parkway. Driving down Flatbush, I ran through a check list of things to do to clear out of Brooklyn and get back into the Army. I had packed up my stuff, given the key to the landlord, and cleared out of the DA's Office—what a good boy I was. Feeling proud of a job well done, I looked at myself in the rearview and realized my hair was completely out of regulation, and that I needed a haircut.

Never, never, never show up to formation needing a haircut. Better to show up dripping blood than make formation with noticeably long hair. I don't care if you're a Nobel Prize winner, Audie Murphy and Joan of Arc all rolled into one, if you don't have a squared-away haircut the sergeant major will Lose. His. Mind.

I pulled off of Flatbush Avenue near the intersection with Ditmus, where I saw a barber's pole out of the corner of my eye. The barbershop was on the corner, with large windows facing both streets. Painted on the windows in broad, sweeping cursive was the name of the establishment: "Mike's 'Look Sharp' Barbershop."

I looked in and saw one barber and three customers. They were all black men, laughing and talking in an animated manner. Standing at the center of this group was the barber—tall, solidly built, with bright, intelligent eyes and a big broad smile. He wore a white smock with the name "Mike" embroidered on his chest. He was chewing on an unlit cigar, and on his head he wore a black felt derby hat.

For black men, the barbershop is kind of a private gentlemen's club. There are many rules, rituals and social graces that must be respected; on the other hand, the very purpose of the club is to serve as a stage for the combative dance of masculinity. That being said, I needed to get my hair cut, and I knew I had to go in strong. I heaved open the door and stood in the doorway with my hands on my hips—Eastwood style. The talking subsided, and I walked up to Mike and said in an overly loud manner, "Hey, Mr. Mike, can you cut a white man's hair?"

It was on.

The three men kept repeating what I said, "The man just come in here and asked Mike if he can cut a white man's hair."

"He did! He just said that!"

"That's what he said!"

Mike looked indignantly at me and said, "Of course I can cut a white man's hair. I can cut any man's hair."

"Well, I don't know, Mike," I said, turning slowly and dramatically to the three men who had taken seats in the waiting area. "What kind of barber wears a hat while he's working? Makes me think you're hiding something."

"Oooooh!" the men let out a collective gasp of mock pain. "He got you good with that, Mike," one of the men said.

"You know, he's right," said another. "You're all the time wearin' that hat. Makes me think you don't have pride in your workmanship."

"Let me ask you fellas," I said, "you see a barber wearing a hat, doesn't exactly instill confidence, does it?"

"Hell, no! What's a barber doin' wearing a hat on the job?"

"I *know* how to cut hair," said Mike defensively. "Been cutting hair for 25 years. This here derby is just me styling."

"That's you styling?" I said. "Well, maybe that's a fact, and maybe it isn't. But barber wears a hat, that's like a baker who won't eat bread."

"Whoo!" the men said. "Mike like a baker won't eat bread!"

"If I'm going to get my hair cut by Mike the 'Look Sharp' barber," I continued, "I'm going to have to look at a sampling of his work."

"Yeah, that's right," the group responded. "We need an inspection."

Mike saw my game, and he began to smile. "You don't trust me, then I don't need to be your barber." Mike looked around at the others. "That's like living in a house, when you don't trust the carpenter who built it. Question is, which one's the fool, the shoddy carpenter or the man who hires him?"

"Oooooh!" the men responded. "Mike got you on that!"

Mike pressed his advantage. "You come into a man's place of business and tell him, 'you ain't but a no-count barber, but give me one of your no-count haircuts'—what kind of man does that?"

"I didn't ask for a 'no-count' haircut," I said. Everyone was smiling now, knowing it was on. "I want one of them 'Look Sharp' haircuts. A man can ask questions of his barber, can't he? Especially when that barber is wearing a hat."

Mike looked at me for a moment, then nodded. "Get in that chair . . . *white* man."

"Bam!" I said, easing into the barber's chair. "That's the answer of a true professional. Now, let's get ole Sergeant Redmond one of those 'Look Sharp' haircuts everybody in Brooklyn keeps talking about."

"*Sergeant* Redmond?" the man on my right said. "We got us a sergeant up in here!"

"So, is you a Marine or is you Army?" the other asked.

"Sir," I said, "you are lookin' at 210 pounds of steel-eyed, barrel-chested United States Army Special Forces soldier, on his way to Fort A.P. Hill and then bound for glory."

"A.P. Hill?" the man to my left said. "What you know about

Bowling Green, Virginia?"

I looked at the man with raised eyebrows. I could see that he was drawing me in, and I could see that his strategy was elaborate. "I know the Richmond Turnpike well enough," I said. "And I know Caroline County High School."

The mention of Caroline County High School brought a smile to the man's face, and I figured I needed to introduce myself—but that I had to do so in an elaborate manner. "Sorry," I said, "but I didn't get your name."

"Not sure I gave it," he said with a challenging smile.

"Well, I'm sure you didn't," I said. "That was just my way of introducing myself to a stranger in Brooklyn who, for some reason, has a Southern accent."

He stood up and shook my hand. "Name might be Loving, Bobby Loving." Bobby then introduced me to the other men in the barbershop.

"You already met Mike. He's the big man in the barbershop—I let him think he runs the place."

Bobby then turned toward a lean, handsome man looking to be in his late 50s. He was wearing two-tone chocolate and white tasseled loafers, brown pants with a razor sharp crease, a matching brown and white argyle sweater and a crisp white T-shirt underneath. "This here is Sportin' Life," Bobby said. "He's good with a pool stick and better with the ladies."

Sportin' Life shook my hand. "Don't listen to all that mess he's talkin'," Sportin' Life said, "but if you do want to play some pool, I know just the spot. . . And maybe you want to bring your girlfriend with ya'—you know, just to get her out of the house."

To the left of Sportin' Life was another man, darker than the others, bigger and stockier than everyone except Mike. "This here's Talley," said Bobby. "Talley can drink him some wine, and he can fix a car like no man's business." Talley just grinned. "But he ain't much of a talker, are you Talley?" Talley smiled and nodded quietly.

"Talley's dark, too," Sportin' Life said with a smile. "Talley so dark, when he went to night school . . . they marked him *absent*."

We all settled back down and Mike went to work. "So, Bobby," I said, "tell me about Bowling Green."

"Born and raised there. Caroline County," he said nostalgically. "I got people all around there-bouts."

Talley and Sportin' Life both grew wistful as well. Sportin' Life spoke of the South Carolina low country where his roots lay. "My peoples are from Beaufort," he said, "and Lord, I love to go home. Try to make the reunion every year. I just like the fishing and the relaxing, and I like having my people with me is all. I'd like to retire and move back down there some day."

"*Back* down?" replied Mike. "You were born and raised right here on Flatbush Avenue. You talkin' about going 'back down'? How you goin' *back to* a place you ain't never *been from?*"

Sportin' Life brushed his hand at Mike, like he was talking nonsense. "Oh, you don't know what you talkin' about. Beaufort, South Carolina, that's me." Mike smiled, not wanting to wound the man's pride with the particulars.

Talley agreed with Sportin' Life. "Yup. Meridian, Mississippi, that's where my peoples are from. That's what I call home. Born in Harlem, raised in Brooklyn, but ain't no place but Meridian, Mississippi that I call home."

I listened intensely to these men as they spoke about the people and places that meant so much to them. And as they spoke of their homes down south, I realized that I was listening to an oral history of the greatest intra-migration in the modern era, the great migration of African Americans from the rural south into the industrial northern cities.

The men spoke fondly of their family reunions—great annual pilgrimages back to the town of family origination, invariably commemorated with a custom-made T-shirt. As I sat in that chair, Mike working around me with his scissors, an unexpected sense of patriotism came over me. *This is America,* I thought. *This barber shop, these people are worth fighting for.* When Mike finished cutting my hair, I thanked him, and, of course, pretended to walk out of the shop without paying. It was a predictable bit, but it got a laugh. After I came back, Bobby came up to me, grabbed my hand, leaned in close and said with his eyes moist with tears, "When you get down to Bowling Green, mention my name, would ya?" He looked out the window. "Mention my name around town. Up here I get no respect. I can't go out at night or I'll get mugged. I can't keep a nice car, cause it'll get ganked by the kids in the neighborhood. There's no respect up here, but down in Bowling Green people still respect me. People still remember that I played shortstop at Carolina High School, first year they let colored folks in the school. I batted .500 my senior year. People still remember that. People still remember that."

Driving out onto the Brooklyn Queens Expressway, I couldn't get

Bobby out of my mind. I felt like I owed him something. *This man deserves respect,* I thought. *This man deserves to sit in his barbershop and enjoy the life he has lived.* I felt proud of the fact that I was a soldier, and that I had the opportunity to serve a nation that let Bobby Loving play high school ball.

THE COMPANY YOU KEEP

"Hey, you cheese-dicks," the team sergeant said to us as Jiggy, Crunk, Boy Band and I were eating dinner in the chow hall. "Team meeting tonight at 1900 in the hooch."

"Team sergeant," Boy Band said, "can we—"

"Not till 1930. I've got some important stuff to put out, but after that the drinking lamp will be lit."

At 6:55 p.m. I walked back into the hooch. Crunk and Boy Band were already there. They were playing "Flinch," a game in which you formed a circle with your thumb and index finger, and if the other guy looked at it, you got to punch him. But if he can poke his finger through the circle, then he punched you. I used to play this game too—when I was 11. These men are both in their 30s, they held steady jobs, mortgages and families. It boggled the mind.

"Hey, Crunk, I got one for ya," Boy Band said.

"Let's hear it."

"Why do black people drive so fast?"

"I don't know, why?"

"Because they're *late!*"

Crunk stared at Boy Band silently for a moment, obviously thinking about a retort. "You know what you're going to be when you finally grow up?"

"What?"

"You're going to be one of those weirdo, middle-aged white guys."

"Which one?"

"Trying to figure that out."

"Brews-His-Own-Beer guy?"

"No, not Brews-His-Own-Beer guy."

"Model-Train-Set guy?"

"No, not Model-Train-Set guy."

"Recumbent-Bicycle Guy?"

"Yes!" Crunk said with triumph. "You're going to be Recumbent-Bicycle Guy—walking around in your cycling outfit and your pot belly."

"LOVE Recumbent Bicycle Guy," Boy Band said. "Wearing my

cycling helmet around when I shop at Whole Foods, clacking around in my bicycle shoes. Chicks dig a guy like that."

Team sergeant Lawton walked in with the team leader, Captain McMann. Frank Lawton was no longer the young shit-kicking cop he once was, but he remained intimidating. White and from the rural South, Frank Lawton wanted to play college football, but the only team that would take him was Norfolk State University, an historically black university. He started quarterback all four years, and graduated with some sort of sociology degree he cared nothing about. But he never forgot every one of the overly-articulating, angry, black professors who tried to sabotage his college career. He would tell us about them over the campfires, and explain to us the various ways he outflanked them all, getting them to renounce the things they had said to him in class, and making them make public apologies.

After that, Frank went through his "bodybuilding phase," and won Mr. Virginia. A police officer for Norfolk, he was on all their toughest units—SWAT Team, Scuba Rescue Team, whatever. If it was the toughest, he wanted to be on it. Now 50, he had lost a step and slimmed-down as well, but he once told me about the old days. "Back then, the cool thing was to come back to the station at the end of the shift with blood all over the hood of your car. . . . I always had blood covering the hood of my car." But the one thing about Frank, you didn't call him Frank. You called him team sergeant or you called him Dragline. He was not your buddy. He was not 'Frank.'

Captain Michael McMann was the antithesis of the team sergeant; where Dragline led by force of personality, Captain McMann led by character. A perfect reflection of another more genteel time, Captain McMann was a Virginia gentleman. The McMann family was a scion of one of the great tidewater families that first established the Virginia colony, like the Lees, the Randophs and the Fairfaxes. A fourth generation VMI graduate, service to the country ran in his blood. Although Captain McMann never discussed his personal life openly (such a thing would have been seen as vulgar), every member of the team listened to the tidbits he dropped and we pieced them together like patchwork. At VMI he had done well and was well liked. Upon graduation he accepted a commission in the Army, and after his time of service returned home to Virginia to earn his law degree at "The University"—UVA. Of course, such a disciplined, well-ordered and likable man was attractive to the ladies, and he married well, took a position with the appropriate Richmond firm, and began a family.

It was impossible not to like Captain McMann, not because of his successes, but because of his humility. He at all times thought of dignity, not just his own, but that of whomever he interacted with. He was a rare thing, a young man moving forward, but being particular about not bruising others in the rush. Jiggy pegged him best when he said, "Captain McMann is an officer you don't want to disappoint."

Still, there was something lonely and wistful about the captain. For, although he was a team leader on a Special Forces A-Team, he clearly longed for his days back in 'Division'. When a soldier uses the word 'Division', dropping the article 'the', there is only one unit he is talking about—the 82nd Airborne Division. At the age of 25, Captain McMann had taken command of an airborne infantry company. And you couldn't help but sense that everything in his life after that post had an element of the banal.

Jiggy sat down next to me, and the team sergeant began the meeting. "We're all here, so let's start."

"Spooky's not here," Jiggy said.

"Spooky's at an intel brief," Captain McMann said.

"Alright," continued the team sergeant. "The company commander and the sergeant major just came back from Fort Bragg. Looks like we're going to be incorporated into 2nd Battalion, 3rd Special Forces Group."

"D'oh!" sighed Jiggy. "I was hoping to get back in 1st Battalion." Jiggy had done 4 years in 1st Battalion, 3rd Special Forces Group.

"You all know," continued Dragline, "we've got positions in the team for twelve guys, but there's only seven of us—so we're a little light. I don't mind that, we know our jobs, know our equipment and know each other. There are five teams in the company, and the most men any of them have is nine. Major Brenner has been the company commander for over a year, and he'll lead us in Afghanistan—and bring us back. Sergeant major is still sergeant major, so we'll have complete continuity." Dragline stood, put his hands on his hips and looked at me. "Jet Set, you're the only one who hasn't been to the Advanced Urban Combat Course—you're goin' in March." I was glad to hear that. They were introducing a whole new approach to urban combat at the SFAUC school and I wanted to be trained up.

"Tomorrow," the team sergeant continued, "we'll be on the range all day dialing in our aiming optics. And don't ask me, because, yes, you will bring your issued weapons to Afghanistan. Each of you will have your same M-4 rifle. Tomorrow night you'll all be working with your night vision equipment, and, yes, you will all have the exact same Night Vision Googles (NVGs) you've been using for years. You're also going to dial in your infrared night lights, and you will have them lined up on your weapons with the upmost precision."

The team sergeant fell quiet, and Captain McMann cleared his throat. "Oh yeah," the team sergeant continued. "Right now you're on state orders—Title 32 orders—for three weeks. On December 17, you'll get released, go home for Christmas, then come back January third on federal mobilization orders. At that time, we'll pack up all our stuff and move to Fort Bragg." Dragline dropped his eyes. "Now, they wanted to put us on buses and drive us down there, and not allow us our personally owned vehicles." We all groaned at the thought, but Dragline looked back up and said, "The good news is Major Brenner raised hell about that and got them to let us bring our POVs."

We all cheered, and even the captain smiled.

"Sir, anything else?" the team sergeant said.

"No, team sergeant," Captain McMann replied.

"Then, boys, the drinking lamp is lit."

Just then, Spooky came in, walked over to the sofa and sat on the arm, hovering over us like a bird of prey.

Tall and lean, and with an angular face, Martin Schmidt—former sniper with the 5th Special Forces Group—and now an investigating officer for Immigration and Customs Enforcement (ICE), stood looking at me with his enigmatic, searing, black eyes.

Spooky was our intel sergeant. In an A-Team, the intel sergeant had a unique position. He was usually the guy waiting to take over the team sergeant's job—equal in rank, but not authority. This often led to unnecessary tensions within an A-Team. But if the team sergeant and the intel sergeant worked well together, it was like rocket fuel. Spooky and the team sergeant worked very well together, but where the team sergeant was fierce, Spooky had a more dark and menacing presence. He always seemed to be sizing you up, determining your motivation. He knew about people—their fears, their desires, their motivations—and you got the feeling he wasn't overly impressed by most of them.

THE UNBLEMISHED RED HEIFER

Ira Glass's *This American Life* is one of those radio shows I love and hate and love to hate. The show is smug and self-righteous, but Ira's got this laid back, just-hangin'-out sense of humor that I can't help but love. And the stories are very compelling. Besides, I secretly enjoy listening to the navel-gazing hipsters as they wryly comment on the world, then wryly comment on each other's wry comments.

Ira, who looks like the kid you used to beat up in elementary school, has a knack for creating gripping stories from a pastiche (yeah, it's a word) of interviews and voice-overs. Last week he told a story about the close, friendly relationship between a group of Orthodox Jews and a group of fundamentalist Christians. You would assume these two groups would be diametrically opposed to one another, but they have formed a close bond with the goal of sanctification of the Temple of Jerusalem.

The Old Testament says that the coming (for Jews) or second coming (for Christians) of the Messiah can only occur after the Temple of Jerusalem is rebuilt. One part of that rebuilding is the sanctification of the Temple through the sacrifice of an unblemished red heifer. At first blush, it would seem terrific that these two groups are working together and pursuing a common goal—you know, celebrating diversity and all that. But these guys aren't holding hands and singing the Coke song. The reason they want this heifer is to bring about the end of the world. As they both see it, the Messiah will not come (return) until there is a temple, so it is their duty to build it. The big problem for these guys is that when the Muslims took Jerusalem, they built a mosque on the Temple Mount—awkward, right?

It was an interesting story, filled with great interviews of the people involved, and it left me feeling deeply uneasy. The idea of people actively, diligently, and eagerly working for the end of the world was unnerving. The day after I'd heard the radio program, we were out on the range, and I was up in the observation tower giving direction to the firers: "Right side is ready. Left side is ready. Firers, switch your selector switch from safe to semi, and *watch* your lanes." But I kept thinking about the unblemished red heifer. So, when I had a break, I called over to Jiggy—the most religious man I know—and said, "Hey, do you know anything about this unblemished red heifer?"

"What?" he said with confusion. "No, I don't know what you're talking about."

"I do," said Dragline. He was at the ammo table, loading his magazines with 5.56, and he had an enormous chaw of chewing tobacco in his mouth. I had forgotten that Dragline had gone through a period where he was a deeply devout Christian. This was sometime after his "Bodybuilding Phase" and before his "Who Gives a Shit Phase." He used to read the Bible all the time, and was surprisingly well-versed. Once, when we were out in the woods on a training mission, the company commander found a reason to go home, and Dragline said under his breath, "Uriah the Hittite wouldn't do that."

"Yeah," he said in a disinterested manner, "the Messiah ain't returning until the Temple is restored and sanctified. The only way to sanctify the Temple is with the blood of an unblemished red heifer." With that Dragline spit out a mouthful of tobacco juice.

"Well, team sergeant," I said. "Doesn't it worry you to know people are diligently working to bring about the end of the world?"

He just laughed. "Nah," he said, "who gives a shit? Before they can sanctify the Temple, they've got to actually *build* it, and—last I checked—the Muslims are in possession of the Temple Mount. If the Jews ever take the Temple Mount from the Muslims and start building a temple, the whole world is going to go bat-shit crazy, and you're gonna have a hell of a lot more to worry about than that the hicks and the Jews Frankensteined a super cow."

"I'm so glad you're my team sergeant," I said. "You bring such comfort."

THE HIDE SITE

"It's called a 'hide'," Boy Band said. "Not a 'hide site'."

"Not according to Field Manual 7-93," I said. "It's a 'hide site'."

"Did you go to sniper school?" Boy Band asked. "Because *I* went to sniper school, and *I* was instructed that it was called a hide." The issue of nomenclature would seem ridiculous to anyone who had never spent a day in the Army. But both of us had, so this was going to be a pissing contest.

A hide site is a small position that offers good observation and concealment, and an adequate area for team rest, maintenance, and personal hygiene. In other words it's a tiny hole you dig in the ground and cover back up with natural vegetation so no one can see you, and you look out of the tiny slit you made to observe your target. You have to maintain eyes on a target for at least 24 hours before you hit it, so Boy Band and I would be in our hide a long time taking turns looking out the binoculars—the binos—taking notes of what we saw, and basically just farting on each other.

It took all night to build the hide site, but we concealed it well, and in the morning the Opposition Force—OPFOR—couldn't detect us. Boy Band took the first shift, and I racked-out for a few hours. I don't like eating in a hide site, because everything that goes into a hide site has to come out, not just the food, but when you're . . . um, *done* with the food. I did my shift, and we switched out again, and now it was high noon, and the sun was out. We were lying under a poncho with branches and dirt camouflaging us, but we both got sort of sleepy. Trying to stay awake, I looked around the hide site. It was about 24 inches high, and ten feet by four feet. In the back were both of our rucksacks, and I noticed that Boy Band had a baseball mitt sticking out of his ruck. "Why do you have a baseball glove in your ruck?" I asked.

Boy Band looked around at his ruck. "Oh," he said. "When we get released for the weekend, I may not have time to go home, so I can go right to the game."

"You're still coaching little league? How can you do that when you're here at Bragg?"

"Just assisting," said Boy Band. "Just for fun."

"I never understood that," I said. "Why you coach little league even though your son is five and too young to play."

Boy Band pulled his eyes away from the binos and looked up thoughtfully. "I like kids," he said. Then he spit on the ground way from the binocular tripod. "Hell, kids are the only good thing in this screwed-up world."

"Kids grow-up," I said. "And they get screwed-up."

"Yeah," he replied. "But when they're kids, they're still kids." Boy Band nodded, as if agreeing to himself. "Yeah," he repeated, "they're the only good thing in the world."

I looked at the building 400 meters to the west we were observing, then looked back to see Boy Band still looking up at the hide site ceiling. "I think God is a kid," he said. "Everybody thinks God is this old guy with a white beard, touching fingers with that guy with the little dick. But I think God is a kid." Boy Band kept his eyes glued on the ceiling. "He never gets old—God—because he doesn't do wrong. He only does what's right, so how can he get old?" Boy Band looked back into the binos. "That's why every day *happens*, that's why babies get born. God likes seeing wonderful things happen over and over again." Boy Band turned and looked at me. "You ever show a magic trick to a kid?"

"Sure."

"What's the first thing the kid wants ya to do?"

"I don't know—"

"He wants to see it again," replied Boy Band. "You show a kid a trick and he's like, 'do it again', 'do it again'. He never gets tired of it."

I laughed. It was true, all my nieces and nephews were exactly that way. "I think God's like that," said Boy Band. "God likes people—as screwed-up as we are—he likes us. And when he sees a person being born, God says 'do it again', 'do it again'."

"Some people don't believe there is a God," I said. "They say, 'How can there be a God if He lets all these terrible things in the world happen'?"

Boy Band scoffed. "Yeah, that's our whole relationship with God. He loves givin' us stuff, and we love screwing it up—then blaming Him for our screw-ups." He spit again away from the tripod. "That's what we do, 'Oh, God, everything's so screwed-up, help us!' And God hears us and He says, 'Oh, goodness, my children are in need. I'll give them the greatest thing in the whole world, I'll give them a baby—an innocent human being. Nothing's greater than that.' And, of course, we screw that up too. And so God says, 'Well, obviously they need more', and boom, boom, boom, he gives us more of the greatest thing there is. And we manage to screw that up as well—yeah, we humans, we're a real piece of work." I looked over at Boy Band. This was the meanest son of a bitch I'd ever known, and he was talking like a philosopher.

"I remember about two years ago," he continued. "This kid, Randy, didn't get picked up by his parents after baseball practice. I think they just forgot him. Anyway, the kid was no athlete, uncoordinated, a terrible fielder. I mean this kid couldn't catch his dick in a zipper."

"Nice metaphor," I said.

Boy Band brushed me aside. "But I picked up the bat and said, 'Randy, run out there to center field and I'll hit ya some fly balls.' Kid was scared shitless, had those big frightened eyes weak kids get. But he said, 'Okay, coach'. And he runs out to the field." Boy Band pulled away from the binos and rolled over on his back. "I had about 30 balls, and I just started plinking'em out to him." Boy Band swept his hands across his torso, like he was lazily swinging a bat. "Sun was starting to go down, you know, and we were the only ones on the ball field. And you could smell that fresh-cut grass. That first one Randy ran under, then did that thing nervous kids do, where his feet hop around like he's not sure what to do. But he steadied himself, raised his mitt and bam, he caught it." Boy Band smiled. "Kid pulled it out of his mitt and held it up in the air like a trophy. So I kept hitting to him, the ball going up in that long arch over the infield, dropping down into his glove. For 20 minutes all you could hear was the plink of the bat, then silence, and finally the slap of the leather as Randy caught the ball. I hit him 30 balls, and he caught every one. Round about that time, we see a minivan pulling into the parking lot with its lights on, and Randy came up to me with that look kids get, where they're suddenly incredibly serious, where you see in them a focus you couldn't have in a million years. And he looks up at me and says, 'Thank you, coach. Thank you'." Boy Band rolled back over and looked again through the binos. "Randy probably forgot about it the very next day, but I'll never forget. I'll never forget that day when I saw a kid who was perfect, who was perfectly perfect."

Later, I took the watch position and it was Boy Band's chance to be bored. "Didn't you used to box?" he said, casting about for things to talk about.

"Yeah," I said. "I boxed for a couple years."

"Were you any good?"

"Yeah, I was good. Basically found a *niche* and exploited it."

"How did you find a *niche* in boxing? I mean, isn't it just beatin' people's asses?"

"Pretty much," I said. "But it's like anything, there are windows you can take advantage of."

"You sound like a foreign field goal kicker on a football team, 'I have skill-set, is useful in your *American* football'."

"Yeah," I said. "Just put that field goal kicker in the ring with me, see who gets the extra point." I rolled over away from the binos. "No, I won because I was in better shape than the other dudes. I fought Heavy Weight," I said. "In amateur, Heavy Weight is 201 pounds—over 201 is Super Heavy. The thing is, not many 200 pound dudes can go three three-minute rounds. Even one three-minute round is a lot. You have no idea what it's like being in the ring for three minutes—it's an eternity. But what I had over the others is that I was always *way* more in shape than the guys I went up against. They were mostly these powerful but overweight black guys."

"Why's it got to be black?"

"You tell me? That's just what it was. Me fighting big black guys."

"So, how did it go?"

"Oh, I'd beat the shit out of them—if I could make it out of the first round."

"What?" Boy Band said with a laugh.

"Well," I said, "I wasn't some genius fighter, I just had stamina, and if I could make it through the first round with these guys, they were done." I punched up into the air, maybe a little too hard, letting Boy Band know it wasn't nothing to me. "I did have a good jab, and a good straight right. But I was stiff, and I wasn't good on my feet—the usual white guy problems." Boy Band rolled his eyes. "You ever step into the squared circle with the entire crowd screaming for your blood?"

"No."

"That's what it was," I said. "It was just me, the *White Guy*, in the ring with these big, black guys, and a crowd, at least 95% black, all screaming for my blood." Boy Band went silent. "And you climb those steps with your crew. There are four ropes that create the ring, and your seconds pull up on the third rope and step down on the second rope, and you climb in. And it's on." Boy Band was suddenly interested.

"All you want to do is kill that man across the ring," I said, "and all he wants to do is kill you. And it's lonely, it's really lonely, but it's beautiful too."

"What do you remember most about boxing?" Boy Band asked, a note of sincerity in his voice.

I thought about it. It was a question I had never asked myself before. "When I think about boxing, I think about wrapping my hands."

"What?"

"When you're training, you wrap your hands with 'wraps' made of heavy cotton. And there's a science to it, and it takes time. So, while you're staring at your hands, threading the wraps around your wrists, between your fingers and over your knuckles, you're thinking about fighting, you're thinking about climbing into that ring and killing the man across from you." I rolled over on my back a second time, and stared at my hands, and started miming wrapping my hands. "You always start on the left hand, because combinations start with the left— it's a superstition. The wrap has a loop at one end, you hook the loop around your thumb and pull it down diagonally across the hand to the wrist, and you encircle the wrist once, twice, three, then four times— your wrist has to be sturdy or you'll snap it." I looked up at Boy Band who was listening intently. "Then you arch it up, between the thumb and pointer finger, across the palm of the hand, and you wrap your knuckles four times. Then you bring it down from between the pointer finger and the thumb across the palm, wrap your wrist once, and bring it up over the back of the hand, then down between the pinkie and ring finger, then down the palm and around the wrist again, then up between the ring and index fingers, then down again around the wrist, then a second time around the wrist and you come up on the other side, and you 'X' the back of your hand and run the wrap between your index and your pointer finger, then you go one time around your knuckles, one time around your wrist and you tie it off."

"That's a lot of wrap."

"120 inches."

"Sounds like a lot of work."

"You're preparing to kill. You need your hands to be ready, and it puts you in the right frame of mind."

"What was your favorite fight?"

"The night I won the Golden Gloves, I guess. The night I TKO-ed Levron Brent."

"You won the Golden Gloves?"

"The Regionals," I said. "I won DC, Maryland and Virginia."

"Doubt it."

"Look it up, bitch. 1993 in the Heavy Weight Division. Nationals were in Little Rock that year, and I went."

"How'd ya do?"

"Um, you know. . ."

"Got your ass beat, didn't you?"

"No, went all three rounds. He beat me up pretty good in the first, but he lost his gas in the third, and I almost knocked him out. Thing is, the fights were only six minutes long, three two-minute rounds. That threw my whole game off. Most of what I really had was stamina, and when they cut the fight time by one third, I lost my edge."

"Okay," said Boy Band. "So tell me about the big fight, Champ."

I laughed, "Okay," I said. "Let me set the stage. It's Hillcrest Heights auditorium, in Prince George's County—deep in the hood. I think I'm the only white guy in the whole place. So when we go to weigh-in, Levron sees that I'm white and—I shit you not—he turns to his people and says, 'Buy me my plane ticket, 'cause I'm goin' to the Nations'."

Boy Band laughed. "I can see that."

"Yeah," I said. "His people laughed all over themselves. Did that thing black guys do when they fall all over themselves laughing. It didn't go unnoticed."

"Okay, so anyway, tell me about the fight."

"Well, Brent was solid. Shorter than me—which meant I could tag the shit out of him with that jab—but he was built. His legs were like tree trunks, and his arms were like . . . well, they were also like tree trunks. The guy was solid." I turned over and looked again through the binos. "While we were prepping, my people were telling me to use my jab, stay outside of him and keep my distance. 'Just keep snappin' that jab', my trainer kept repeating. But, of course, I was out for blood after what he said. So when the bell rang the two of us just walked into the middle of the ring and started slugging."

Boy Band started to laugh in earnest. "So, 'screw all that' you said, 'we gonna throw down'."

"Pretty much. My corner was screaming at me, but I didn't give a shit. We just stood in the middle of the ring goin' toe to toe. And he had a solid punch—I mean, I *felt* each one—but I just returned everything he gave me. And the crowd was loving it. I mean, they were on their feet the entire time. Usually, Heavy Weights are sort of boring, but we stood there in the center of the ring like two battleships delivering broadsides."

"Can you do that for three minutes?" asked Boy Band.

"Well, *I could*," I said. "Round about 2:30 in the round ole Levron started to flag. He was getting tired, and, because we were so close, he started leaning his head against my shoulders. Just before the bell rang, I started thinking I could drop an upper-cut right to his chin. But the bell sounded and we went back to our corners. And, man, was my corner mad. 'Stay on the outside', my trainer keep shouting, 'you got the jab, stick with it'!"

"Of course, you didn't listen."

"Natch," I said. "I was only interested in killing the guy."

"So, round two."

"Round two started exactly the same way. We walked right into the middle of the ring and went to town. The crowd was on their feet, and the corners got to yelling. But about 30 seconds into the three minute round, ole Levron started flagging. Now, we've got two and a half minutes of close quarters combat, and he's running out of gas, and he starts leaning on me again. The thing about an upper-cut is that you don't just drop your hand down and punch up, you drop at the hips, you squat down, and drive that punch up. It comes from the legs, that's why it's devastating. Watch Mike Tyson, he drops and delivers from the thighs. That's what I did. Levron had his head resting on my shoulder, and I dropped down and came up from my legs and put that upper-cut right on his chin—right on the button. And, man, he lost his shit! His head went back and his arms splayed out like Christ on the Cross. But he didn't go down. I give him that. He never went down. But the crowd went crazy. As soon as I connected, the entire crowd let out this gigantic, 'OHHHHHHHH!'"

Boy Band was now riveted. "Not a knock down, though," he said.

"He got a standing eight," I said. "And not only that, but he was completely out on his feet. The referee saw it, but he wasn't going to let some white boy walk away with an easy victory. He counted the eight, then sort of walked around between us, trying to give the guy a few extra seconds. After that drama, Levron and I went right back to it. For about 20 seconds he was as game as ever, but then he started resting his head against me again, and I just thought, *hell, let's do it again.* So I dipped down low again, and, BOOM! came up with that same upper-cut! The crowd went crazy, and Levron's hands splayed out, and he got another standing eight. And at this point, Levron's been given a count twice in a single round. You get three counts in a round and it's over. Nobody can contest that. So there's still more than a minute in the round. And we get back together, and for about 15 seconds we're going toe to toe, but then ole Levron starts tuckering out, and, again, he starts resting his head on me and, BLAM! I drop that upper-cut. Levron's head pops up, his arms splay out and the ref rushes in to stop the fight."

"But you never dropped him?" Boy Band said.

"No," I said. "It was amazing. The guy never went down."

"So that's not a knock out."

"It was a Technical Knock Out," I said, with a bit of annoyance.

"But he never went to the canvass."

"I won the Golden Gloves," I said. "What did you ever win, 'Miss Congeniality'?"

HEAVY WEAPONS

"Hang it. . . . Fire!" The sergeant major shouted, and I dropped the 81 mm round down the mortar tube. The round hit the bottom of the tube, rocketing it out and, seconds later, 1800 meters away, a denuded hilltop exploded. The sergeant major smiled and congratulated me even before the explosion could be heard. "Geez," said the sergeant major, "I've never seen so much ammunition on a practice range in my life. Back in the 70s they used to tell us to pick up a stick and point it down range."

The sergeant major was in a good mood. "Last day of training," he told us on the bus ride to the range. "It's been good training these last two weeks—aggressive, but safety-conscious." It had been good training. Tomorrow we would be released for Christmas. When we came back after New Year's, we would pack up and head to Fort Bragg—and from there we'd be bound for glory.

"I haven't used a mortar since I was stationed in Alaska," I told Jiggy.

"Yeah," he replied. "When I was a private, I used to have to hump that big ole base plate on top of my rucksack—it gets heavier with every mile." I laughed. "Add that to your issue equipment," he continued, "and you're humping over 100 lbs. It gets old in a hurry."

The mortars were a blast, but the real fun began when we started working the Mark 19 and the M 2 .50 caliber machine gun. The Mark 19 was the latest thing in the Army inventory—and it was a shit-kicker. It worked in tandem with the .50 cal, and the two together could be an unstoppable combination of death and destruction. The Mark 19 was basically a machine gun that fired bombs—what's not to like, right?

The M 2 .50 caliber was for direct fire—if you could see it, you could kill it. The .50 fired an enormous bullet, and it had a mountain of gunpowder behind it, so it had a range out to, like, forever. Marine legend Carlos Hathcock had confirmed kills out to 2,500 yards. The Mark 19 was (mostly) for indirect fire—when the bad guys ran behind the hill, you just aimed the Mark 19 at a high angle and rained death down on them.

The heavy weapons range was not like the rifle range. It was massive in size—over a mile in every direction—and it was not all brush and grass. It had mature trees and even acres of woods within "the box." As soon as Jiggy got behind the .50 cal, he started picking out medium-sized trees—10 to 12 inches in diameter—about 800 meters away. And then he began mowing them down with the .50 cal. After he cut down about four trees, everybody wanted to do it. The .50 caliber ammunition we were using had tracer rounds in it to help see where the bullets were going, and these tracer rounds started setting fire to the brush. I was on the Mark 19, so Jiggy said, "See if you can put those fires out with the Mark 19."

I swung the Mark 19 around and walked the rounds into the fire, smothering the flames with high explosives. Since cutting down trees was all anybody on the .50 wanted to do, blowing up fires was all anybody on the Mark 19 could do. This went on for hours.

Later in the day, as it was growing dark, the sergeant major started easing things back so we could close down the range. We began cleaning up the brass and breaking down the weapons. With the sun beginning to set, we only had one .50 cal and one Mark 19 still in action. Unfortunately, we ran out of Mark 19 rounds before we ran out of .50 cal rounds. So when the sergeant major gave the word to break down the last two weapons there were no fires visible to the naked eye—but there was a good degree of smoke still rising from the hillside.

The Range Control Safety Officer came and cleared us from the range just as the sun was beginning to set. Even before Range Control left, you could start to see fires sparking back up along the far ridge line. I nudged the team sergeant. He looked over and said, "Just get on the bus, you didn't see shit."

By the time we were all on the bus and a good headcount was taken, the entire ridge line was in flames. When the major got on the bus, every eye was on him. If we had to go out there and put out those fires, we'd be there all night. Tomorrow we were going home, and this could very easily turn into a serious goat screw. The major and the sergeant major looked at the fire, looked at each other and they both shrugged— "We're cleared from the range," said the major. "It's not our problem." The entire bus burst out cheering.

"Let's go home, boys," the sergeant major said. "You got your Christmas present early this year."

The sun was now behind the hills, and as our bus drove along the gravel road parallel to the burning ridge line, we saw the entire west side of the horizon in flames. We had spent the day in an orgy of high explosives, and now with night settling in, the eerie orange glow of fire reflected off faces. Boy Band turned to Crunk. "Remember *Full Metal*

Jacket?" he said. "At the end of the battle of Hue, when the whole city was burning?"

"Yeah," replied Crunk. "They started singing the *Mickey Mouse* song."

Boy Band began, and Crunk joined in, "Who's the leader of the band, who's made for you and me—"

Everyone heard it, and everyone got the reference. The entire bus was about to break out singing along with them, but just then the sergeant major jumped up, visibly angry. "No fuckin' way!" he shouted. "No fuckin' way are we singing that loser song!" The sergeant major was the only one in the unit who'd fought in Vietnam. He had won the Distinguished Service Cross, lost many friends and been wounded twice. We were in high spirits, but his word was the law and I thought we'd have to sit in stoney silence all the way home. But just then, the sergeant major let out a single, clear note, his voice a crystalline tenor, beautiful, mournful, pure as he sang 'The Ballad of the Green Berets':

"Fighting soldiers from the sky
  Fearless men who jump and die
  Men who mean just what they say
  The brave men of the Green Beret"

The sound was so haunting it had us stunned. Then Captain McMann came in with him, with a youthful, tempered voice:

"Silver wings upon their chest
  These are men, America's best
  One hundred men will test today
  But only three win the Green Beret"

We all joined in, the bus vibrating with song now, the bus driver looking bewildered.

The song over, the bus made the long drive back to the barracks. It was now completely dark. No street lights, and a pitch black sky. The only lights were the headlights of the bus as it wound slowly down the gravel road of the range. Every man on the bus remained absolutely silent, afraid to disrupt the perfect unity we felt. We stayed silent even when we got to the barracks. The next day no one mentioned that voice or the song we sang. It was too exquisite a thing to ruin with words.

MARYLAND MY MARYLAND

All of Maryland is divided into three parts: the region of the Potomac, where the people cheer for the Redskins; the region of the Chesapeake, where the people cheer for the Ravens; and the region of the western mountains, where—inexplicably—the people cheer for Penn State.

I'd been staying with my folks in Maryland since we left Fort A.P. Hill. My old neighborhood was once the outer edge of the Washington suburbs. The post office called it "Rockville," but the house was nowhere near the City of Rockville. It was once so rural a neighborhood that the idea of putting your dog on a leash was abhorrent. When I was a kid, we thought it was normal to have a pack of dogs at the school bus stop, chasing cars and biting tires. As the years rolled on, and the area became engulfed in suburban sprawl, the neighborhood remained unchanged—a quirky collection of sporadically built homes, each on at least a one-acre plot. It was a place where grand mansions sat next to two bedroom bungalows with chicken roosts and vast vegetable gardens.

The family home was a nice place to spend Christmas, but still there was tension with me heading off to Afghanistan. A couple of days before Christmas, I was helping my mom set up the Nativity scene, and as we worked, my mom started casually telling me the story of her eldest brother, Uncle Richard, who was a bombardier in World War II. "I was just seven years old when Richard went away," my mother said, "but I'll never forget it." Her eyes, of a sudden, flashed with bitter memory. "Your grandmother—my mother—would march us all down to Queen of Victory parish in Chicago every First Friday—Lillian, Anne, Jack and I." As my mom began to tell the story, she reached into the box of figurines covered in old newspaper and uncovered the figurine of the Blessed Virgin Mary. My mother never even looked at the figurine she had pulled out, but, as she remembered those hard times, she began to unconsciously shift it from one hand to the other. "We would pray the rosary for Richard," she said, the vivid, long lost memory returning to her. "Not just five decades, but the whole thing, 15 decades. And then we would go to Mass." My mother wiped something away from her eyes. "And the entire time your grandmother would be on her knees praying for Richard to come home safely." My mother looked at anything but me as she spoke.

"Three times, we completed the Nine First Fridays," she said, now clutching the Virgin Mary to her chest. "And three times Richard's plane was almost shot out of the sky. They lost an engine over the Channel and had to crash-land in a field; they lost most of a wing over Stuttgart, but straggled home to England, safely; and last they lost all their hydraulic fluid from a strafing, and landed on their belly." My mother unconsciously jabbed the figurine into her heart. "But not one man on Richard's plane ever received so much as a scratch—not one was scratched!"

My mother dropped her hands to her side. "But *God* the toll it took on my mother. I remember the waiting, the not-knowing." She began to thump the figurine against her chest. "She used to march us down Agatite Avenue, with that Chicago wind howling at us like a *banshee*, and those gold stars mocking us from the windows on every side—row after row of gold stars, and every one like a dagger in the heart." My mother stiffened. "And after '44, those gold stars spread like cancer. Not one apartment building was without a gold star, sometimes you'd see three or four of them in a single building. And the wind always howling, always howling like a *banshee, * like *ban-shee* it screamed at us every time we walked down the avenue."

My mother looked at me angrily, took the figurine of the Virgin Mary and jabbed me with it. "You think about that," she said. "You think about what it's like for a mother to hear the keening of the *banshee*, when you run off to war with your rowdy buddies."

The Christmas party was in full swing by the time I came home from Mass. My Uncle Ron was in the kitchen, and, of course, he was telling a joke: "So, there's this guy, right? He's sitting in his kitchen on Sunday morning, drinking a cup of coffee, and the doorbell rings. He— you know—puts the coffee down, goes to the door, opens the door, and there's no one there. He looks left, nobody. Looks right, still nobody. Looks on the ground, and there he sees his newspaper. 'Oh, yeah, the paper' he says to himself. Then he sees that on top of the paper is sitting a snail. So he takes the snail and chucks it into the neighbor's yard." Uncle Ron paused and smiled.

"Ten years later," he continued. "Ten years later, the same guy is sitting down in the same chair, in his kitchen drinking a cup of coffee. And the doorbell rings. Guy gets up, puts his coffee down, goes to the door and opens it. Nobody's there. Guy looks left, nobody. Looks right, nobody. Then the guy looks down and there he sees a snail. And the snail is lookin' up at the guy, and the snail says, 'What the fuck was that all about?'"

We all laughed. But when the laughter died down, my uncle turned to me with a concerned look. "Timmy," he said, "your dad says you're going to Afghanistan. Is this for real?"

"Yes, Uncle Ron, this is for real."

There was hesitation in his voice, and he looked at me in a way that was disapproving. "This is not good, Timmy," he said. "You have a family that loves you. Hell, you're an attorney, Timmy. Can't you figure a way out of this?"

"I don't want to figure a way out of this, Uncle Ron," I said. "I want to go."

"Why would you want to do that?" Uncle Ron said. Years of Jesuit education, devotion to the Catholic Worker movement and the writings of Catholic peace activists Daniel and Philip Berrigan had made him intrinsically averse to the military. This was going to get ugly.

His son, my cousin, Matt, was standing next to me, and he could see the signs of an awkward conversation. Matt and I grew up together. He was now a fourth grade school teacher. Matt threw an arm around me and said, "Hey, come on, Dad. Timmy's going off to seek his fortune. Good on ya, Timmy. We're all real proud."

"Thanks," I said. "I'd like to think people were proud, but it doesn't always come off that way."

"Oh, no," said Uncle Ron. "We're proud of what you're doing. It's the government we're not sure of. War is a deeply moral issue, and the way we've just jumped into this thing causes deep moral concern for thinking people."

"And I disagree with you," I said, "so therefore I'm not a *thinking person*?"

My uncle laughed. "That's a trick I learned at Fordham."

"I get it," I replied, a little bit too emotionally, "but last I checked *they* hijacked four jet planes filled with innocent people and flew them into three buildings filled with innocent people."

"The Afghan people did that?" replied my uncle. "I don't think that's correct."

"Their government harbored those who did," I said. "The Taliban supported it, and that's who we are at war with."

"Let's assume *arguendo*" (Uncle Ron loved his Latin) "that your

96

premise is correct. Moreover, let's accept that the Taliban and bin Laden are equally guilty—which I do not agree with. Even so, the Afghan people are not. The Taliban conquered the country along with bin Laden and other foreigners, and their rule is deeply oppressive. Our invasion will lead to many innocent lives being lost, prevent humanitarian assistance from reaching starving Afghanis, and will create a horrible refugee crisis."

I didn't like what my uncle was saying, but I always enjoyed arguing with him. "Those aren't arguments *against* war," I said. "Those are simply factors to weigh when *contemplating* war." Now I was going to get him. "I'm afraid you are arguing *petitio principi,*" I said with a smile. "Your point is 'because eggs will be broken, it is wrong to have an omelet'. This is a fallacy."

It was on.

My use of the Latin must have awoken something in his dormant Jesuit soul, because he came alive: "Well," he replied, "your premise is an *argumentum ad ignorantiam*—you are arguing that 'certainly, what I say is true, no one has proven it is not.'"

I had wanted to keep things light, but I got pissed off just the same, and went a little sideways. "*De profundis!*" I exclaimed, a bit too emotionally. "*De profundis clamavi ad te*—'from the depths I cry out to you!'" I said. "From the depths, I cry that we will be avenged!"

"Avenge what?" said Uncle Ron. "The Afghanis did nothing."

"The Afghanis harbored those who did this to us," I said. "That place is a viper's nest, and we will crush the head of every viper in that forsaken land."

"So an *argumentum ad baculum*—and appeal to force," said Uncle Ron, triumphantly. "And we call ourselves a nation of laws."

"Whoa," said Matt, playing peacemaker. "It's Christmas, Timmy, leave it for another time. We've got to give our parents some slack. My dad's just worried about you."

I laughed nervously. "Yeah," I said, shaking off my emotions, feeling slightly embarrassed. "I know, and I appreciate it."

Uncle Ron came up to me and gave me a hug. "We are concerned, Timmy. We want you to be safe."

I wasn't in the hugging mood. "I'll be fine," I said.

Uncle Ron looked at me with an awkward pride. "Where'd you learn your Latin?"

"From you," I said, "and my dad." I thought about the many times when I was a kid that they used to throw Latin phrases at each other,

97

both being altar boys and both being Jesuit educated.

Matt got me out of the kitchen, and he said in something of a whisper, "Hey, I've got a story I'd like your opinion on." We walked into the living room.

"Okay," I said, "I'm listening."

"Well, right after September 11th a crazy thing happened in my classroom."

"What, someone hide your chalk?"

"We use whiteboards now."

"Whatever."

"No, after 9/11, I was leading a 'current events' discussion with the class. And, naturally, it was all about Mohammad Atta and the terrorist attacks. And the kids knew the facts, because a lot of them have parents who work at the Pentagon. None of my kids lost any parents, but it was a big deal to them." Matt took a big breath. "So, we're talking about Mohammad Atta and the other terrorists who hijacked the flights, and just about then Shamina Khan, the perky little Pakistani girl in the second row, raises her hand and cheerfully tells the class, 'Oh, no, you have it all wrong. It was the Jews who hijacked those planes, and it was the Jews who killed all those people. Then they made it look like Muslims did it, because that's what Jews do.'"

"Wait. What?"

"That's what I said."

"What did the other students do?"

"Oh, the room went silent. All the other kids were just looking at Shamina like she had snakes in her hair."

"Wow, what did you do?"

Matt picked up his cup of cider and took a sip. "Well, I tried to mollify the situation, of course. I figured she was just confused. So I said, 'Gosh, Shamina, where'd you hear that?' You know what she said?"

"What?"

"'My parents told me. Also my uncle and my cousins as well. Everybody knows it was the Jews. The *Imam* has put it out at the mosque as an article of faith.'"

"Man," I said. "That is nuts." Matt and I started to laugh, but the laughter died away and we were left just shaking our heads. After a long while, I said to Matt, "You know, it's genius, really."

"What do you mean, genius?"

"Well, you have to admire it for what it is, strategically brilliant," I said. "It's a battle of the narratives. The *Imam*, the family, even the little girl, they all just said, 'Fuck it, we don't care what the truth is. This isn't about the truth. This is about choosing sides.' It doesn't matter what actually happened, it only matters who wins out. Once you win, you can make up the truth."

"No," said Matt, incredulously. "It's a lie, and it will never become true. Lies do not become truth."

"That's not what they're betting on," I said. "I think they see it as a contest that they can win. Think about it, you don't explain, you don't apologize, and if you're asked for particulars, you stick to your story."

"That seems," said Matt, "inhuman."

"What do you call what happened on 9-11?"

"But they were terrorists."

"And they just sprung up from the ground? They fell out of the sky? They weren't nurtured in an environment? What do you call it when an *Imam* in a middle class suburb of the United States puts this out to the entire mosque? What do you call it when successful professionals blithely go about their business saying, 'Oh, the Jews did it?'"

"But still," Matt said, "you're talking about some great conspiracy."

"Who needs a conspiracy," I said, "when everybody already agrees on the general outline."

I looked around the room at my cousins, my brothers, my family. It was beautiful, and warm—it was Christmas. But they didn't see things the way I saw them. To them, little Shamina was a one-off, just a weird story. To me it was the brilliant strategy of a resilient opponent: ten year old Shamina believes it was the Jews who attacked us on September 11th, and all the other girls roll their eyes and make "gag me" motions when she talks; four years from now, Shamina believes the Jews committed the terrorist attacks, and all the other girls believe in unicorns and *Tiger Beat Magazine;* four years later, and Shamina believes the Jews did it, and the other girls believe that these jeans make them look fat; at 22, Shamina's still talking about the Jews, and that stunt they pulled off back on September 11, 2001, while all the girls in her class believe they are vegetarian lesbians; at 35 Shamina stays with her belief, while the other girls don't believe anything at all, they just wish the Jews hadn't attacked us on 9/11.

"I don't know," said Matt. "I can understand some level of cognitive dissonance in the Muslim community, but you have to remember we are two totally different cultures trying to learn to live together."

"Matt," I replied, "what have they done to make you think they're trying?"

The party was a great time, my brothers and their wives and family were all there. The thing is, no one in my family shared my enthusiasm for going to Afghanistan. In fact, they were dubious about it—it almost felt like an intervention. All of them, from my parents down to my youngest brother, *assumed* that, first off, I *could* get out of the deployment, and secondly, that I *wanted* to get out of the deployment. I felt like I spoke a different language from them.

I told them, like, a hundred times that I *wanted* to go and it didn't register with anyone in my family. The last day was the worst day of all. I was with my dad at the mall shopping, and he said, "So, what have you done to get out of this?" Talking to me like I was a college kid with bad grades—like the problem was that I wasn't 'putting forth the effort'.

"Dad," I said, "I'm not getting out! I'm a soldier, don't you get it? I'm not going to disgrace myself. I'm glad to go to war. I want to do my duty."

My dad didn't bat an eye. He just looked at me like I must have misunderstood his question. "But you're an attorney?" he said.

"I'm also a soldier in the United States Army, and I would never try to get out of this opportunity."

"Opportunity?" he replied. "Opportunity for what, getting your legs blown off, getting killed?"

"Opportunity for honor, for promotion, and for serving my country."

"But what about your future?" he said.

"What about our country!" I replied. "Don't you get it, Dad? This is war. This is what I've been waiting for."

Naturally, my dad spoke to my mom. And when we came back from the mall, she was very quiet and circumspect with me. We had our last dinner together and after it was over, while I was at the sink cleaning dishes, out of nowhere, my mom blurted out, "Do you feel like you are finally living your life now?"

Her question took me completely by surprise, but I knew what she was asking. After I thought about it, I said, "I feel like things are laid out in front of me in a way that I can finally understand. And that all I have to do is perform the tasks given to me correctly. All I have to do is my duty."

"Well," my mom said, tears streaming from her eyes, "I don't understand you at all. But I would like to think that I raised my children to be free and brave." She paused and wiped the tears from her eyes. "But you can't control men who are free and brave." She put down the dish she was drying, and turned her face away from me. "Just promise me that you will go to Mass on Sunday, and that you'll confess your sins as often as possible. I couldn't stand it," she said, "I couldn't stand it if I were in Heaven and there stood a great gulf between us."

SERGEANT FIRST CLASS

When we returned after Christmas, I was promoted to sergeant first class. The sergeant major called me into his office and said, "Congratulations, Jet Set, you got promoted." Then he grabbed me by the collar and pulled me close to his face—so close I could smell the garlic on his breath. And he said, "With promotion comes responsibility, Jet Set. Greater duties. Higher standards. Duty—it's all about duty."

At first formation, Major Brenner called me out, and the command "Attention to Orders" was given, and my new chevrons with double rockers were pinned on. The other staff sergeants were actually angry with me. Boy Band and Crunk shook my hand, but they wouldn't look at me. Even Jiggy was visibly upset that I had been promoted above him.

The sergeant major sensed there was unease, so he spoke to the company. "Listen, you pissants," he said. "Promotions are coming down the pike to all of you. You are all considered to be in slots above your grade, and you'll all get promoted. Jet Set beat you out because he had his shit wired tighter than you guys." The sergeant major put his hand on my shoulder. "What I would recommend you panty-waists do is quit your belly-aching and get your shit squared away so you can get promoted."

After lunch, Jiggy and I were loading up the ICU-90, which is a sealed container for carrying sensitive items like weapons. Jiggy was silent for the longest time, but finally he said, "Dude, I got two things to say to you: number one, congratulations. Number two, what the heck. I got more time in grade than you, and I'm a better shot than you. How the heck did you get promoted over me?"

"Jiggy," I said, "you mistake the Army for someone who gives a shit." I shrugged my shoulders. "Look, the secret to getting promoted is having your paperwork in order and always maxing your Physical Fitness Test—it's even more important than marksmanship." Jiggy turned away, still pissed. "Look," I said, "the Army has a test: two minutes of push-ups, two minutes of sit-ups and a two-mile run. And that, along with the weapons qualification test, is the only across-the-board standardized test in the Army."

"Well why don't they make marksmanship more important?" Jiggy said, as he picked up his M-4 and took aim at something.

"It *is* important," I said, "and, yeah, you shoot better than me. But I still shoot at the highest level the Army measures. You shoot at a level the Army doesn't even grade—way to go, it gets you a case of beer every quarter. But I'm the one who made sergeant first class."

"Well, I usually max out the PT test," said Jiggy.

"Not consistently," I said. "Let's face it, the Physical Fitness Test isn't that hard to pass—every swingin' dick in the line should be able to pass the test on any given day. Moreover, it is something that a soldier can easily improve upon with a dedicated effort. The lazy Army sees the PT Test as a quick-read indicator of a soldier's commitment to his job, to his career, and to the Army itself."

"What?" said Jiggy. "It's just a standardized test."

"It's a lot more than that," I said. "What the Army wants to know is do you take the Army seriously? If you always get a perfect score of 300 on your PT test, you manifestly take the Army seriously."

"But there's a lot of guys in this unit that consistently max the test," said Jiggy.

"Yeah," I replied, "but they don't have their paperwork in order."

"Okay, I agree with that," said Jiggy with frustration. "And almost every time it's because some clerk-typist loses their stuff."

"Exactly," I said, with some irritation, "but that's *their fault.*"

"Their fault? said Jiggy. "How is it a soldier's fault when he gives his documents to the person in charge of documents, and the guy just freakin' loses them?"

"Because they always lose them," I said, "and any soldier who's been in the Army more than a day knows that, and yet they still get angry when they hand their paperwork to some slack-jawed, rear-echelon clerk-typist who immediately loses those documents."

I picked up my weapon and pointed it at some invisible clerk typist in the corner of the ISU-90. "The fact is," I said, "that the clerk-typists don't put things in your file when you give things to them. They *lose* things when you give them to them. The way to succeed with these people is to always have three copies of everything on your person when you deal with them. The first copy you give to the clerk because he will tell you he will put it in your file—which, of course, he won't. The second copy you have with you when you have your promotion packet reviewed by that same clerk."

Jiggy rolled his eyes. "Yeah, that never goes well."

"Of course," I said, "during your review, that clerk is going to look at you with condescension and say, 'Packet can't go forward, Sarge, you don't have your DA Form Whatchamajiggy'—the same form you personally handed to him not a week before. That's when you whip out your second copy and say, 'Bam! There it is!'"

Jiggy was laughing now and nodding his head. "I know that guy."

"At that point," I said, "you stand there and watch him physically place that necessary document in your file and then follow him as he physically carries it to the next clerk."

"You're right," said Jiggy, with ironic laughter. "That's the key." He was now grudgingly on my side. "You got to make sure he delivers that document to the next guy."

"And it's so often neglected," I replied. "Every clerk is going to tell you he'll take the file to the other clerk."

"It's a head fake," said Jiggy. "Don't take the head fake."

"Exactly," I said. "And sometimes he'll even give you his phone number and tell you to call him in the afternoon to follow-up—don't fall for that one, either."

"Oh, totally," replied Jiggy. "He won't be there in the afternoon. And if he's there, he won't answer the phone."

"Right, and if you leave him a message, he will absolutely not return your call. In my entire military career, not one person has ever returned my phone call."

"Why would they?" said Jiggy. "You're not their rater."

"What you do when a clerk-typist tells you he'll forward your packet," I continued, "is you smile and say, 'Well, I've got nothing to do. I'll just sit here until you do.' This will completely blow his mind. Look at it this way, when you get his stamp on your document, it's 10:30 a.m., he's already planning on slipping out a little early for lunch (which lasts, like, four hours anyway). Telling him you'll just wait will almost always get you immediate action."

"Okay," said Jiggy, "so, now that the file is on clerk number two's desk. What do you do?"

"First thing you do with your third copy of the document is you make more copies, because this crap is going to go on, like, forever. Next thing you do is give the new clerk that same document, because, let's face it, that thing just evaporated from your file the moment that guy laid hands on it."

"I know what you're saying," said Jiggy. "But did you ever notice that officers always seem to get their stuff wired tight?"

"Sure, why not?" I said. "That's because officers have their own way of doing things—they just call each other up. If Captain Bob needs his paperwork to go through Major Jerry's office, he just calls Jerry and says, "Jerry, it's Bob. I need a fav.""

"Yeah, it's ridiculous," agreed Jiggy. "When I was in basic training, our entire platoon was not getting paid for, like, three months. We complained enough about it so that a lieutenant from the paymaster's office came to hear our complaints. He'd come every couple of weeks, listen to us, write stuff down, then nothing would change. Finally, I said, 'Sir, we have a serious pay problem here.'"

"What did he say to that?"

"He said, 'No, Private, we don't have a *serious* problem at all. Why, I got paid just this morning."

GREETINGS FROM FORT BRAGG

My second year of law school I began a relationship with a classmate, Rachel. Rachel was sweet and attractive. She had beautiful brown hair and bright blue eyes. At school she wore Ann Taylor, but on the weekends she rocked more interesting outfits.

Rachel also—how shall I say this?—was of a type. Dedicated to "social justice" (whatever that is), she was very political (guess which party), and enjoyed nothing more than being offended. We had good times together, and would work-out at the gym, and sometimes cycle the Baltimore and Annapolis trail. But Rachel had that girl-in-graduate-school habit of going around telling people, "That's not funny."

One day Rachel and I were studying, and she saw a postcard a buddy of mine sent me. The postcard was an aerial photograph of Fort Bragg. Pictured was the long, sweeping arch of Ardennes Road and Grubber Road as they ran perfectly parallel to each other for miles. Laid out along these roads, running four deep, were identically built concrete barracks, row upon row of them. They seemed to go on forever. And above all that, written in bright, cheerful letters, were the words, "Greetings from Fort Bragg."

Rachel looked at this postcard, with its depiction of endless barracks, and her face went blank. She could see that she was looking at what was essentially the nation's warehouse of trained killers, and she said, "When I look at that picture I see the apocalypse."

I just laughed and said, "You should."

Having loaded up our team connex, ISU-90, and other cargo containers with our team gear, the team sergeant formed us up in the parking lot and gave us the safety briefing. "Listen-up, Numb Nuts," he said, "Major Brenner jumped through his ass to get you guys authorization to bring your vehicles to Fort Bragg, so don't screw it up."

Having set the proper tone, Dragline transitioned into his sergeant-as-facilitator mode. "We're all driving down as a team. None of you will be out of my sight at any time. And I want us going the *actual* speed limit, not what everybody else is driving." In our hands we each were carrying an MBITR radio—an intra-team radio with earpiece and microphone attachment for hands-free communications. "Our comms are up, so you pricks will be able to talk all the trash you want." I let out a low cough.

Giving me an irritated glance, Dragline continued: "For some dicked-up reason, Jet Set has to get his undergraduate transcripts from VCU, so *we're all* gonna have to drive alongside him into Richmond."

"What the—" said Boy Band.

"I don't know," replied Dragline. "He needs his transcripts to un-fuck himself with the New York State Bar or something."

"Thank you, team sergeant," I half-shouted, "for giving me this opportunity to un-fuck myself. . . You guys can watch if you want."

"We should be in North Carolina before 1100," continued the team sergeant. "We can stop off and get lunch in Rocky Mount, and still be at Bragg before 1300. We have incorporated into our travel plan ample time to fart around Fayetteville before the battalion formation." He continued: "I'm going to go to the Soldier's PX. You're all invited to come along, but wherever you go, you need to have your bright, shiny asses standing tall in Sniper Stadium at 1500 for battalion formation."

After that, we each went towards our cars to convoy out of Fort A.P. Hill. It was a remarkably warm day for January, and we all drove with our windows down, wearing our green berets and Oakley sunglasses. "How do you feel, Jet Set?" The captain asked me over the radio.

"Like a mean motherfucker, sir!"

We drove south down Route 301, gassed up at the truck stop, then merged slowly onto southbound Interstate I-95. I was second car from the front. In front of me was Jiggy, behind me was Boy Band, then Crunk, then Spooky, the team sergeant and lastly, Captain McMann.

A brightly painted red Mini Cooper came alongside the convoy, clearly intending to pass. "Hey, Boy Band," said Crunk, as the small vehicle passed him. "What's the most difficult thing about driving a Mini Cooper?"

"I don't know," said Boy Band, the car now passing him. "What?"

The Mini was now alongside me. It was being driven by a slim, clean-shaven young man wearing a tennis-sweater.

"Telling your parents you're gay."

By the time we were near Ashland, I realized I hadn't been to the South—the real South—since I left Fort Bragg four years before. I could smell false-spring in the air. A feeling of nostalgia came over me, and I sang the words of an old song over the radio, "Take me back to the place where I first saw the light/ to the sweet sunny South take me home."

"Meh," said Boy Band, "not a big fan of the South."

"Me neither," replied Jiggy.

"What's wrong with you people?" said Crunk. "The South has the best food, the best women and the best weather. The people are respectful and pleasant to be around. I love the South, gonna retire there."

"I dunno," said Jiggy.

"I thought you were from Cajun Country," Captain McMann said.

"From there, sir," Jiggy replied. "Never goin' back."

The radio erupted. "Uh-oh! Sounds like there's a 'Jiggy Junior' running around lookin' for his dad!" Boy Band said.

"Sportsman's Paradise indeed!" Crunk replied.

"No, it's nothing like that" Jiggy said. "I just . . . it's a long story."

"Well, we got nothing but time," Dragline said.

"It's a stupid story," Jiggy replied.

"Them's the best kind," Spooky chimed in.

"Well, sir," Jiggy finally replied, "I'm from a small town in Louisiana—as you all know. And, growing up, I wasn't the only Jason Molineux in my class. There was another Jason Molineux—smart, handsome, fun-to-be-around Jason Molineux."

"*Good* Jason Molineux, is what you mean," said Boy Band.

"And you're *evil* Jason Molineux," said Crunk.

"Well, no—" said Jiggy.

"Goofus and Gallant?" I said.

"No, I wasn't a jerk. I just wasn't him," replied Jiggy. "I didn't dislike the guy, it's just that people would always compare us—and he always won."

I turned up my radio to hear better.

"So, it's our senior year," continued Jiggy, "and by now I'm a full blown skater punk. I'm winning skateboard competitions every weekend and traveling around with a skater team. The other Jason is—you know—class president, straight 'A' student and all around super-nice-guy."

"Such a disappointment you are," said Boy Band with a Jewish-mother accent.

"Anyway," continued Jiggy, "one weekend in the spring of our senior year, I go to Dallas for a skateboard competition, and smart-guy, captain-of-the-team Jason Molineux gets killed in an automobile accident."

"What, ya cut his brake lines?" said Crunk. "And now you want to confess. You're in a safe place, Jiggy. It will never leave the team."

Ignoring the comments, Jiggy continued, "And, naturally, that was the weekend my car decides to break down in Dallas, and I can't get back to school on Monday. So, anyway, Monday morning, Principal Boudreaux gets on the P.A. system and says, 'Class, I have a tragic announcement to make. . . your schoolmate, Jason Molineux, was killed in an automobile accident over the weekend.'" Jason paused, and you sort of knew where this story was going. "Now the whole school is freaking out," he continued. "They don't know which one of us is dead." I could see Jiggy driving directly in front of me, and I noticed that he was starting to pull away.

"And, of course, I know absolutely nothing about Jason's death or the simmering freak-out that's about to blow up in my high school when I come be-bopping into class on Tuesday morning." Jason's car picked up more speed. "Tuesday morning I roll into school and the place goes nuts. Girls were crying, guys were slamming lockers, even the teachers were pissed. Some cheerleader bitch came up to me and she's screaming at me, 'Why couldn't it have been you? Why couldn't it have been you?'"

Jiggy went silent for a long time. "Man," he said at last. "Those people can screw themselves."

No one said a word. The teasing stopped, the laughter died away. Jiggy then noticeably picked up speed, and we all followed along. He moved into the left hand lane and began passing people. The team sergeant didn't say a word. We hit 90 mph and nothing was said, we just stayed with him.

Eventually, Captain McMann got on the radio. "Jiggy," he said, "you know we're right here with you, right? You know that we're not going to leave you, right? You're on the team now, Jiggy. You can't run away from us, but we can't leave you either. You're on the team, and the team is all that matters. You're not going anywhere, but neither are we."

Jiggy's brake lights flashed on a couple times, and I could see he was slowing down gradually. "Yes, sir," he said, "I'm on the team."

In Richmond, we exited off I-95 onto Boulevard. We could have exited closer to the university, but I wanted to take a scenic drive through the

Fan District. I'd always loved the Fan, with its Edwardian and Victorian townhouses, and distinctive walk-up apartments. But most beautiful of all was Monument Avenue. We drove down Monument with its broad cobblestone pavement, elegant houses, and grand statues to the heroes of the Confederacy—Lee, Jackson, Stuart and Jefferson Davis.

"What do you think of that, Crunk?" Boy Band asked. "The most magnificent street in the city is lined with the statues of slave-ownin' stale, pale, male, Confederate heroes. That piss you off?"

"*Heroes*?" said Crunk. "Looks more like the largest collection of second place trophies in the world. Last I checked, these guys *lost* the war."

Boy Band laughed. "Yeah," he said. "Still, my wife would kill to live in one of these houses."

"Agreed," said Crunk, "mine too."

I got my transcripts and we continued on through the city towards downtown. As we navigated down Broad Street, we saw a group of white, professional-looking men jogging alongside us.

"Hey, Boy Band," said Crunk.

"Yeah."

"Let's say you're a middle-aged white professional."

"Okay, let's say that I am."

"Would you take off your shirt in the middle of the city, in the middle of the day, and just—I don't know—*amble* your ass around?"

"Not in a million years."

"Then how come when you're white, and you're *jogging* it all the sudden becomes acceptable to take your shirt off in the middle of downtown? I mean, you're a middle-aged professional man and you just run around with no shirt on all the sudden. Do white people have some miracle white-people shirt that only they can see?"

"I don't get it either," replied Boy Band, knowing he was getting bested.

"I mean," continued Crunk, relishing his victory, "if the question is 'Where's your shirt, white man?' is the answer really, 'Oh, it's okay, I'm jogging?'"

You could hear the laughter coming from every microphone.

"My dad always asked one question when we would see white folks do shit like that," continued Crunk. "He'd say, 'Is white people crazy?'"

As Crunk said that, we came up to a red light on the intersection of

110

Broad and 7th Street. Standing on the corner was a middle-aged black man wearing a baseball cap sideways. He was clad in a Lakers jersey three sizes too large for him, and untied Timberland boots. He was dressed, in a word, like a twelve-year old, and he was standing on the corner dancing.

"Well, there's your dad now," said Boy Band. "Why don't we ask him?"

We drove out of Richmond and on to North Carolina making comments—positive and negative—about everything Southern. "And here's another thing," said Boy Band, feigning irritation. "What's up with 'unsweet tea?' You have 'sweet tea,' and then you have 'unsweet tea'. The opposite of 'sweet tea' isn't 'unsweet tea', the opposite is just 'tea.' Saying 'unsweet tea' makes it sound like there's some process—unknown to Yankees—that turns sweet tea into unsweet tea. It's ridiculous. Take a hot dog and a bun; if you don't have a bun, it's not an 'un-bunned hot dog' it's just a hot dog."

Two hours later we pulled into the Cracker Barrel outside of Rocky Mount, North Carolina. "I'm going to get that big hamburger they have here," I said to Jiggy as we adjusted our berets walking through the parking lot. Just as I said this, a woman came up to me—terribly excited—and said with a deep Southern drawl, "I just want to thank y'all for what y'all are doing."

I was completely thrown off guard, and couldn't imagine what she was talking about. "I'm just going to get a hamburger, ma'am," I replied.

We went inside and Jiggy gave me a friendly shove. "'Just going to get a hamburger.' What the heck was that?"

"Dude, I don't know," I said. "No one in New York ever thanked me for being in the Army. Not in Baltimore either. I'm not comfortable with people thanking me 'for my service', I'm not used to it."

"You did nothing wrong," said Jiggy.

"I guess not," I said. "But I don't know how to reply."

"So, why can't you just be appreciative?"

"I am," I said. "But it always puts me on pins and needles."

"That sounds gay."

The team was seated at a large round table, and people kept coming up to thank us for our service. The first thing the captain did when the waiter arrived was tell him that under no circumstances would we allow

111

anyone to pay for our lunch. The waiter mentioned that two people had already offered. The waiter was good at his job and very friendly toward us, which we all commented on. "You won't see that in Fayetteville," I said.

"I know," agreed Captain McMann, "everybody in Fayetteville is rude and surly."

"You'd hardly think you were in the South at all when you're in Fayetteville," said Dragline.

"Fayette-nam ain't the South," said Crunk. "Fayette-nam is an entity unto itself, ain't nothin' but a town full of hustlers and brawlers."

"Yeah, but I kind of like it," I said, to general agreement.

"Me too," said Boy Band. "The thing about Fayetteville is that it's just got so much energy. It's bustin' with life. Sure, everybody's got a chip on their shoulder, but that town is built for speed, there's always something happening in Fayetteville."

Captain McMann laughed. "What can you expect from an economy based on the desires of a 20 year old paratrooper?"

"Liquor stores, strip clubs, gun stores and used car lots—what else could a PFC ask for?" said Dragline. "Hell, I'm a master sergeant, and it's pretty much all I want."

We got into Fayetteville a little before 2:00 p.m. and Jiggy and I went immediately to 'Kim's Number One' on Yadkin Boulevard (not to be confused with 'Kim's Number One' on Bragg Boulevard or Kim's sister, 'Yon's Number One' on Reilly). We got haircuts at Kim's, and while there, I also got my boots shined, one of my uniforms pressed, and had some patches sewn on to another uniform—all for under $15.00. Sitting in the barber's chair getting his after-haircut back message, Jiggy said, "Let's go to the gun store."

"I'd rather check out a pawn shop," I said.

We both looked at each other, realizing we were back in Fayetteville, and we said in unison, "Let's go to Jim's!"

Jim's was an enormous gun store/pawn shop on Yadkin Boulevard. It had an endless selection of guns, power equipment and sports gear—the greatest second-hand American dream store in the world. After I did a tour checking out the power equipment, I wandered back to the gun section where I found Jiggy haggling with a dealer over the price of a Glock 17. The two went round and round about the price, the quality and the limitations of the Glock. Jiggy had no intention of buying the weapon, he just liked guns. The dealer knew Jiggy wasn't going to buy the gun, but he really didn't care. He liked guns, too. They were both in heaven.

As we left Jim's, I said to Jiggy, "You ever notice that no matter what gun store you go into, anywhere in the country, there's always one morbidly obese guy working the counter? I mean, one of the clerks is going to be this enormously fat guy, and he's going to know *way* too much about guns, and he's going to want to tell you everything he knows."

We got down to Sniper Stadium about twenty minutes before formation, and already there were about 300 guys there—it was like one big reunion.

"Hey, Jack! Panama Jack!" I shouted, seeing my old teammate. "I didn't know you got out of Group!"

"Yeah," Jack replied. "The wife was sick of me being gone all the time."

"So now you're in the Nasty Guard, like the rest of us."

"Best move I ever made. Hey, heard you went to law school or some shit. You half-steppin' Irishman, still tryin' to get over aren't ya'?"

"Natch," I said. "Still shammin'! What about you, still hanging around playgrounds with action figures sticking out of your pockets, you filthy degenerate?"

"Seen anybody else from our class?" Jack asked.

"Just got here. How about you?"

"Yeah, Eddie's here with me. We're in the same company. You remember Drop-Kick Eddie don't ya?"

"Sure," I said. "Guy with the droopy eye?"

"Hey, Jet Set, where are they tellin' ya you're goin'?" Jack continued, a note of concern in his voice.

"The Stan, man," I replied. "We're goin' to the Stan. How about you?"

"Man, you lucky bastard. They're telling us Colombia," replied Jack, "but it seems a little hinky."

"You think they'll cancel the mission?" I asked.

"I don't know, doesn't make sense." Jack dropped his voice and took on a leadership tone, "'Men, there's a war in Afghanistan, so, naturally, we're going to need you in Colombia.'"

"Yeah," I agreed. "Sounds like the Good Idea Fairy had too much free time."

Jack looked at me with pure envy, and he shook his head. I felt bad for him. We were going to the show, he was just gonna get jerked around for a year.

The battalion came to formation in companies. I was in the rear of the company and couldn't see or hear the battalion commander when he took his place in front of us. All I know is that he got a lot of cheers. And when the formation was given the order of "fall out," we were issued barracks. We were staying over by the 82nd's All American parade field, in what was known as "The World War II Barracks"—small, wooden, open-bay barracks with completely open bathrooms, so the guy at the sink, the guy on the toilet and the guy in the shower could all keep an eye on each other.

After we unpacked and got our bunks squared away, Captain McMann and Dragline decided they were hungry. Dragline announced, "We're going to Luigi's. Jet Set, you drive, and I'll drive, too." We piled into the two cars; Captain McMann, Dragline and Spooky into the team sergeant's car, and Jiggy, Boy Band, Crunk and me into my car. It never occurred to anyone to wonder which car they were to ride in.

Driving down the road Crunk said, "Remember that hooptie you used to drive, when you first came to the unit?"

"That 'hooptie' gave me 320,000 miles," I said.

"I remember that thing," said Jiggy, laughing. "Remember how the door locks used to just pop on and pop off when you were riding down the road? You'd be sitting there and 'pop' the locks would go up, then 'pop' they'd go back down again. I swear, that car was possessed."

"I rode that car all across Alaska and the Yukon Territory, then down the Frasier Pass and across the U.S."

"Oh no," groaned Boy Band. "Not another 'my big trip out of Alaska' story?"

"Right," said Jiggy, "with his brother, the *successful* lawyer."

"Hey, let's keep the punches above the belt," I said. "But, yeah . . . that's pretty much right."

"Remember," said Crunk, "how he had that—what was it—a trashcan lid? Propping up the front seat?"

"And you had that replacement front light," Boy Band said, "that you just bolted onto the bumper—looked like a popped-out eyeball."

"Okay," I said. "It was a beater, I admit it. When I lived in Baltimore," I continued, pulling out of the parking lot, " I used to park that car in a parking deck. And the last week I had the car, the muffler fell off, and that damn car was so loud it used to set off the car alarms of every car I passed getting out of the parking garage."

"Whatever happened to that car?" said Crunk.

"It was such a piece of junk that I started leaving the key in the

114

ignition," I said. "Some kids eventually stole it. I called it in to the police, then forgot all about it. About three months later, the cops called and said, 'Mr. Redmond, We have some good news and we have some bad news. The good news is we found your car. The bad news is it has been horribly vandalized.' I went to check the car out—it was exactly as I'd left it."

We drove down Ardennes Road, passing the 82nd Airborne Division's Museum, when all of a sudden the team sergeant stopped his car in the middle of the road. All the other cars on the road stopped as well, and people began to get out. I pulled over as well, but I had no idea what was happening. Just then I heard the sound of "Retreat," and I realize that they were lowering the flag. Jiggy, Boy Band, Crunk and I got out of the car and, facing the music, came to parade rest. I looked down Ardennes Road, and there were hundreds of soldiers frozen in place, standing exactly where they were when they heard the music. Retreat ended, and I heard the report of the cannon. Old Glory was being lowered. I came to attention and snapped a sharp salute. The sun was setting, a mild breeze was in the air, and I had only one thought, *God, it's beautiful. God, but it's a beautiful thing to be a soldier.*

THE ADVANCED URBAN COMBAT COURSE

"Hey," said the young buck sergeant standing in the doorway of the small wooden barracks. "Name's Chuck, but everybody calls me Mooney. I'm with Alpha, 3rd of the 20th."

"You in Ocala?" I asked.

"Yeah, we drill there."

"Name's Redmond, but they call me Jet Set." I pulled my rucksack and duffel bag out of the back of the minivan and dropped them on the gravel driveway.

"Grab a bunk before the others get here," said Mooney.

I took a look around at the grounds of Fort McClellan, just outside of Aniston, Alabama. "This was a once proud post," said Mooney.

"Yeah," I replied. "Used to be the home of the MPs. Now there's nothing—no PX, no bowling alley, no chow hall."

"It belongs to the state of Alabama, now," said Mooney. "Only thing they got now is the weapons range, the shoot house and the MOUT site."

"Have you seen the MOUT site?" I asked.

"Yeah, it's actually pretty awesome. It's an entire six block urban environment with buildings two and three stories high. It's got two wide boulevards that intersect, and a number of smaller roads and even some alleyways. The buildings have multiple rooms—some with doors, some without."

Mooney came over and picked up my duffel bag. "Thanks," I said. "I'm with Bravo, 3rd of the 20th." I looked Mooney over. He didn't look to be more than 25 years old, thin and wiry with a broad toothy smile. He had freckles on his face and I half-expected to see a slingshot sticking out of his back pocket. Still, there was something predatory about him. He walked like a pit bull.

I threw my gear on a bunk, and a small cloud of dust puffed up from the mattress. The room smelled stale, like an attic. The barracks were small, with only eight bunk beds, a bathroom with two showers to the left as you walked in, and a coal-burning stove on the wall across from the bathroom. The building was square, made of wood, with two windows on each wall. This would be my home along with Mooney and a couple other soldiers for the next three weeks.

I was nervous about attending the Advanced Urban Combat Course. It was mandatory that I pass if I wanted to stay on my A-Team. Moreover, our instructors, and the other soldiers attending the course, would be some of the best soldiers in the country. All of them were Special Forces qualified and they'd be a mixture of former Marines, Rangers, SEALs, and various other high-speed units. This would be no walk-over.

I looked at Mooney, trying to figure him out. I wanted to ask a few questions, but didn't want to come off sounding like I cruised men's rooms.

"Been into Aniston?" I said.

"Nah, just flew to Alabama today. Got a rental, though. So we can definitely check it out if there's any time."

"I hear the training is non-stop," I said. I'd read over the schedule; it was 21 days straight. The days spent on the range, the shoot house and the MOUT site, the nights spent in classroom until 10:00 p.m. every night—they were definitely going to be feeding us with a fire hose.

"Yeah, I think we get a half-day off one Sunday," Mooney said, "and that's about it."

I looked at Mooney's uniform. An Army uniform is like a resume; when it doesn't say anything, it's just told you everything. Without being too noticeable, I looked Mooney over. As young as he was, he already had a "triple canopy," that is, he was already Special Forces qualified, had graduated from Ranger School and was in an Airborne unit. He was also a jumpmaster, a very rare skill for such a young man. He had an Expert Infantryman's Badge as well as master blaster and Pathfinder badges. He did not have a right shoulder patch, so I knew that he had not been deployed to a combat theater, but obviously that was coming. From his age and what his uniform told me, I knew the exact trajectory of his career. "Were you in the Ranger Battalion?" I asked.

He nodded, "1ˢᵗ Bat, Hunter Army Airfield." It was transparent. He went into the Ranger Battalion right out of high school. He went to Special Forces Selection his last year in the Bat, got selected and let his enlistment run out. He then joined the National Guard, got his orders and went to the Q Course. When I asked him what he did for a living, his answer was exactly what I expected.

"Sheriff's department."

The one thing I didn't understand was why he was just a buck sergeant. I was hesitant to ask, but I slowly said, "So, how is it you're…"

"Soldier abuse, soldier abuse and dehydration," Mooney said with a big grin. He had clearly been watching me size him up.

"Soldier abuse?"

"Yeah, when I was in the Bat, I had a couple bitch privates accuse me of whipping their asses."

"Did you do it?"

"Oh hell yeah I did it, I beat the shit out of them—two separate incidents. Seemed like every time I was about to get promoted, one of my privates would get sand in his vagina and I'd have to stomp him." Mooney threw a couple upper-cuts. "But I only hit 'em in the body, doesn't leave too many marks that way. The last time, though," continued Mooney, looking down with exasperation, "was all me. I dehydrated on a run. I'd gone to the beach on a four-day pass and drank a lot. The morning I came back we had a hellacious PT run and I fell out, sweating alcohol and barely breathing. When I woke up all my shit was piled on the curb and I had my walking papers, right out of battalion."

"That seems harsh."

"That's the Bat. They don't bullshit around. You screw up, you're gone."

A van pulled up outside and two soldiers got out. Mooney and I went to help them bring their gear in. Mooney introduced himself, then gestured to me, "This is Jet Set. He's an E-7, so I let him think he's running shit."

A tall, lanky, staff sergeant got out of the van and in a deep Georgia accent said, "Name's Petey, and this here's Bro Nameth."

A swarthy, stocky staff sergeant got out of the van and looked at us with a shrug. "Name's actually Rocco, but since I met up with 'Petey' over here, at the airport, he's been calling me Bro Nameth—freakin' hicks. I don't get 'em."

"Oh yeah," said Petey. "Bro Nameth don't cuss or use 'pro-fan-it-ee.'"

"If George Washington was against cussin'," Rocco said, "so am I."

"George Washington was against cussin'?" Mooney asked with a grin.

Rocco gave him a stern look. "He said, 'How can we hope that God will bless our arms, if we insult him and say impure things?'"

"Well," said Mooney, "I'm pretty far down the road on that one. I'm gonna have to rely on God's forgiveness."

"Yeah," I said, more to myself than anyone else. "Me too."

Petey was in his late 20s, and he had a goofy, friendly quality about him. He was the kind of guy who's always looking for his glasses, as they perch on top of his head. I was surprised to see that he also had a triple canopy and an Expert Infantryman's Badge.

Rocco was in his early 30s. He had a brooding, serious Italian disposition. He reminded me of a high school gym teacher going around telling people to 'knock it off.' Rocco came from New Jersey, something he was—for some reason—proud of. Rocco's uniform was something of a puzzle. He had his Special Forces tab and his airborne wings, but he also had a combat diver badge, which you don't see too often.

We got their stuff inside and I racked out on my bunk. Rocco and Petey spent the next 20 minutes unpacking and making small talk. "So," said Mooney, "what are your units?"

"Well," replied Rocco, "the hick's with Alpha, 1st of the 20th, and I'm with Charlie, 1st of the 20th."

"Where'd you get that combat diver badge?" Mooney asked him.

"In the Corps."

"That makes sense," I said. "So, you did four years with the Marines, then got out and joined the Guard?"

"Yep."

"Where were you stationed?"

"Lejeune. And I spent some time in Hawaii too."

Petey went over to his wall locker and put his shaving kit on the overhead shelf. "What about you, Petey?" asked Mooney. "Where'd you get that Ranger tab?"

"In the Bat," said Petey.

Mooney looked at Petey with surprise. "*You* were in the Bat?"

"Second Battalion, Fort Lewis."

"All due respect, Petey," said Mooney, "but you don't seem like a Bat guy."

"What's a 'Bat guy' like?" I asked.

"They're wrapped tight," Mooney said. "They don't like nothin' that ain't like them."

"No doubt," Petey laughed. "That's the real Ranger Creed—'You are different, and therefore wrong.'"

"It has to be that way," said Mooney. "Everybody has to know everybody inside and out. You can't be off script in the Bat or people

119

die."

"Yeah, I know," said Petey, "but that's why I made it. After months of daily torture from my squad leader and others, I realized I either had to leave or I would stay and become the mascot. I decided to become the mascot. I maxed every PT test, I shot expert, and I was never found sleeping on guard duty."

"Yeah, but you were still a goof. I can see that."

"I became *their* goof," Petey replied, "they adopted me. Sure, at first they wanted me out. We were in England working with the Royal Marines—and you know the Brits can drink, right? So we got to drink with them, and my squad leader got drunk and tried to PT me to death in front of his friends." Petey's bright complexion grew dark, and he clenched his fist and slammed it down on the table. "I wouldn't quit. I passed out and he threw water on me to wake me up. He was laughing and put his boot on me, like a conquering hero. He didn't know I was a wrestler in high school. I cupped my hand around his heel and drove my shoulder into his foot. He went down like a sack of shit, and I jumped up and went right back into PT-ing. It embarrassed him—and I won." A smile came back to his face and he walked over to the window. "When my enlistment ended, even the battalion commander came to my going-away. He shook my hand and said, 'Petey, you're a one of a kind Ranger.'"

"What is this 'Ranger' stuff all about, anyway?" said Rocco. "I never could understand it. You've got guys who are 'Rangers' and you've got guys who are '*in* the Rangers.' What's the story?"

"The tab is a school," said Petey, almost robotically.

"The scroll is a way of life," Mooney finished his thought.

"One more time," said Rocco. "What's the story?"

Mooney got up from his bunk. "Okay, there's the Ranger School, it's a 61 day gut check testing your small unit tactics, leadership and infantry field skills."

"But it's really not 61 day," continued Petey, "because you're not going to get through it without screwing up and having to recycle. You better figure you'll be there 90 days."

"And, of course," said Mooney, "there's going to be shit loads of 'pre-ranger' training you're going to have to go through before you even have the *honor* of going. So, figure four months of patrolling and living in the dirt—"

"Eating one meal a day and not being allowed to sleep at all."

"That's Ranger School," said Mooney. "And when it's over, you're

120

given your little black and yellow Ranger tab to sew onto your uniform." Mooney rubbed the Ranger tab on his left shoulder. He had a look of nostalgia in his eyes. "So now you can call yourself a Ranger."

"But that ain't being in the Bat," said Petey with surprising emphasis. "You went to school—way to go—but when you're in the Bat it's another world."

"What do you keep talking about, 'the Bat?'" Rocco said.

"He means," said Mooney, "being in one of the three battalions of the 75th Ranger Regiment—having the scroll of the 75th Ranger Regiment as your shoulder patch. The 75th is the premier light infantry unit in the U.S. Army. It does not fall under regular Army command, but falls under the Special Operations Command. When you're in the Battalion, it is everything to you. You are the Battalion, and the Battalion is you."

"Yeah," said Rocco. "Sounds like it's almost the Corps."

"The 75th is better than the Corps," said Mooney.

"Nothin's better than the Corps," replied Rocco, jumping up from his bunk.

I stepped between them. Rocco and Mooney both grunted stiffly, searching for some clever thing to say, but just then—as if on cue—the sound of "Taps" wafted mournfully through the room. We strained to hear the slow, plaintive notes float across the desolate post. The day was done, there was no reason to say another word.

MEET THE CADRE

"My name is Master Sergeant Greer, and I am the chief instructor for the 20th Special Forces Advanced Urban Combat Course." We sat on metal bleachers in a warehouse near the shooting range. There were about 120 of us. Master Sergeant Greer was speaking to us from a raised podium. He looked young for a master sergeant, not even 35 years old. Narrow at the shoulders and lean, he looked like a runner. His hair was long, almost beyond regulation, but his eyes were fierce and stern. "In the next three weeks you will be trained in the newest and most fluid manner of close quarters combat. You will begin your training shooting from the static position, learning by rote the three tap drill—two to the chest, and one to the pelvic girdle." Master Sergeant Greer pointed his finger at his belt buckle. "That is right, we do not instruct you to go for the head-shot. Put that round in his dick and he'll bleed to death, put it in his head and it will bounce off—you'd be amazed at the survivability of a shot to the head."

Master Sergeant Greer pointed his remote at a laptop sitting on the podium and a montage of pictures of people who survived shots to the head appeared on the screen behind him. There were pictures of men looking at the camera with enormous wounds on their foreheads, deep gashes running across their skulls, and even a guy smiling with a .22 caliber bullet protruding out of his skull just above the ear. "Blow their balls off. That's how you kill your enemy," Master Sergeant Greer said with finality.

"The first thing we need to do is break you of your obsession with reloading your primary weapon once it has run out of ammunition. You are soldiers of the Special Forces. There is a reason you are issued both an M-4 rifle and an M-9 pistol."

Master Sergeant Greer put up his hands as if he were pointing a rifle. "All your military career you have been taught to drop to one knee when you are out of ammunition and reload, but close quarters combat is a fast and a fluid thing, and you need to lose this habit. It sounds easy, but when we get out on the range, and the bullets are flying, and the cadre is helping you develop through the use of negative reinforcement, you will find that your brain is going to shit all over itself." Master

Sergeant Greer looked up at us. "Once you have proven that you can actually think while you fire your weapon, you will move on to the walk-while-chewing-bubble-gum phase of the course. You will be shooting and moving on the range. In various scenarios and under various conditions, you will have to move to covered positions, acquire and hit targets and transition to the weapons issued to you. None of it is brain surgery." Master Sergeant Greer was making it clear that this was entry-level stuff.

"From the range, we will move to the shoot house. In the shoot house you will be using live ammunition, and we will be walking the balcony directly above you. If you shoot one of us you will not be recycled for another class, you will most likely be killed. Yes, we also carry weapons and we cannot wait to kill one of you." Master Sergeant Greer smiled, but none of us laughed.

"In the shoot house, you will be shooting and moving from room to room, firing live rounds. You will be using high explosives, and be instructed in making and deploying shape charges, linear charges and other types of explosive breaching devices." Master Sergeant Greer walked over to the display of breaching devices we would be using. "You will be trained in a number of breaching techniques, some of them classified." He lifted up a number of demolition charges, then a shotgun, what looked like a chainsaw with a steel disc instead of a chain, and a huge iron bar with a wedge on one end and a barbed hook on the other. "Other breaching techniques, like the shotgun, the Husqvarna, and the Hooligan Tool are just a lot of fun."

Master Sergeant Greer rubbed his hands together in joy. "Once you have shown that you can manage to conduct yourselves safely in a room-to-room environment, we will move onto the real battle—the MOUT site. We will teach you how to storm an entire village, a neighborhood or maybe even a small town, and take it from the enemy. You need to understand that the might of the U.S. military is absolute in the open theater. No one can match us in the field . . . but the real fight will be in the cities, where the might of the U.S. cannot be unleashed."

Master Sergeant Greer again placed his hands on the speaker's stand. "We are in the business of killing," he continued, "and business is good. But you, as Special Forces soldiers, are in the business of being highly discriminatory killers. You will have to make split-second decisions on whom to kill. It is our job, as your instructors, to give you the tools you need to make the right decision, but ultimately it will be your job as soldiers on the ground to decide to pull the trigger. We will teach you speed and violence of action, but your aggressiveness on the battlefield will be your salvation." Master Sergeant Greer stared at us sitting on the bleachers. "We don't want any unnecessary kills, but neither do we want any of you unnecessarily dying. And the one thing we will not accept is anything less than victory."

After the talk, we filed out of the auditorium and assembled at the loading tables by the shooting range to reconfigure our holsters, ammunition pouches and our "quick-release" rifle slings. These slings would allow us to drop our rifle but not lose it so we could transition to the pistol.

We then loaded the magazines for our rifles with various numbers of bullets—sometimes eight, sometimes three, sometimes one. Similarly, we loaded the magazines of our pistols with different numbers of bullets. The purpose of the exercise was to get us to learn to fire quickly, accurately and mechanically, then, when we'd run out of bullets, to drop the rifle and transition to the pistol. This simple exercise—which on paper seemed easy enough—was at first all but impossible.

Since we'd entered the Army, all of us had trained that when out of bullets, drop to the knee and reload a fresh magazine. I was by no means the worst of our bunch, but I wasn't looking like I'd make the Dean's List either. "Oh, hell, no, Redmond!" shouted an instructor on day three. "This shit is not rocket science, is it? Your monkey-ass has been out here already three days, and you're still doing this bit where you drop your magazine, go to a knee and . . . 'oh, I've got a pistol, I should actually use the thing!' No, shitbird! People die when you get a brain fart—pull your head out of your ass and figure out that you have a killing device that is every bit as capable as your rifle in a close quarters environment."

I was rehearsing in my mind what I needed to do to the point of obsession. Master Sergeant Greer—whom I'd come to fear—was watching all this, and he pulled me to the side. "Look, Redmond," he said. "You're over-thinking it. Just remember, 'slow is smooth, and smooth is fast.'" I was surprised by how low-key and matter-of-fact he was. I'd thought of him as a fire-breather, but here he was talking to me like he was the tennis coach teaching me the backhand. "It's no big deal," he said. "Just take it as a mantra, 'Slow is smooth and smooth is fast.'"

I repeated the slogan, "Slow is smooth and smooth is fast. Slow is smooth and smooth is fast."

"Alright, Redmond," the instructor shouted over to me, "give us one more display of your confusion." He put his finger to the stop watch, mashed down hard on the release device, and I calmly put two rounds in the torso with my rifle, then attempted to put one in the pelvic girdle. There was no third round and I saw that my bolt remained to the rear. For a split second, I thought about going to one knee, but then I repeated the mantra in my mind, 'Slow is smooth and smooth is fast'. Instead, for the first time, I dropped my weapon in front of me, and went for my holster. I drew my M-9 and fired a round into the dummy's groin.

"Well, hell yes!" shouted the instructor, with unconcealed delight. "I knew your monkey-ass could learn to transition." It was a small victory, but it was my victory. On the third day of just shooting rounds, I'd finally figured out that slow was smooth and smooth was fast.

That was the beginning of week one. The days were spent on the flat range and the nights in the classroom learning the new technique for clearing rooms and buildings. "Most of these techniques have been developed post-Somalia," Master Sergeant Greer explained to us in one of the evening instructional blocks. "The biggest lesson learned in Somalia was stay out of the streets! Almost all the casualties in 'The Mog' were taken while the men were in the streets. It's sort of like being in a tunnel." Master Sergeant Geer explained, pushing his open hands forward forming a tunnel: "The bullets ricochet off the walls of the buildings and funnel into—uh—into you. The other thing that you might be hearing," he continued, "is the reports coming out of Afghanistan that the bullet for the M-4—the 5.56—is too small, too pointy, and too high-velocity. Many of the guys are reporting shooting Taliban six, seven, even eleven times and not taking them down." Master Sergeant Greer folded his arms across his chest as though thinking in a deep scholarly manner. "There are two schools of thought on this matter. First, that the 5.56 doesn't get its famous 'tumbling action' going until a couple hundred meters out of the muzzle—well beyond the point of most hits. Also that the Afghanis are extremely thin and not well hydrated—which ironically helps them in battle. Lastly, it is thought that the 5.56 travels too fast, and just rips right through the target without the knockdown power of a slower bullet, like the .45. . . . Then, of course, there is the other school of thought, which says that the people reporting all these failures are just really lousy shots."

Most of the men in the course were from the South. The 20th Special Forces Group has most of its units spread out in the deep South, but there's one company up in Massachusetts, and this class had about 15 guys from up there. Everyone at the school was a character, but there was a Sergeant First Class named Mark who was extremely funny. I knew his name because back in the barracks the night before, Petey had been doing an imitation of him. "Name's Mahrk," said Petey, dropping his Southern drawl and picking up a pitch-perfect Boston accent. "I heard him tahkin' with his buds when he was getting some wahteh at the bubbler."

"Hey, Frank," Mark shouted to his buddy the next morning in a manner that let us know he wanted to be heard by everybody. "How y'all doing over there?"

"Why, fiddlee-dee," replied Frank, in the voice of an exasperated southern belle, "I do believe I'm comin' down with a case of the vapors."

Mark turned to the group. "That's what I don't get about you hicks. You say 'y'all' when tahlkin' to one person. If one person is y'all, what the hell do you say when you're talking to a group of people?"

Petey was on it. "Listen to the Yankee," he said. "Struttin' around here like a barnyard pimp and talkin' all that mess. If you were an American, you'd know that the plural for y'all is all y'all."

That got a laugh, so Petey went on the offense. "Hey, Mooney, why should you never try to run over a Yankee riding a bicycle?"

"I don't know, why?"

"It's probably your bicycle."

"Hey, Frank," said Mark in response. "What's a Southern get on his IQ test?"

"I dunno, what?"

"Drool."

Petey let it go at that, but somebody from another loading table shouted up, "Keep talkin' that shit, Yankee, but one day the South will rise again." A cheer went up from the table.

"I hope so," said Mark. "Then we'll be two and Oh."

BARRACKS ROOM BALLAD

The days were a grinding pattern, on the range till dark, then dinner, then a couple hours in the classroom. After that we'd sit in the barracks cleaning our weapons and telling stories. This was always the highlight of the day.

Today we began training at the shoot house, working on our "dynamic entry" into buildings. We used the linear charges and the Hooligan Tool to gain forced entry into the hit points. "What was up with you and that Hooligan Tool, today?" Rocco asked Petey. "We go to the last rally point to put the assault team together, and you just charge off at the window."

"I felt that iron rod in my hands," replied Petey, "and I couldn't help myself."

"That's what she said," replied Mooney, just as we all knew he would.

Rocco picked up the barrel of his weapon and began brushing the muzzle with a toothbrush from his weapons cleaning kit. "Such a knucklehead," he said. And then he looked away, oblivious to the rest of us. "Today's the fifth,, right?"

"Yeah," I said, "the fifth of March, why?

"No reason. . . . Hey, Petey, tell me one of your knucklehead stories about life in the Bat, why don't ya?" Petey was busy working on his lower receiver and didn't respond. Rocco looked impatient, like he wanted to be entertained. "Hey, how come none of you knuckleheads is telling a story tonight? Petey, tell us about the time you put on the gorilla mask and hosed down your team leader with the fire extinguisher."

"I already told that story. And besides, when I told it, you called me a knucklehead."

"I always call you a knucklehead, it don't mean nothing." Rocco looked over at Mooney. "Come on, Mooney, tell us about the time you beat someone up—gave them those 'kneecaps of death' you're always bragging about."

"Nah," said Mooney. "Hell, Rocco. Why don't you tell us a story for once?"

"I don't have any stories. I don't do dumb stuff."

"Come on, you enlisted in the Marine Corps when you were 17," I said. "Don't tell me you didn't do some stupid stuff."

Rocco chuckled. "Well, there was this one time. . ." Everybody looked over, anticipating Rocco's first story. "When I was in Hawaii, I used to drive around this little Ford Fiesta. You remember, in those things you sit pretty low, and they've got the emergency brake on the console between the two front seats." Rocco straightened up and extended both hands like he was driving. "Well, I used to think I was the baddest ass in the valley, and my signature move was to drive right at someone as fast as I could, then pull that emergency brake," Rocco mimicked pulling the brake. "I'd put the car into a fish-tail, do a 90 degree turn and come to a stop almost on a dime right in front of them."

"Yeah," said Petey. "That's pretty stupid."

"Geez, Rocco," Mooney said. "Even I wouldn't do something as shit-all stupid as that."

"That's why we wouldn't have you in the Corps," Rocco said, as he stood up and walked toward the window. "Anyway, you know in Hawaii it rains like crazy, then—boom—the sun comes out and it's beautiful. So, one day I'm sitting in my car with my best buddy, Gonzo Pinacho. We're at an intersection going eastbound, and across the street, on the westbound side, I see, like, fifteen people standing at the bus stop. And right in front of the bus stop, there's this enormous puddle of water—I mean, it's like six inches deep and 30 feet wide." Rocco looked out the window like he was expecting to see an old friend. "Now, there are no cars on the other side of the street coming westbound, but I look, and about 200 meters away at the next intersection I can see that the light has changed and the cars are starting to approach our intersection." Rocco turned toward us. "And as soon as I see it all in place, Gonzo sees exactly the same thing. And he says to me, 'Rocco, you ain't got a hair on your ass if—' But before he even finishes, the light changes, and I pop the clutch on that little Fiesta. And I'm freakin' jetting across the street straight at those people at the bus stop. And they see me comin', and I can see the panic on their faces. And about 15 feet in front of them, I pull that brake," - Rocco's right hand flew up as if he was pulling the brake - "and the car goes into a slide and all that water just comes roaring up in one enormous wall, and I could see them through the sheet of water, and they all had that same look of disbelief, and they all were doing that slow motion 'NOOOOOOOOOOOO!!'"

Rocco was smiling bigger than I'd ever seen him smile before. "And when the water came crashing down on them, you should have seen Gonzo. He was laughing so hard snot was coming out of his nose. He was laughing so hard he couldn't breathe. Even as I was pulling away, he was laughing so much his face was beet red." Rocco laughed to himself, then walked over to the window. "That's how I'll always remember Gonzo Pinacho."

"'Remember'?" I said. "What do you mean, 'remember'?"

"Oh," Rocco said, as if waking up from a dream. "Gonzo was killed five days later in a helicopter crash. He died March fifth, this very day." We all looked at Rocco, no one saying a word. Rocco just stared out the window. "But in that old Ford Fiesta, man, I had him laughing like he'd never laughed in his life. He was sitting right next to me laughing like a human being ought to laugh, laughing like there was no tomorrow." Rocco looked out the window like a sentinel, scanning the darkness, watching, waiting. "You know," he said, "you choose a way of life, and you live by the code of that way of life. Never leave a fallen comrade, that's our code, that's what we live by. But nobody tells you the rest of the code. You never leave a fallen comrade, because that fallen comrade is never going to leave you."

THE ANGEL OF IRONDALE

The last week in the shoot house had not been easy. I completed all the tasks assigned, but nothing came naturally to me. I had to work at things other soldiers seemed to take up instinctively. One soldier was reprimanded, and that was heartbreaking to watch. He was a very solid and well-liked staff sergeant—perhaps a bit too aggressive. I forget the details, but we were stacking up before an open door, leading from the room we had just cleared into another room. For some reason the lead man in the stack lowered his head and the staff sergeant—standing behind him—saw a target and shot it, shooting directly over the head of the lead man. This was a huge safety violation, and the staff sergeant very publicly and embarrassingly had his rifle barrel removed and had a "blue barrel" put in its place—a barrel that could only fire soap rounds. Some of the other guys made fun of this staff sergeant, but I wasn't about to—there but for the grace of God.

Sunday morning, we had a half-day off and I went into town to find a Catholic church. I like going to Mass in towns I've never been in before; it's always a mini adventure. When I was in North Pole, Alaska, I went to . . . wait for it . . . wait for it . . . Saint Nicholas'; in Cape May, New Jersey, Our Lady Star of the Sea. In Manta, Ecuador, Iglesias La Paz; in Montreal Notre-Dame-de-Bon-Secours and in Santa Fe, New Mexico I saw the famous stairway of Loretta Chapel.

I got the keys to the van and headed into town, and as soon as I got onto Greenbrier Dear Drive, I saw a sign for Sacred Heart of Jesus School—which I thought was odd, because who has a school without a parish? I drove up a steep, straight road, but didn't see a church, so I continued into town and pulled into a gas station. Entering the store, the sting of stale cigarette smoke caused my eyes to water. An older white woman in hair curlers was standing behind the cash register looking less than enthusiastic. I had to get some intel from her, so I put on my best Top-O-The-Mornin' face and said, "How are you doing this fine Sunday morning, ma'am?"

"I'm doing well, and you?" she said without interest.

"Great, ma'am, thanks for askin'. Hey, could you tell me where I can find a Catholic church hereabouts?"

The woman paused, more for appearance than for contemplation. "I don't reckon we got a Catholic church in Aniston," she said, taking a drag on her cigarette.

"Oh," I said, playfully. "God wouldn't put up with that." The woman did not see the humor in my statement. "Are you sure?" I said, now more seriously. "I've never seen a town big enough for its own daily newspaper that didn't have a Catholic church in it."

She crossed her arms and narrowed her brows. "Well," she said, "there's Saint Michael's about four miles down that road," she pointed westward. "That might be a Catholic church."

I found St. Michael's—actually called St. Michael's and all the Angels. It was, of course, Episcopalian. At this point it became a matter of pride; Anniston, Alabama had a Catholic church and I was going to find it. I drove deeper into the city and found that I was in a, how shall we say, "less than affluent" part of town. There I saw a distinguished looking older black man dressed in a well-pressed suit, meticulously clean white shirt, sharp tie and parade polished shoes. He was walking with a proudly-dressed, older black woman wearing a bright yellow dress and a very regal bonnet. I pulled up alongside the couple, and noticed that the man clutched the woman closer, as honor required.

"Excuse me, sir," I said. "I'm looking for a Catholic church. Do you know where one could be found?" The man left the lady on the sidewalk and approached the car.

"A Catholic church?" he said. "Well, there's Saint Michael's up the road apiece."

"No," I said. "That's actually an Episcopalian church." The man looked away, as if he knew it was, but didn't think I'd know the difference.

"Well, there's All Saints over on West, but that church is for colored folk."

"Really?" I said. "What color are they?"

"Why, they black folk," the man said with a look of incomprehension. He then looked over toward me and saw that I was smiling at him.

"That's for tryin' to send me to Saint Michael's," I said. "Now please tell me where I can find this colored Catholic Church."

"Hallelujah," said the woman wearing the resplendent bonnet. The impeccably dressed man gave me directions to All Saints, and I rode off—but not before getting a smile and a "have a blessed day" from his companion.

It was one of the smallest chapels I had ever seen—I don't believe it could have fit 40 people. There were about 14 people in attendance. I looked around the chapel and breathed in the air. There was a smell of freshness about the place, as if someone opened the doors every day, brought in fresh-cut flowers, and let the breath of life surge through it. The chapel was simple yet tastefully decorated. The walls were white, as were the exposed rafters. The pews and the vaulted ceiling were of varnished, but unstained wood, as were two panels on either side of the altar. The floor was covered in deep, vibrant blue carpet. The Stations of the Cross that decorated the walls were plain but reverent. The windows were not of stained glass, but were opaque with color. The sanctuary was meticulously clean, and at its head stood the altar, constructed of wood, as was the crucifix that hung solemnly above it.

As soon as I walked in, all heads turned. I was the only white person in the chapel, and I was being looked at with curiosity and concern. I noticed an elderly black woman preparing the Eucharistic vessels for the Mass at the tabernacle. She turned and saw me, and her face lit up with a broad, welcoming smile. When she had completed her tasks, she walked over to me excitedly. She threw her arms around me and said, "Welcome, stranger to our humble house of God. What brings you to All Saints?" I could see that all the parishioners were listening, but I didn't care.

"I'm at Fort McClellan and I just wanted to come to Mass." The woman was visibly proud of the chapel, and I figured she was the caretaker. "It's a beautiful little place," I said. "Whoever keeps this church so nice must have a special place in Heaven."

She beamed. "When I came here from Irondale, fifteen years ago, I said to myself, 'Dorothea, the black folk in this town need a witness. They need to see a proper black Catholic church—Amen." Dorothea laid her hand on my arm and lowered her voice. "You see, the Bishop didn't want a colored folks' church and a white folks' church. He wanted everybody in one church." Dorothea paused, and looked me in the eyes, to let me know she understood his thinking, but more importantly, to let me know his thinking was all wrong. "I hates to say it, but colored folk don't want to go to church with white folk. They really ain't all that much fun." Dorothea let out a laugh.

"So there's a regular Catholic church in Anniston?" I asked.

"What? This isn't a regular Catholic church?"

"You know what I mean, Dorothea," I said. "A Catholic church that I can walk into and the entire congregation doesn't do a double-take on me."

"Why, sure they is, honey," she said. "They got the Sacred Heart of Jesus right up the road."

"That's weird," I said, "because I saw the sign, and I went up the road, but I couldn't find it."

"That's because God brought you to our little church," said Dorothea. "You think that's an accident? Don't you know that the Lord works in mysterious ways?"

"I don't believe it was," I said. "This place is something to see, a small miracle, and it brings you honor."

"It brings the Lord honor."

"But," I said, "I'm mostly impressed that you convinced the Bishop to keep this little place open."

"Well, we's a 'satellite church,'" Dorothea said. "No pastor, just a visiting priest."

"But you still convinced the Bishop to stay open."

"He wasn't gonna convince himself," Dorothea said with a laugh.

"You're quite a woman," I said.

"No, I'm not," replied Dorothea, the smile removed from her face. "I'm just a woman who said yes to Mother Angelica of Irondale."

"Oh, I forgot," I said, "Mother Angelica lives not too far away."

"The one and the same," said Dorothea. "That woman is God's own dynamo. I started out in her mail room—just lickin' stamps and mailin' out letters. I wasn't even a Catholic back then, but Mother Angelica brought me to the Church." Dorothea paused and it seemed she was crying. "I remember what she told me when I had to move here to Anniston. She said, 'Dorothea, we're all called to be great saints, don't miss your opportunity.'"

And so that was my Sunday morning, sitting in All Saints Chapel in Anniston, Alabama—the only white man in the house, receiving the Eucharist, and singing right along with everybody else:

This world is not my home,
This world is not my home.

WHY WE FIGHT

Sunday morning with Dorothea didn't last long. By noon, training had started up again. And after that the week ground on, with me growing in confidence. When I came to the Advanced Urban Combat Course, I was concerned that I would not measure up to the others in the class, but every day I could see more clearly that it wasn't about being the best, it was about doing my best. I came here thinking the class would be a pissing contest, but it wasn't. It was a training ground. The Army didn't need me to be John Wayne, it only needed me to fire my rifle with intelligence and precision.

Some of our training included assault techniques from civilian vehicles. This training required the blue barrels, which fired a .22 caliber soap round. These bullets were like paint balls, but they hurt like crazy and would cut you if you were shot in an area of exposed skin—something I learned at the MOUT site when I forgot to put a bandana over my mouth and was cut in the cheek from a bullet to the face.

The MOUT site was a six block urban environment with avenues, side roads, alley ways, multi-story buildings, multi-room buildings and interior connector hallways. We'd been there the last ten days, and our final exam was a 24-hour, full-class operation, assaulting, then taking control of the MOUT-site—that is, storming a small town. We used our blue barrels because we were fighting OPFOR, an opposing force. We helicoptered into a landing zone 400 meters out, then patrolled toward the town. The OPFOR set up an ambush about 200 meters from town, and a fierce exchange of gunfire ensued. From that point our officers directed us in a bound-and-over-watch technique, and I think one element flanked the OPFOR, but we overran their position before the flanking element deployed.

We hit the outskirts of the town and took small arms fire. I think there were a number of trip flares simulating land mines, but they were pretty obvious to see, and few of them were tripped. The point of the exercise was to work in a coordinated manner to take out the town house-by-house and room-by-room—which we did.

At one point I entered a room at the head of a stack of soldiers four deep, and saw an OPFOR soldier on his knees loading his weapon. I put about three rounds into him, and kept moving. Everybody else shot him as well as he writhed on the floor shouting "Ah! Ah! Ah!" We couldn't stop laughing.

It was dawn when the exercise came to completion, and Master Sergeant Greer told us all to rally around a small house at the edge of the MOUT site. "You men did an excellent job, and I'm proud of you," he said, taking a knee. "I know it's been a long three weeks—working days and nights with little time off, but we wanted to give you this skill before you go over and face the enemy." Master Sergeant Greer stood up. "There's one more thing I want to show you. Get your gear, and be at the auditorium in ten minutes."

We filed into the auditorium and took our seats. The overhead projector came on, and a gigantic picture of the first plane smashing through the World Trade Tower appeared on the screen—then another picture of the same event, then a picture of the Twin Towers burning furiously. In the third picture you could see things falling out of the building. The next picture was a close up, the picture after that was an even closer close-up. The objects falling from the building were people. Master Sergeant Greer took the stage. "This is why we fight," he said, using a pointing stick to show a woman falling through the sky—you could see the ribbon in her hair. "This woman here did nothing to these people. She woke up that morning, put on her outfit and went to work. She has every right to be alive today, but she's dead!" Master Sergeant Greer smacked the pointer against the screen angrily. "Now, she has a right to be avenged!"

The picture changed to one of the Pentagon in flames. "They attacked our home. They came without warning, without provocation, and they slaughtered thousands of innocent Americans. They slaughtered YOUR brothers, YOUR sisters, YOUR sons and YOUR daughters!" The picture then changed to a soldier from the Pentagon carrying a dead body in his arms. "YOUR comrades in arms!"

I could feel a rage coursing through my veins, and I looked around and saw it in everyone around me. "And why did they attack us?" Master Sergeant Greer continued. "Because we exist. They attacked America because our existence is a slap in their face, because we are beyond their control. They hate us because they can't bear the thought of a happy and a free people going about their business without regard for them."

Master Sergeant Greer lifted up his head. "But now it's time to pay the piper. Don't listen to what the politicians say about this war, or what the media says about this war. This war is about revenge." Master Sergeant Greer glared at us. "I'm not saying that you should violate the rules of war—rules they do not abide by—what I'm saying is that you have an opportunity. You have an opportunity to show the whole world that civilized men will fight and die for a civilized world."

Master Sergeant Greer went over to the laptop plugged into the overhead projector. "I'm going to show you something," he said. "I want you to understand the people you are going to be fighting. This is a video taped by the good people of Al Qaeda of Chechnya, who are at war with the Russians right now. They made this video and then they emailed it to every single Russian email address they could locate. The Chechens thought that they could frighten the Russians into leaving Chechnya—but it only pissed them off."

The video opened on a group of about eight Chechen fighters, bearded and armed, standing over three young Russian prisoners of war. Two of the Russians were lying face down in a pool of blood, but the last Russian was on his knees with his hands bound behind his back. The camera zoomed in on the Russian soldier as the Chechens laughed. You could see he was just a boy no more than 18 or 19 years old, and that he was scared.

One of the Chechens kicked the boy to the ground, then put his boot on his neck. The Chechen drew a dirty, dull, fighting knife from its scabbard, and plunged it into the boy's neck all the way to the hilt. The boy made this guttural scream, but the Chechen then started sawing through the boy's throat and although the boy was alive and clearly trying to scream, there was no sound.

The Chechens took turns sawing into the boy's neck. They laughed and jostled each other playfully—hamming it up for the camera. At one point, one of the Chechens picked up the skin of the boy at the point of the wound, and pulled it away. The skin drew taunt and separated from the neck and face of the boy. It became like a solid sheet, and the boy's eyebrow was on it. I think the boy was still alive.

Master Sergeant Greer froze the picture, and for the longest time there wasn't a sound in the room. Then the lights came on and Master Sergeant Greer said his final words, "Your training is complete." He walked over to the door and we lined up and I could see that he was shaking everyone's hand as they walked out into the gray dawn.

When I came to the door, I shook Master Sergeant Greer's hand and simply said, "Thank you." I then crossed the threshold, ready to kill.

SPLENDID ISOLATION

It had been a couple of weeks since I graduated from the Advanced Urban Combat Course, and now we were at Fort Pickett, Virginia, again training our asses off.

Walking toward the barracks from the chow hall after dinner, I looked up and the thought hit me, Geez, everywhere I go—Fort Bragg, Fort McClellan, even here—it's always the same, open bays, open toilets, open showers. Climbing the steps, I saw Crunk sitting at a desk directly behind the door. "You're kidding me," I said, "don't tell me we've got to pull guard duty our last stop before Kandahar. Our last two weeks in country, and we're gonna pull CQ duty?"

"'Course not, Jet Set," replied Crunk. "This is just my clever ruse."

"What are you talking about?" I said.

"Boy Band's old Ranger buddy is driving up from Fort Bragg to give him that steak dinner he owes him, and I'm gonna punk the guy out."

"Oh yeah," I said. "The illusive Rodriguez." I'd forgotten about the bet—Rodriguez and Boy Band had bet a steak dinner on who would go to the war sooner.

None of us on the team had ever actually met or even seen pictures of 'Rodriguez', but everybody felt like we knew him. We'd heard about the bet, just as we'd heard everything about Rodriguez, indirectly through Boy Band. I sat down on the steps heading to the second floor of the barracks, and looked over Crunk's elaborate set-up—the desk in the hall, the white board on the wall noting the weather conditions and uniform of the day. He hadn't missed a thing, and I had to laugh, because I'd never seen Crunk go through such efforts just for a joke. And then I realized it; Crunk was jealous of Rodriguez.

Boy Band and Crunk were like brothers; they did everything together. The one wouldn't even go to the PX if the other didn't want to go. Still, everybody on the team had gleaned from his stories about his time on active duty in the 7th Special Forces Group that Boy Band had a BFF before he met Crunk. He never talked about Rodriguez, but he never told a 7th Group story that didn't make mention of him.

This was going to be the clash of the titans, and I wasn't going to miss it. We heard the sound of a car pulling up onto the gravel driveway

137

beside the barracks. Crunk's ears pricked up and his shoulders shot back. "Now, you gonna watch a brothah show a punk he just a punk," Crunk said to me. We both looked out the window to see a beautifully restored 1964 Impala Super Sport. Crunk's jaw dropped. He looked like he'd been punched in the stomach. "You got to be shittin' me!" he said. "How'd that son of a bitch get a whip like that?" It was one fine automobile: hunter green, with white, tuck-and-roll interior. The chrome was pristine, and the car had all the right edge-dressing. The Six-Four idled for a few seconds before he shut it down. It sounded throaty, with a rumbling idle. Rodriguez turned off the engine, and Crunk whispered to me, "Whatever you do, do not compliment him on that car—you didn't even notice his ride."

Rodriguez got out of the car. He was tall, lean and athletic. With a name like Rodriguez, I'd always pictured him as Mexican, but he looked more African, like he was from the Caribbean. He wore a Yankees T-shirt, loose fitting shorts and Fila flip-flops. We continued to watch as Rodriguez fairly swaggered across the parking lot. "Look at that cocky son of a bitch," said Crunk indignantly, "he struttin' around like he's the last Coke in the refrigerator."

Rodriguez bounded up the steps, opened the front door and stared down at Crunk with astonishment. "ID, please," Crunk said with feigned boredom.

"You're bullshittin' me," said Rodriguez with a laugh. "Since when does an SF unit pull CQ duty?"

"Since people with more rank than you decided it should be so," said Crunk. "ID please." Rodriguez grimaced, but he produced his ID, threw it on the desk and Crunk picked it up as if it were diseased.

"Do you have a vehicle on the post?' Crunk said, with studied indifference.

"Of course I do," replied Rodriguez. "You see that wicked-ass Six Four out there bringing up the property value of your broken ass old barracks? That belongs to me."

"You do realize, Mr—" Crunk studied the ID for a long moment, raised his eyebrows and said, "'Rod-ree-geez', that being on a military installation is not a right, but a privilege. And that I have the authority to search your vehicle if I deem it necessary."

"Who the hell?" Rodriguez exclaimed.

Dropping the topic, Crunk lazily half-turned his head back to the bay and shouted in that sing-song voice that a kid uses when calling his brother to the phone, "Boy BAND, your Puerto RICAN friend is here."

"Puerto Rican?" Rodriguez shot out. "I ain't no Puerto Rican. I'm Dominican."

"Oh, Dominican, is it?" Crunk said dismissively. Then, looking over at me, said with a grin, "Dominicans . . . the only people in the world who aspire to be Puerto Rican."

Rodriguez's eyes flashed, but just as quickly he read the entire set-up. "Oh, I see," he said. "You're Boy Band's buddy—his Negrito friend. He told me about you. And he was right, you are one sweaty son of a bitch. You sweat so much, you look like you been sprayed with Armor All."

It was on.

"Hey," Crunk said, "you better check yourself. You ain't in Guachington Heights no more!"

Rodriguez didn't raise an eyebrow. "What do they call you, again?" he said. "Oh, I remember. They call you 'What-Not,' ain't that right?"

"'What-Not'?" replied Crunk. "Ain't nobody call me 'What-Not'. My name is 'Crunk'."

"Are you shining me?" replied Rodriguez. "Don't you shine me. Your name is What-Not. Boy Band said so."

This was not how Crunk had planned things, and I got the feeling it might even come to blows. Just then Boy Band, oblivious to the drama, shouted out from back in the bay, "Rodriguez, you wild man!" Coming at Rodriguez at a full run, Boy Band almost tackled him. "Brother, how the hell are you?" he exclaimed. "And how is Josefina y Juanito?"

Rodriguez broke into a big toothy grin. "Somos Buenos. La familia esta feliz."

"Bastante bien! Estas listo por otro nino?" inquired Boy Band.

"Por supuesto! Siempre listo!" responded Rodriguez. "But right now I'm just getting acquainted with the guys on your team," he continued, nodding toward Crunk.

"So you met Crunk?" replied Boy Band. "Crunk is the shit, man. You should see him on the 240 Bravo. He can take out a target at 1,100 meters." Crunk and Rodriguez looked at each other hesitantly.

"Yeah," said Rodriguez with a shy smile, "I feel like I know him already." That brought a smile to Crunk's face, and the two shook hands aggressively, almost pleasantly—the complicated ritual of their meeting having been successfully negotiated.

Boy Band then turned to me. "And this here is Jet Set. He's our Demolition guy—and our shit house lawyer."

"I heard about you," replied Rodriguez. "I'm surprised Boy Band didn't use you to get him out of the war—claim he was some sort of Conscientious Objector, or some shit."

"I tried," I said, "but the judge determined he lacked a conscience."

Boy Band looked out the window and saw Rodriguez's car. "There it is!" he exclaimed. "You brought the Six-Four?"

"Well," said Rodriguez, "I was going to take the truck, but I figured your bitch ass is probably going to shoot yourself or something, so I better give you a dignified send-off."

"Nice. I appreciate your concern. You hungry?"

"I'm pretty damn hungry. If you want that steak, we best get to steppin'." Boy Band and Rodriguez headed out to the car and drove off in that stunning Six-Four. Crunk and I watched through the window.

"Man, that thing is wicked," I said.

"Yeah," replied Crunk, "but don't ever tell him that."

An hour later I was lying on my bunk, a soft breeze blowing through the window screens, and I heard Crunk's cell phone ring. Crunk was lying on his bunk not ten feet away. He picked up his phone and the entire team listened to his stilted conversation: "The name's not What-Not," he said in a loud whisper. "No, it's too late to go out. . . . No, I know we got tomorrow morning off, but I got to call my wife, and . . . Where? . . . Okay, I'll be there in half an hour, but y'all better take it easy. I ain't getting' locked-up because of your mess."

Crunk then got up, went to the sink and washed his face. He changed his shirt and—as casually as he could—said, "So, um . . . I'm ah gonna' go out for a bit, team sergeant. Next hard-time is zero twelve hundred, check?"

"Check," said the team sergeant, with open curiosity. "You, ah. . . you make sure Boy Band and you are standing tall tomorrow. Be in the right place at the right time in the right uniform."

"Roger that, team sergeant," Crunk said, and then he was off.

A cab pulled up to the barracks around midnight, waking up the team. We all pretended to be asleep as Crunk, Boy Band and Rodriguez stumbled out of the back seat. They came in banging doors and making exaggerated shushing sounds to each other. Boy Band hit his bed and immediately began snoring. Crunk found an empty bunk for Rodriguez and helped him climb up. As he was turning toward his own bed, Rodriguez whispered loudly to him, "Crunk . . . hey, Crunk."

"What?" Crunk replied.

"Listen," Rodriguez said, sitting up in his bunk. "When you guys are in The Stan, do me a favor."

"Sure," said Crunk.

"Keep an eye on Boy Band, would ya?" Rodriguez said. "He gets a little reckless. Sometimes he does stuff without thinking."

"I know," said Crunk.

"Yeah, of course, you know," replied Rodriguez. "But Boy Band can be . . . heedless. He's a good guy, but he . . . doesn't understand caution."

"Yeah," said Crunk. "He's basically an idiot."

Rodriguez grunted a laugh. "He's not basically an idiot. He's completely an idiot." Rodriguez rubbed his eyes. "But the world needs idiots—guys like Boy Band—who never think about the danger. And it needs guys like us, too, who do think about the danger. A guy like that needs to be unleashed, that's what he's born for. But a guy like that also needs to be reigned in . . . that's what guys like us are born for."

Crunk had begun to snore, and Rodriguez was now talking to himself. "I don't know why, but I just felt like I should come up here before you go off. Wanted to ride in the Six-Four with Boy Band one last time."

At noon the next day, the company filed into the lecture hall. We filed in from the back, and filled the seats that cascaded down to the white board, the podium, and the unknown man standing before the microphone. The man held a laser pointer in his hand. The company was no more than 60 men, so we didn't do that regular Army bit where the sergeant major yells at you until the entire front row, the next row, and the next row is filled in. Instead, he just lazily motioned us forward, saying, "Come on, fellas, I don't want you hanging out in the back like hoodlums in church."

"Look at this dude," I said to Jiggy, tossing my head toward the man at the podium. "Everything about him says CIA."

Jiggy laughed. "He screams it."

"J. Crew Khakis and mountain-climbing boots?" I said. "Who does that?"

"Yeah," replied Jiggy. "That's not a tell? Rockin' that polo shirt too, and what's with the hair?" The guy had the classic 'undercover' haircut—a high-and-tight that hadn't seen a barber for two months.

"That hair," I said, "it looks like it's trying to minimally adhere to a memorandum it disagrees with."

"And check out that dive watch," Jiggy said. "Ever notice how these guys gotta' have the big clunky dive watch?"

"Yeah," I said. "It's got to look like a Rolex, but it can't be a Rolex. They're real particular about that."

Spooky sat down in front of us, but turned around and said, "Don't ask a bunch of dumb ass questions, got it? We got things to do, and I don't want to make a career out of this briefing. You show these CIA boys the least bit of interest and they get a hard-on and want to talk for hours."

"Hey, fellas," the guy said with enthusiasm. "My name is . . . Mr. Lynch and I want to tell you about Afghanistan before you go over."

Mr. Lynch put the flat of his palms on the table in front of him. "You men are really lucky," he said. "It's only been—what—six months since we smoked the Taliban out of Tora Bora. Big Army isn't even there yet, there's only like 3,500 U.S. troops in the whole country, and most of those Mopes never go outside the wire. You men are going to have the opportunity to ramble all across your sector of Afghanistan. The country is wide open and it will be for some time—you guys got it pretty good."

"I like this guy," I whispered to Jiggy.

"Yeah, he's cool," he replied.

After Spooky's little talk to us about not asking questions, I was surprised to see his hand shoot up. "When did you get to Afghanistan?" he asked.

"I came in with the first crew," replied Mr. Lynch. "Been in country on and off since late October 2001."

This was an exciting admission. Clearly Mr. Lynch was the real thing. He'd have been there when we brought down the Taliban. Spooky practically leapt out of his seat. "Did you work with any of the boys from 5th Group?" he asked.

"I did," said Lynch, smiling to see a look of recognition in Spooky's eyes. "I worked with ODA 5XX."

The entire room went silent. ODA 5XX had been spoken of only in hushed tones since November. We weren't even sure if we could discuss what we knew, but here was a guy who was there (ODA, or Operational Detachment Alpha, was the proper term for an 'A-Team'). Spooky stayed standing—ODA 5XX was his old team when he was in the 5th Group, a fact of which he was intensely proud. "Were you at Mazar-e-Sharif?" Spooky asked hesitantly.

Lynch paused for a moment. He was thinking about what to tell us.

"I was," he said at last, and the room exploded into loud applause. The sergeant major looked over to Major Brenner, and Major Brenner nodded to him.

The sergeant major came forward and quieted us down. He turned to Lynch and said, "Sir, if you don't mind, everyone here is vetted Secret at the minimum. We will listen to your briefing about weapons caches and Specter Gunships—but we don't want to. We want to hear about the battle. Tell us about the victory at Mazar-e-Sharif." The entire company came to its feet, clapping and shouting to hear the story.

Lynch smiled sheepishly. He seemed delighted to be among men who wanted to know about this extraordinary victory that was barely covered in the newspapers. As he told the story of the battle, we listened to him spellbound, because the men he was talking about were us, and we were them—this was our battle, or at least we wanted it to be.

"Mazar-e-Sharif began like many great battles begin," he said. "With one side digging in. It was the Taliban who chose the time, the place and the circumstance of battle. It was here that they were going to show us who was in charge of Afghanistan—and we punished them for it."

After Mr. Lynch told us the story of the battle, Major Brenner stood up. It was surprising to see him ask a question, as he was usually so remote and stand-offish. "Mr. Lynch," he said, "what about the prison riot after the battle?"

"Yes," said Lynch solemnly, "the victory was so complete we had problems with all the prisoners. There were only a handful of us Americans, and there was the language issue as well."

"What about Mike?" Major Brenner asked with a little too much passion. "Did you know Mike?" Before Major Brenner came to the 20th Group, he had been a Marine officer on active duty.

"Who's Mike?" Jiggy leaned over toward me and whispered.

"Mike Spann, the CIA guy who was killed in the prison riot. . . Brenner and Spann bunked together in Officer Basic at Quantico."

"Yeah, I did know Mike," Lynch said, uneasily. "I helped recover his body. And I can tell you this, Mike didn't go down without a fight. He took three of those bastards with him." The room was dead quiet, except for the slow whamp, whamp, whamp of the ceiling fans, and the haunting sound of a helicopter flying lazy circles in the distance. We knew what Lynch meant. It hung in the room like a challenge, like the purpose to our lives. If we were going to die, we would take the enemy with us.

The reason we were at Fort Pickett was specifically so that we could isolate ourselves, and each ODA would work on their specialty. Our training would cumulate with a complex two-day, company-sized operation in which we would take down two separate buildings where hostages were being held—each team using their specialty. Captain McMann had instructed the team sergeant that he wanted us to be doing a lot of live fire exercises. "I want you shooting and moving," the team sergeant said, "on your own and with the team."

On the last day before the final exercise, we spent the entire day land navigating or firing the heavy machine guns. But the most important training event was practicing the 'Australian Peel.' The Australian Peel is an infantry movement initiated when a small unit runs into a much larger unit and needs to break contact as quickly as possible. In this scenario, the point man drops to a knee and opens fire on full automatic. When he has expended his entire magazine, he turns around and runs like hell a good distance away, gets into position, reloads, and covers the others as they follow. As soon as the point takes off running, the next guy opens up with his weapon on full auto, and when his magazine is expended, he turns and hauls-ass back to where the point man is, reloads and takes up a position in line with the point. This goes on until the entire unit is back in line with the point man. Once they're all back and accounted for, the point man starts the whole thing all over again.

"The trick about the Australian Peel," the sergeant major explained to us, "is to peel two and even three times." Since he was the only Vietnam veteran, we always listened to what the sergeant major told us. "Anybody can peel one time. And you get—what—200 meters away from the enemy? You got to figure you're running from at least a company, maybe even a battalion. You better Dee Dee your ass at least a klick away. Those bastards are gonna bring up their mortars and unleash hell on your ass. You need to be able to peel one, two, even three times away." The sergeant major looked at us fiercely, and we could all tell he was speaking from authority. "And you've got to do it right, too—it's important to get this shit right!" The sergeant major grabbed his collar stiffly. "This is one of those 'Hail Mary' things. This is what you do when everything goes to shit."

As we rehearsed the drill, the sergeant major turned to the team sergeant. "This thing is always chaotic, Dragline," he said. "It's a bunch of guys shooting on full auto and running at top speed."

"Roger, sergeant major," said Dragline. "It can be a real goat-fuck, if we don't watch out."

"That's right," said the sergeant major, with unusual severity in his voice. "It's a total goat-fuck, and that's why I want you fuckin' this goat. These other guys are just here to hold its head."

We were on a grassy plain that stretched out to a high berm 300 meters to the south. It was well into spring now, and the trees were in full bloom. It was mild, in the mid 70s, but the team sergeant had been running us so much we were smoked. He had us rehearsing the peel over and over again in full body armor, and, like some football coach, he harassed us if we ran too slowly. "Looks like we don't have much daylight left, team sergeant," Captain McMann thankfully said. Although training was inherently a sergeant's job, many officers stepped in and took it over. Here, our Team Leader let the team sergeant go on almost exhausting us, but when it really was time to step in, all the captain said was, "Hey, it's getting late." The way he did things was very respectful.

"Yeah," said the team sergeant, "well, I hope we're ready. Boy Band, take point. The rest of you take your positions." I put a magazine into my weapon and chambered a round. I took up a position about 40 meters to the right of Boy Band and about 15 meters behind him. I looked across and saw Jiggy directly in line with me 80 meters away. When we were in position, Boy Band gave the hand-and-arm signal to move forward. We walked silently forward, slowly rotating our torsos around, scanning the scene, our eyes and weapons moving as one. After about 60 meters of patrolling, Boy Band came to a halt, put up a clenched fist and we all went to a knee just as Boy Band unleashed a furious barrage of fire ripping through the silent twilight. Then Boy Band jumped up, spun around, his weapon pointed downward, his hand covering the trigger well, and took off running to the rear. As soon as I heard a break in fire, I opened up on full automatic, the cordite filling the air around me with an acrid yet invigorating smell. When my weapon stopped firing, I took a quick look and saw the bolt to the rear and the chamber empty. I stood up, turned around and took off running as I heard the report of Jiggy's rifle spitting out rounds. I couldn't see Boy Band right away, but after running about 200 meters, I saw him lying prone on the grass some ways up. I picked out a spot in line with him and raced toward it.

Dropping into the prone, I released my magazine and slapped in a fresh one, chambered a round, and brought my rifle up. Just then, I saw Jiggy running in my general direction. When the team had all peeled away, and we lay in line about 200 meters from the initial contact, it all

145

started again—this was the time when undisciplined teams lost control. Boy Band opened up and spent his magazine. He then turned and took off running. Then it was my turn, and I did just the same. I turned and began running, but looked to my left to see Jiggy lighting up the enclosing darkness with his rifle. We pulled back another 200 meters and formed up a line. When we got a good count, the captain stood up and shouted, "ENDEX! ENDEX! ENDEX!" The exercise was over. We could have done it again, but it was getting dark and, I thought, we had done well.

"Well, no one got shot," was all the team sergeant said, but he said it with satisfaction. We collected up our magazines and policed up the area as best as we could, and we walked back together toward our van and the tree where we had left our equipment. The gentle twilight was giving way to darkness, and we all walked along in silence, all of us afraid to speak before the captain and the team sergeant gave their evaluations. At last the captain said, "I'm happy. Team sergeant, whatcha think?" Approaching the tree where our equipment was stored, it was now fully dark.

"I cannot say," said the team sergeant with ponderous hesitation, "that I'm at all displeased." No one of us could see another, but we each knew exactly where the other was. "No," he continued. "I cannot say I am displeased at all." It was the highest praise I had ever heard from him, and I beamed an invisible smile.

Still, the toughest and hardest test would come the next day. We were jumping-in for our final exercise, a company level assault on multiple buildings.

THE FINAL ASSAULT

"Picture Perfect," shouted the captain, as we made our big loop around Fort Pickett. In the distance you could see the small town of Blackstone. It was evening, so the town's idea of rush hour could be witnessed—five cars waiting at the town's only light.

We were riding a CH-47, Chinook helicopter. The temperature was downright balmy so they never bothered to lower the rear gate. Just as the sun was arching past the tree line in the west, we were issued our final jump commands—"Stand in the door!" When I exited the aircraft, I went through my usual spectrum of emotions—concealed but extraordinary fear, followed by fragile but triumphant masculinity, followed by the usual maniacal laughter. And then came the WHUMP of the opening parachute. After that it was just happy me, screwing around in mid-air, looking at various stuff, glad to know I was getting paid just for jumping out of a perfectly good aircraft.

I hit the ground hard but not incorrectly, and unsnapped my chute and quietly gathered it up into my bag. I deposited the parachute with the ground crew and found the team rally point. When I got there I found Jiggy and Captain McMann both on one knee facing away from each other, about 20 meters between them, pulling security. I silently took up a similar position—there would be absolute noise and light discipline from this time on. It was by now dark, so I put on my NVGs. Soon afterward we moved-out to the west.

It had been warm and spring-like the entire time we'd been at Fort Pickett, but now the temperature began to drop precipitously. Ice was forming in the brooks and streams we patrolled silently past. Coming up out of a ravine, we came over a small, sloping hill, and just then an enormous full moon came out from behind a group of pine trees, flooding a small field with a muted light. I took off my NVGs. Patrolling, for me, was always both a solitary and group-oriented activity. The very silence of patrolling made it intensely personal— almost like delving down deep into a bottomless lake—but it was entirely a group action, you were constantly keeping visual contact and communicating with hand and arm signals. The silence offered you the opportunity for profound contemplation, but the intense unity required you to remain constantly vigilant. That was the joy of patrolling, stalking a kill, moving completely alone, and yet not alone. When you patrol with a loaded weapon, you feel like a venomous spider— completely vulnerable, but utterly able to kill.

This mission was going to be complicated. We jumped in about ten klicks away from our link-up point with ODA 20XX. We were to use map and compass to travel overland to the link-up point and make contact with 20XX, who were coming in from about ten klicks out in the other direction. It was my job to navigate—get us to the link-up. Boy Band would be on point, but I would steer the patrol. Boy Band, the captain and I had spent almost an entire night during the planning phase map-reconnoitering the route. I knew my checkpoints and my backstops, and at exactly what distance on the pace-count I would see them. Once at the link-up, the plan was for our combined elements to establish an "ORP" (patrol base) in a draw with thick vegetation. From there, we would send out a two-man element to put eyes on the target.

Our team cleared off the drop zone and into the wood line at exactly the spot I had pinpointed on the map during isolation. We moved through the forest the way a venomous spider walks across your arm. My first checkpoint was a road we had to cross at 200 meters. We hit a road at 200 meters, and I checked to see that it was running in the same direction as our road—a common mistake. I was glad to see that it was, and that my pace-count was right. The patrol was a long one, but I gained in confidence every time we hit my checkpoints. At around 1:30 a.m., I made a hand-and-arm signal to the captain that we were within 200 meters of the link-up. We pulled-up into a tight 360 degree security position. The captain and Spooky went out to make contact with the other team at exactly 2:00 a.m.

Now that we were no longer moving, I noticed that an incredible late-spring cold front had hit us. I began to shake violently, but I couldn't stop laughing, thinking that here in southern Virginia, late into April, the creeks were freezing over with ice. The coldest April this place must have seen for years, and we had to be out in it. Jiggy was lying in a prone position behind a tree about 20 meters away, and I could see that he was shaking as well. He looked over at me with a look of amused befuddlement. "WHAT THE HELL!" I mouthed to him. And he laughed.

At 3:00 a.m. Spooky and the captain returned. But instead of leading us to the link-up, the captain signaled for me to come over. He pulled out his poncho liner and his map, then threw the poncho liner on the ground and crawled under it with the map and a red-lens flashlight. He signaled to me to get under the poncho liner, the team sergeant too. We lay prone on the ground covered by the poncho liner, and the captain pulled out the map. "Where do you think we are?" he calmly said.

I picked up a pine needle and pointed it at what I thought our location was. Something about the captain's frustrated tone made me doubt myself for the first time in that night. "Alright," he said, "so if we're here, then there's a road about one hundred and fifty meters to the East, check?"

"Roger, sir."

"And that road runs . . . North, South, check?"

"Roger."

"I want you to take Jiggy, and go 150 meters to the East and see if there's a North, South road."

"And both of ya keep pace-count," whispered the team sergeant. "That's probably what's not right here."

Jiggy and I headed east. This was not good. I prided myself on my land navigational skills, and I was confident we were exactly where I said we were. Jiggy could see that I was starting to ping, and he nudged me in the shoulder. I looked over and he gave me a face to say, "Don't worry about it."

At exactly 150 meters we came upon a North, South traveling road. I gave Jiggy a cocky, triumphant look, and he looked back with the same "don't worry about it" look. His look said, "Don't fret too much when you're down, and don't preen too much when you're up. Neither one will last too long."

I shot a 180 degree back azimuth, and we returned to the team. When we got there, 20XX was with them and they were rucking up to go to the ORP. I looked at the team sergeant questioningly, and he moved his fingers like a man walking, as if to say, "their pace-count was off." Vindication! I thought. I was not the weak link on the team!

Soon, cold darkness gave way to gray dawn. The sun came up and the day grew warmer. The next many hours would be a waiting game. My role would be just holing up in the ORP, making sure I was silent and keeping an eye out for enemy patrols, which were not expected. That's the thing about a patrol base, it is by definition going to be in a crappy place. You want to be where no one else wants to be. If guards are roving around, they're going to take the easy route. They're not going into the draw with the snakes and the vines and the whatever. So that's where you need to be—it's not rocket science.

Sitting in a draw all day long can get boring, but you do get to know all the insects and small animals around you—they have personalities that practically yell at you. There's going to be that same black ant always running around frantically looking for whatever stuff he can bring back to the colony. And everywhere he goes, he's always saying, "What do we got here? What do we got here? What do we got here?" Then there's the big pincer insect that likes to stay down in his hole. But he comes out all aggressively every fifteen minutes shouting, "Who wants some shit? Who wants some shit? Who wants some shit?" Of course, Mr. Salamander rolls into the neighborhood whenever he feels like, saying, "I'm gonna eat all you bitches!" But wait till nightfall—especially in the spring—that's when the frogs come out, and GEEZ, then it's a freaking orgy. Frogs don't care about anything except getting laid. Frogs don't care if they're eaten, if they're rude or if they're captured by cruel, torturing little boys. They come out at night and it's like Spring Break. All the females are shouting, "HOT STUFF! HOT STUFF! HOT STUFF!" and all the males scream, "BIG MAN HERE! BIG MAN HERE! WHO WANTS SOME OF THIS BIG MAN!"

That's the thing about nature, it's just so embarrassing.

At midnight we moved from the ORP to the LRP (Last Rally Point), where we did our final preparations for the assault. I primed the breaching charges with the blasting caps and made sure the charges were sticky and would cling tightly to the door. Explosives are funny things. Unless they're pressed directly to the target, they do not destroy it. If the charge is even a quarter inch away, it will not breach (that bit of demolition knowledge was just for your edification. You're welcome). Then we ran into a problem. We all knew by heart the layout of the building, and we knew it had a small shed attached to it. But the shed was only about four feet by four feet, so we didn't think it needed to be a priority to clear. But now when we brought the recon team in for the assault, they told us that over the last two hours someone had been coming and going numerous times into the shed. "When we pulled out," whispered Spooky, "no one was in the shed."

"If there's someone in that shed," whispered the team sergeant to Captain McMann, "he's liable to come in after we make the breach and smoke the shit out of all of us. Maybe we should detail someone to clear that shed at the same time as we blow the door."

A line creased Captain McMann's forehead. "We're already thin."

He wiped the sweat from his face, heavy with the weight of command. "No. We can't spare it," he said. "We've got a plan. We rehearsed the heck out of it. We stick to the plan. If we're wrong and someone is in that shed, then we'll have to deal with it, but we have a plan and we stick to it."

"Roger that, sir," said the team sergeant, "but you know what Mike Tyson said about having a plan?"

"What'd he say?" said the captain.

"'Everybody's got a plan . . . until they get hit.'"

We crept silently up to the entry point. I slapped my linear charge against the locked door, then we stacked up against the building 10 meters off. "Fire in the Hole," I whispered to myself, and mashed the plunging device on the detonator. The door exploded with a shattering roar, and wood and glass and debris careened violently within an angry little circle. We raced to the breach, flooding into the building. Three men were inside about 20 feet from the door. Two of the men were standing and holding assault rifles, the third man was tied to a chair with a blindfold covering his eyes. We shot the two standing men, then Jiggy pointed the muzzle of his weapon at the man in the chair and shouted, "Shut up, and sit still!"

We swept the room with our weapons and each pronounced it "clear." Everyone but Jiggy moved forward down a darkened hallway with numerous doors on both sides—some open, some closed.

The minimum number of men needed to secure a room is two, but that number, 'while authorized, is highly discouraged' as they say in the field manual. Captain McMann and I quickly stacked up on the first door on the right, which was closed. The best breaching device for an inside door is a shotgun, but since real men could be on the other side of the door, it was determined that just a kick would suffice. Captain McMann gave me the signal and I kicked in the first door. He swarmed in first, me behind him. The room was dark, but we had our "Sure Fire" lights on our weapons, and saw that it was empty. "Clear!" we both shouted as we moved back out into the hallway. Crunk and Boy Band where taking down another room, as Spooky and the team sergeant took down a third. Captain McMann and I entered the fourth room and two men were waiting for us. I took a round to the chest and another round grazed off my helmet. I put two rounds into one man, and Captain McMann finished off the other one. The rounds that hit me were only soap, but it made me appreciate my helmet and body armor. Once we had cleared the building, Crunk ran out to secure the shed.

Having cleared the building and set up security, we returned to the man in the chair. By now Jiggy had released him from the chair and zip-tied his hands.

"I am a hostage!" the man shouted at us. "I am the person you have come here to free! Release me!"

"Shut-up, shit bird!" Dragline said. "We don't know that. For all we know, you're one of them, you just got caught stealing from the till. We'll sort this out when we're out of here."

We got a head count and made a hasty retreat back to the ORP. From there, we rucked-up and rapidly ex-filtrated to the Landing Zone to board a helicopter. When we arrived at the LZ, we began to take enemy small arms fire. Although the fire was sporadic, the chopper pilot insisted the LZ was too hot, and that we needed to go to the alternate LZ. So we laid down suppressive fire, and Dee Dee-ed westward 400 meters (Note to future Special Forces soldiers: the first LZ is always going to be 'too hot," and you're always going to have to go the the 'alternative' spot).

Again it was Boy Band on point with me navigating. We arrived at the alternate LZ, prisoner in tow, and the helicopter landed with the usual sound and fury. We leapt onto the deck like fish landing in a boat. Head-count was taken, and we stole away into the night.

The night before's cold front had completely gone away, and the evening was warm. The doors of the Blackhawk were open, and the rush of the wind was refreshing. All our eyes were on Captain McMann, as he nodded to Dragline with a look of satisfaction. Dragline beamed with delight. "Hell yeah!" he shouted, slapping everyone within arm's reach.

We careened though the darkness, just above the tree tops, the prop blast ripping around us, the fields and houses just feet below us. It felt magical. I looked over at Jiggy, and shouted above the rotor wash, "Don't let me die," I said, "until I get to Afghanistan. Just let me get to the war: everything else will be gravy."

RHEIN MAIN AIR FORCE BASE

"Ever notice," said Boy Band, casting a sideways glance at Crunk, "that everyone in a McDonald's commercial is—I don't know—vaguely black?"

Crunk raised his eyebrows, but did not respond.

"I mean," Boy Band continued, "they're not, like, black-black, they're more like . . . Soledad O'Brian black. You know, leg-up-on-your-college-application black."

The team was sitting in a row of airport lounge chairs disinterestedly staring across the enormous lobby of the passenger terminal of Rhein Main Air Force Base, looking at a large television on the other side of the room. The television hung from the ceiling, flanked on one side by a German flag and on the other an American flag. The television was playing a romantic comedy, occasionally interrupted by commercials for fast food, denim jeans and big American cars. We couldn't hear the movie, but we didn't care. We just stared at it with bored curiosity.

"That's because," Cronk said with a broad grin, "white folks want to be like black folks. They like to think of themselves as relaxed and fun to be with. They like to think they're athletic and quick with a laugh—white folk wish they was black folk." Crunk tilted his head towards Boy Band and stared at him triumphantly. "But black folk," he continued, "black folk have no desire to be like white folk. We don't want to be all uptight all the time, nervous about everything, physically awkward." Crunk stood up and brushed himself off with dramatic particularity. "See," he said turning toward us, "y'all see how white folks always be imitating us, they always stealing our slang, our music, our swagger. Just look at the high five," Crunk threw up his right hand, "everybody always high-fivin' each other. Who invented the high-five? We did. That's who." Crunk grinned victoriously.

"That's true, Crunk," Boy Band responded in agreement. "You guys invented the high-five." He paused and looked across at the rest of us. "We . . . um, we invented the telephone."

The team had left Pope Air Force Base at 4:00 a.m. and was sitting through a five hour lay-over in Germany. There had been many delays and a lot of tension leaving Fort Bragg. Higher command kept kicking us off our scheduled aircraft and giving those lifts to the regular Army. They were obviously snubbing us, and everyone in the company felt it. But we had our own cards to play, and so when the company commander and the company sergeant major scheduled a meeting with the battalion commander, and a certain senator from Virginia called in to take part in the discussion, it was found that there was, in fact, room on the aircrafts for us after all—but we had to go in teams, not as a company.

There was something about the way we were being treated, not just by the regular Army, but the country. Nobody was taking the war seriously, that's what was bothering me. We flew out of Pope in a C-141 loaded with a battery of 105 mm howitzers. We would pick-up another aircraft in a few hours and head to Kandahar—for some reason routed through Qatar. In Qatar we were scheduled for another four-hour layover, then on to Afghanistan. All we wanted was to get to Kandahar, to at least touch down in the war zone. It was our biggest fear the war would be over before we arrived.

The McDonald's commercial finished and the movie returned, and as we watched, Boy Band started up a running commentary: "Apparently, although handsome and well-liked by his peers, the young man and the beautiful, kind-hearted, young lady absolutely hate each other."

"And yet," I chimed in, "coincidence finds them constantly together."

Boy Band shrugged his shoulders. "Sparks are flying, and hi-jinks will ensue." We watched as the couple got stuck in an elevator together, then collided while jogging in different directions around the Central Park Reservoir. We stared at the movie curiously, observing it like anthropologists studying a strange tribe. At one point in the movie, the likeable young man was in his relaxed, weekend mode—we understood this because we saw him in jeans and a fisherman's sweater.

"Who needs sound?" said Boy Band. "Everything's in shorthand." The young man left his quirky-but-comfortable apartment in a multi-ethnic neighborhood and went grocery shopping at an open-air market. He was friendly and on intimate terms with all the shop venders—all of whom, unexpectedly, were from different ethnic backgrounds. The likeable young man kicked a soccer ball with a bright-faced Hispanic youth. He then folded his arms and spoke sagely with an old Jewish man, who was having coffee with a distinguished Arab gentleman. Later, the likeable young man expressed dramatic enthusiasm about the flamboyantly colorful head-dress of an African shop-woman. And, climbing the stairs back to his apartment, he helped a little Russian girl collect up her Matryoshka dolls. It all seemed a bit much.

Finally, as the likeable young man entered his apartment and placed his grocery bag on the kitchen table, Boy Band started up again, "You know how you can tell if a guy in the movies is 'boyfriend material'?" Boy Band air-quoted the words with his fingers.

"How's that?" Crunk asked.

"A guy in the movies is 'boyfriend material' if he's got a loaf of French bread sticking out of his grocery bag," replied Boy Band. "I mean, there must be something magic about French bread, because all a guy in the movies has to do is have it sticking out of his shopping bag and PUFF, instant boyfriend material."

We picked up a flight out of Germany about 2:00 a.m. and all of us immediately racked-out as soon as we boarded.

"Check it out, man," Jiggy said, shaking me awake.

"Wha…what is it?" I said angrily, rubbing the sleep out of my eyes.

"Dude, I was talkin' to the crew chief," said Jiggy. "He says we need to see the sun coming up over the Nile."

"What?"

"Dude," Jiggy spoke to me like he was speaking to a baby, "we're fly-ing over the Ni-hil Riv-er. Crew chief says we got to see it when the sun comes up. Says we can go up into the cabin, captain won't mind."

I was lying under a pick-up truck lashed to the deck of the C-141 aircraft, in which we were flying. We had boarded the aircraft about three hours earlier at Rhien Main. We were carrying a load of four "technicals" to Kandahar, by way of Qatar. Technicals were a little piece of military inventiveness we learned from the Somalis in the early 1990s. A technical was just a pick-up truck rigged with a machine gun in the truck bed. The pros of the technical were that it was cheap, fast, maneuverable, and an excellent firing platform for heavy machine guns and mortars. The cons, however, were that it had no armor, and that the machine gunner was completely exposed—think of a guy dunking a basketball in the middle of a gunfight.

"Are you sure?" I asked.

"Yeah," Jiggy continued. "Apparently, it's the only thing that makes this run worthwhile."

I rolled out from under the truck, tucked my poncho liner into my rucksack, stood up and brushed the dust off my uniform. The inside of the plane was almost completely dark, the only lights were the red warning lights running along the fuselage.

The crew chief was looking out a window several feet away, and he gave us the thumbs-up. The last time I had been in a cockpit was when a bunch of us enlisted got to look out at Denali as we made the pass over the Alaska Range. It was not what I'd expected. I thought Denali would be all sheer faces and jutting edges, but it wasn't tall-looking at all, just enormous, like a 14 year old second-grader who wanted your lunch money.

The cockpit of the C-141was much larger than I had expected, and the windows wrapped around the entire front of the plane, giving us a full 180 degree view. Even as we climbed the ladder, the windows began to flood with the light of the rising sun. At first there was yellow, then orange, then the eastern sky took on a brilliant white. Jiggy and I both stepped closer to the windows, awed by what we saw. Directly beneath us, and running out into the distant horizon in every direction, was an endless expanse of white, gleaming sand, astonishing in its sameness. Cutting across this vast emptiness was a single meandering ribbon of greenish-blue water stretching out as far as the eye could see. I pushed my face up to the thick glass, and could already feel the heat of the rising sun. For the longest time Jiggy and I just stared out the window—silent—searching, but not finding an end point to these two eternal elements arrayed against each other.

I have viewed many landscapes from the air. Not two months before, Jiggy and I swung from a narrow rope swaying below a Black Hawk helicopter 500 feet in the air as it made lazy circles above the woods and farmland around Camp MacKall, North Carolina. On many occasions I had stood in the open door of a moving aircraft as we made gigantic loops back to the drop zone to release more paratroopers. But those landscapes were tiny and precious compared to this. Those were landscapes of intricate detail—farms, streams, roads and houses. This was something else entirely. What I saw was the Earth awakening to its daily struggle. What I saw was the Great Desert, colossal in its desolation, hurling itself against the battlements of the mighty Nile River—two enormous elements in eternal struggle against each other. What I saw was a limitless sea of emptiness completely surrounding a needle-thin thread of ebullient life, a living river dancing inside the embrace of a brooding dead desert. And it seemed to me that both the river and the desert knew that someday the desert would conquer the river, but every day that it did not the river mocked the desert. And the river knew that it would someday die, but that it would not be on that day, and the desert knew that it would have to wait another day to kill the only thing it really ever cared about.

"Thanks for waking me up," I said to Jiggy.

"You're my battle buddy," he said. "Can't do fun stuff without you."

We didn't say anything after that, but stared out at the entrancing landscape in studied silence. After a time Jiggy said quietly, "I was in Liberia when they had their civil war. It was like being in hell. Nothing made any sense, it was just killing."

I vaguely remembered some chaotic news footage about President Samuel Doe and rebel leader Prince Johnson. "Yeah," I said, "I remember that."

"My team was on the task force to evacuate the Americans," Jiggy said, his eyes still fixated on the river. "It was mostly a Marine operation, but they wanted a recon element, so that was us." Jiggy chuckled and shook his head slowly, as if he was telling me a dream. "The rebels had taken to cross-dressing and wearing, like, little kids' Halloween costumes. We set up a hasty checkpoint at an intersection in Monrovia, and these three rebels kind of just stumbled out of the jungle right where we had set up." Jiggy's face grew quizzical, as if he was trying to remember a long forgotten tune. "The one guy had an M-16 with an extra magazine duct-taped to the loaded magazine. I remember he wore a wedding dress, with, I want to say, a 'Casper The Friendly Ghost' mask on his face. The other guy had an RPG, and he wore a wig of long pink hair and a tutu. The last guy had an AK-47, and, for some reason, he wore an orange life-preserver vest." Jiggy paused, as if lost in thought. "We weren't supposed to engage anyone unless for self-defense, so we just stared at each other. But eventually Cue Ball Eddie, my buddy, raised his rifle and started just barking out cuss words at these guys, and they took off running."

"That's totally nuts," I said.

"Well," replied Jiggy, "it was war." He paused, still staring out at the sun rising over the Nile. "Next day, we go to a house we were told to secure. There was a dead woman lying in the doorway, and then six other dead people in the house—three of them kids." Jiggy was still staring out the window, but his eyes were ablaze with memories. "That was the thing," he said, "that was the thing they used to do. They'd come to the house, knock on the door, and whoever answered, they'd say, 'Give me three feet.' That meant they were going to kill you, and they didn't want to get their clothes spattered with blood. 'Give me three feet,'" Jiggy said, incredulously. "It became like a thing to say all over Monrovia. Some radio disc-jockey made it his tagline, and some local singer wrote a song with that line as the title, Give Me Three Feet. It became a wildly popular hit. It made me sick every time it came on the radio."

I shook my head. "It sounds evil."

"What do you think war is?" Jiggy said. "Jet Set, you're stupid. That's why I like you. The whole reason I woke you up is because you're stupid and you still believe stuff." I coughed nervously. "You believe we're going to Afghanistan to do something good and noble and even glorious." Jiggy looked again back at the sunrise. "But I know we're only going off to war. . . . Still, I like having you around, you know. You remind me of myself. I used to believe in stuff. . . . I used to believe in all that stuff. It's all stupid, but I used to be stupid. I wish I was stupid again."

AMONG THE BELIEVERS

"Alright, numb-nuts," Dragline said, feigning anger, but not looking too sure of himself. "Change number 99: we got pushed from the manifest for the flight to Kandahar . . . so we'll be stuck here in Qatar for a few days."

The entire Team groaned in unison. "What?" Boy Band exclaimed. "A few days? They're trying to screw us out of this deployment!"

"This is bullshit!" Crunk said, practically shouting. "I ain't pickin' up cigarette butts in Qatar for the rest of the war. We got to get to the show!"

"Shut your cock holsters, both of you," said Dragline, relieved now to be actually angry. "We're going to the show . . . but it'll be a few days."

We all knew what this meant. We were being diverted from the war—we weren't going after all. I went red in the face, and Jiggy looked the same way. The regular Army was going to screw us, that was obvious. First at Bragg, where they made us jump through our asses to get a flight, then in Germany, where we were incidental, and we practically had to beg them to let us hitch a ride with the equipment, and now this.

All of us were hostile and humiliated, but it was Spooky, surprisingly, who lost his military bearing. "What the fuck, Frank, are you going to let them dick-dance us out of the war?" he said.

"Don't you 'what the fuck, Frank' me, former captain," Dragline replied, "it's team sergeant to you,"

Spooky regained himself. "Sorry, Drag—team sergeant," he said, "but don't you see what these regular Army douche bags are doing? They're trying to gank us—they don't want National Guard guys showin' them up on the battlefield—which we will, if they let us. They're going to keep us out of theater. Fra—team sergeant, we can't let them brush us aside."

"Spooky," said the team sergeant, "that's not going to happen. We're going to the show."

Spooky gritted his teeth, and lowered his eyes as he spoke. "What I'm saying . . . team sergeant, is that this is not about who's on the

159

manifest. This is politics." Spooky continued as his eyes rose to Dragline's, "I was an A-Team leader in 5th Group—as you just referenced—and I know what these rear-echelon pogues are like. They want to short-dick us because we're National Guard. Everything is a pissing contest with these 'Chairborne Rangers.'" We all nodded our heads in agreement, as if we knew what we were talking about. "Team sergeant," he continued, "what is the captain doing about this?"

This was a slight. Spooky was not asking about the captain, he was doubting the captain. Spooky was just a master sergeant—whatever he had been in a previous life—and he was completely out of line to doubt the captain. Dragline grew livid, and he reached to his side, as if to grab the night stick he carried as a police officer. "The captain," shouted Dragline, "is on top of this!"

Just then Captain McMann stepped out from the tent he and the team sergeant shared. He did not say a word, but only looked at us as if we had struck him a blow.

Spooky took a step back, embarrassed, but then he righted himself and said, "I'm sorry, sir. I meant no disrespect, but they want to keep us out of the war. Sir, team sergeant, may I speak with you in private."

The captain motioned for Spooky to step into the tent, and he and the team sergeant followed him. The tent was directly in front of us, not 15 feet away, and immediately after the three ducked in, we heard their loud whispers. "All I'm saying," said Spooky, "is that the regular Army is looking for a reason to DX us."

"Do you think I don't know that?" Dragline said in response. Captain McMann said nothing, but we could feel the weight of his silence.

"Do you really think Captain McMann and I," replied Dragline, "are just sitting in those planning sessions saying, 'Yes, sir, no, sir. Three bags full, sir'?"

"What I'm saying," replied Spooky, "is that we need to get creative."

After that there was a long silence, and in the silence we all began inching closer to the tent. At last Captain McMann's voice could be heard, "What do you recommend?"

The three began to whisper, and their whispering inched us closer still to the tent, until we were not 18 inches away from the front folds. At times the whispering was agreeable and conspiratorial, and at other times it was excited and angry.

After about ten minutes, the whispering sounded like the whispering of consensus, and we all looked at each other happily. There was some rustling around in the tent, and we backed up to where we were before, as Dragline and Spooky emerged. Dragline was smiling as he emerged, but immediately looked down at the disturbed sand around the tent and frowned. "What the— " he said, then checked himself. "We've got a plan—a good plan. And I promise you, we will see action."

The captain then emerged from the tent, also looking down at the disturbed sand not 18 inches from the opening of his tent, and lifted his head with a look of anger, saying, "You will get your fill of the Taliban—so don't say anything you're going to regret. We're going to war, don't be confused about that." Gigantic smiles came across all our faces. We all knew that if the captain said something would happen, it would happen.

"But," said Spooky, "we will be here a few days longer . . . so I'll need to go into town. And, I guess, I'll need someone to go in with me as force protection. Any volunteers?" We all raised our hands at once.

"What about you, Jet Set?" he said. "I'm gonna need a good intel officer with me where I'm going. You think you have the sack for that?"

"Roger that," I said. Until I recently mentioned that I wanted to become an officer, Spooky had never shown the least notice of me, but now it seemed I was his buddy.

Jiggy looked over at me, his eyebrows raised. "Your stock is rising, Jet Set."

"Oh yeah," I replied under my breath, "I get to go into an Arab souq with a mad genius named 'Spooky'. Things are definitely starting to go my way."

The team took off for the chow hall, as Spooky and I headed back to our tent. "Okay," said Spooky, "we need to get strapped. Go get your KA-BAR and meet me at my cot."

"What?" I said, thinking Spooky was joking. Is this some sort of psychological game he's playing with me? I thought. "You heard the briefing we got when we came here," I said. "If we go into town, we are absolutely forbidden to have weapons on our person."

Spooky laughed. "Are you kidding?" he said. "Two white guys, two obvious American soldiers, ambling down the souq, and you think it's okay to be without a weapon?" Spooky looked at me like I was from another planet. "You want to be the Green Beret who got kidnapped and butt raped because he trusted his Arab allies and went into town with nothing to defend himself?"

"No," I said feebly, "but the regulations—"

"Screw the regulations," he said. "You're in the Arab world now, the world where everything is cool, until it's not. You're among the believers. Get that through your head—you're among the believers, and you're not one of them." Spooky shook his head. "To them you're just a kafir. We don't have our guns, but we still have some serious-ass killing tools, and there is no way we're going into town without having them at the ready."

"You're being dramatic," I said.

"I'm being prudent," Spooky replied.

"What if we get busted at the gate with our weapons?" I said. "They'd UCMJ us to death—so much for Afghanistan and getting in the show then."

"Oh, bullshit," Spooky said. "They'll freak out for a day or two; then, when our flight comes in, they'll put us on board, because—fuck it—who wants to deal with a couple of sergeants who 'forgot' they had knives on them when they went into town."

We entered the tent, and Spooky walked over to his footlocker and took out a roll of hundred-mile-an-hour tape and his KA-BAR. I went to my footlocker and got out my KA-BAR as well. Spooky took off his shirt. "Here," he said, handing the roll of tape to me, "give me two pieces about fifteen inches long." I pulled off the tape, and tore the first piece and stuck it to my belt, then tore off the second piece and did the same. "Tear off two for yourself, as well," he said. The KA-BAR knife is the fighting knife made famous by the Marine Corps. It has a sturdy seven-inch blade made of high-grade steel and a pummel wrapped in leather washers. It is essentially the military version of a Bowie knife, and just holding it in your hands will give you an erection.

"Give me a piece of tape," Spooky said without looking at me. I took the piece from my belt and handed it to him. Spooky laid the tape upside down on his cot. He then placed his KA-BAR on an angle onto the sticky side of the tape. Picking up the tape on both ends, with his fingers keeping the knife in place, he slammed it against his abdomen, and rubbed the tape flat (one sensed he had done this before). He then took the other piece of tape and X-ed it across the knife, the tape extending into his pelvic region over his public hair. Spooky looked at me and laughed, "Yeah, it's gonna hurt when you take it off—but that will brace you, remind you you're in a fight."

I did exactly as Spooky did, and secured my knife to my abdomen, still wondering if this was a good idea. Once the weapon was secure, I got the vehicle.

162

The vehicle was a late model Toyota SUV. We drove up to the gate, and went to the MP's office. There was a young MP at the desk, furiously filling out release documents authorizing various people to leave post. Spooky and I stood in a kind of waiting room, which was being guarded by a lone Qatari soldier with a bored look and an automatic weapon.

"So," said Spooky smiling, "let's check out the future intel officer's situational awareness. Give me a SALUTE report on this room." A SALUTE report is the format in which a soldier describes intelligence he has collected. The acronym stands for Size, Activity, Location, Unit, Time and Equipment.

"Thursday, May 9, 2002," I said, "four maybe five men of the Qatari Army pulling over-watch and perimeter security at the western checkpoint of Doha Airfield."

"Go on," said Spooky, with interest.

"They are equipped with automatic rifles," I continued. "They do not have load-bearing equipment and have only one spare magazine apiece. They do not have helmets or body armor."

"Good," said Spooky with obvious pride. "But any Joe can rattle off a SALUTE report. Go deeper, make inferences. Don't just tell me information, give me intelligence." Spooky tossed his head toward the soldier standing across the room. "What else, of intel value, do you see or could be reasonably assumed?"

I looked over at the soldier. He was in his late teens, and right away I knew what Spooky was talking about. "He's not Qatari," I said. "He's not Arab at all." Spooky smiled. "He looks more like a Pakistani or an Indian," I said.

"Nice pick-up," said Spooky. "What might that tell you about Qatar?"

"It tells me they can't fill their Army with their own people," I said, "and so they have to hire out."

"Yes," Spooky continued. "These rich Arab countries are like that. No one wants to be a soldier, so they hire Pakistanis. Now, tell me about that bad-ass weapon he's pimpin'."

The soldier had a new and very well made assault rifle; it was all black with a hard plastic pistol grip and hand guards. It was made of machined, not stamped, steel, which is a key indicator of a well-engineered weapon.

"Modeled on an AK," I said. "Likely fires a NATO round 7.62. It's too well made to be Russian or Chinese."

"Good pick-up. But twenty bucks says you can't name where it was made."

"Oh, I don't know," I said. Spooky had stumped me. "I'm not that smart with weapons."

"That's a Galil," said Spooky, obviously proud of himself.

"There's no way that's a Galil," I replied. "No self-respecting Arab government would buy Israeli weapons."

"You'd think that, wouldn't you," replied Spooky. "And that's the irony of the Arabs. They hate Jews. I mean, they hate them. It's like a thing they take in with their mother's milk. And yet," Spooky smirked, "they need good weapons."

"But why buy weapons from Israel?"

"Because there's one thing Arabs hate more than Jews."

"What's that?"

"Each other."

The road from the airfield into Doha was straight and clear. We watched the flat baked desert stretching out on either side into the blue horizon as we rode in our air conditioned SUV. Spooky turned on the radio, and the voice of a young, vivacious Indian female poured into the cab. "Noo, Noo, Noo," she said excitedly, "I vill noht play that song again. Anjna, you are my sister and I love you, but I love that song too. And you are trying to get me sick of it." The young woman laughed with an infectious, generous laugh, and Spooky and I looked at each other with quizzical smiles. It was as if we'd just walked into a pillow fight at a sorority house.

"I am on the phone vith my sister, Anjna," the DJ continued, "and she vahnts me to play Underneath it all by No Doubt again—and I vill noht do it. I love that song, but, Anjna, you vill only make me veary of it." We heard the sound of a phone being hung-up, then items being picked up and moved around. Then the sound of a phone ringing. The DJ picked up the phone and we heard one side of the two sisters' playful argument. "Of course I knew it vas you, Anjna, you are my mohst loyal fan. . . . but, no, I vill not . . . I just played it, and 73 minutes before I played it then as vell. . . . No, don't put mother on the phone, I do not vant to speak to . . . Yes, mother. . . Yes, mother. . . Yes mother." The conversation stopped. There was some sound of movement, and then the opening riff of No Doubt's new single came on the air.

Spooky turned the radio dial to the BBC World Wide, which, in a most serious, somnolent tone, told us about the recent UN conference on Something-No-One-Cares-About. And at this conference, the

164

honorable UN Deputy Undersecretary of That-Same-Something-No-One-Cares-About was a "participant in a round table discussion." We listened to the BBC for about one minute, and it was clearly the most un-news-worthy news I had ever heard. Spooky then turned the dial again. An Islamic cleric was giving a sermon in Arabic, and although I had no idea what he was saying, I understood that he meant business. Spooky hit the buttons again, and this time an Arabian soap opera came on—dramatic and tense. Spooky sat back, closed his eyes and listened. I fell silent for about five minutes, but finally I felt I had to say something. "What are you doing?" I said. "Your Arabic is minimal at best. There's no way you understand what's going on."

"You don't need to speak the language," Spooky replied. "Soap operas are the same no matter where you go. I find them calming."

"You find soap operas in unintelligible languages calming?" I asked, shaking my head. "You know that you're out of your mind."

"No," Spooky replied, "Soap operas tell you more about people than anything else in the world—certainly more than the BBC World Wide." Spooky turned to me, his expression animated. "Look at the world," he said. "All you hear about is war, famine, political strife and . . . whatever. But you go to any of these countries, with all their wars, famines and pestilence, and if you turn on the radio, the first thing you hear is a soap opera." Spooky nodded toward the radio. "Soap operas tell you what people are really concerned with—family, love, status and work. People the whole world over are mostly concerned with nothing more than the little world in which they live." Spooky's eyes were alight, and I could see there was much more to him than the racist, psychotic, de-commissioned officer I suspected him to be. "Have you ever noticed," he said, "that soap operas rarely reference the larger world? They are not at all like Hollywood blockbuster films, where giant forces hold the fate of the world in balance. Soap operas are about little things—the conflicts between a man and his wife, the dilemmas of a troubled child, the rivalries that emerge when a powerful patriarch falls ill. In a soap opera, the entire world is never about to end, just the entire world of the people in the story."

Spooky looked mournful, and he stared out the window. "When I pick somebody up to deport them, I'm ending their world. The wife or whatever will be screaming, the kids will be going batshit crazy. I'm taking away their mother or father." Spooky looked down at his hands. "It's not the end of the world, it's just the end of their world."

"And yet you do it," I said, trying to smirk, but failing.

Spooky shrugged. "Order has to be maintained. Somebody has to wield the sickle—besides, they knew the gamble going in."

We pulled into the mall—one of the biggest and most celebrated malls in the Middle East—and I parked in the ground-level parking deck. There was a mosque on the parking deck, which I only noticed because of the hundreds of men's shoes lined up outside the entrance. The entrance doors were open, and behind them I could see the multitude of men kneeling prostrate in prayer. It was a classic image, one found in every high school social studies textbook, but to actually see the men, not 100 feet away, fervent in their prayers, was to understand that you are, in fact, in the minority.

"Look at all those shoes," I said.

"Tell me about them, Intel Officer," Spooky replied. "Look closer, and tell me what you see."

I looked at the shoes lined up in front of the mosque. Here we were in Doha, Qatar, a fabulously wealthy city in a fabulously wealthy country, and the shoes in front of the mosque were incredibly shoddy. There were cheap, flip-flop sandals, and some knock-off tennis shoes, but by far the most popular shoe was the loafer—row upon row of loafers, but none of them were made of leather. "They're all plastic," I said in disbelief. All the loafers were made of plastic.

"Right," replied Spooky, "and tell me about their socks."

I looked in at the praying men. "They're not wearing socks," I said. I was actually in disbelief. "I guess they just go about all day in their plastic loafers without any socks," I said.

Spooky laughed softly to himself. "They go into battle like that, too." We opened the glass doors to the mall, and again he laughed reflectively. "Back in '91, half the Iraqi soldiers wore plastic loafers and no socks." Spooky looked at me, assessing my ability to understand. "You probably know that my team was overrun."

"Yeah, I heard something about that," I said, feeling a little awkward.

Spooky gave me a sideways glance and continued, "When your whole team is sitting in a hide and some ten year old boy sticks his head right into your view box, what are you gonna do?" Spooky was remembering now the cause of his great career collapse, and his hands flew up, trying to articulate his story. "I mean, you could kill the kid—problem solved—but that's a war crime, and it's also a ten year old kid you have to carry with you to your grave." Spooky wasn't talking to me anymore, but to some board of officers from a decade before. "It's totally okay to—you know—fire-bomb Dresden. And dropping nuclear bombs on millions of Japanese civilians is tanto simpatico, but putting a single bullet through a ten-year-old's head is a war crime." Spooky began to walk faster, and he was wringing his hands. "I mean—shit man," he exclaimed, "we could have just tied him up and tossed him into the hide with us, I guess. But that would only have brought the village out looking for him, right? So, okay, maybe I chose a hide-site too close to the village—didn't look too close to the village when higher command agreed to the location." I nodded my head in agreement.

"So, anyway," he continued, stepping on the escalator with noticeable agitation, "as soon as we made the decision not to kill the kid, we called in an extract and explained what had happened." Spooky's hands went up toward his face, with a mock display of outrage. "Well, that got every swingin' dick back at the TOC on the radio, telling me what I should have done. 'Thank you, General Armchair, that's a brilliant fuckin' idea. Sure wished I had your big, fat ass sitting here with me in this hide, instead of back in the air conditioned TOC, drinking Evian water, and eatin' ice cream at the chow hall.'"

Spooky slammed his fist down upon the rubber hand rail of the escalator. "Within an hour an Iraqi battalion was swarming all around us like a hive of pissed-off hornets. We strapped incendiary grenades to what we couldn't take out, and hauled-ass to the pick-up point." Spooky's head was sweating, even though the mall was frigid. "Man," he said, "the bullets were snappin' all around us. I really didn't think we were going to make it out. And I remember this one Iraqi soldier—not 50 meters away from me—running across my sector of fire, trying to get to a better position. One of his shoes came off halfway across. I opened up on his ass with a three round burst, but I missed him."

"Then what happened?" I said, enthralled by the story, and, frankly, honored that I was the one he was finally telling it to.

"Then he and I got into this mini-duel, popping off rounds at each other." Spooky stared off into the middle distance, bobbing his head up and down. "He'd pop his head up every couple seconds, always in a different spot—he was a seasoned soldier—and fired off a couple poorly placed rounds at me. Then I'd come up and fire a few, you know, well-placed rounds at him."

"But you didn't hit him," I said, just to annoy Spooky.

"No," he replied, with irritation. "Like I said, he was a seasoned soldier. Anyway, we were trading shots, and things were not looking good for yours truly. I mean, it was a battalion to, what, eight guys. But just when things looked their bleakest, I heard those extraction choppers coming in—along with a gunship." Spooky smiled, thinking about the moment. "And when that gunship opened-up on the Iraqis, it was all over."

We were on the first floor of the mall now, walking towards the Carrefour, and Spooky stopped in his tracks. "So now the tide has turned," he said, "and it's beginning to dawn on me that I just might make it out of this suck-fest after all. But extractions take a lot of time, and I'm still in this little gunfight with this Iraqi guy, who is well-concealed from the gunship—like I said, a seasoned solder." Spooky glanced over at me, to let me know he'd won that argument. "The guy is only popping up every once in a while now, because he also sees that I'm going to get out of this alive, and it's more likely that he will be the one who gets greased. So, anyway, the two of us are now starting to think more long-term, we're both thinking about what happens after our extraction—and I notice that when he pops up to shoot, he always looks over at his shoe sitting out in the open 20 meters away."

"You didn't," I said.

"Oh, hell yes I did," replied Spooky. "I turned on that shoe and shot the shit out of it." I started to laugh; it was a thing too simple, too cruel not to admire. "I just poured lead into that plastic loafer. And as I did, I looked over at the rock the guy was hiding behind, and I could see his raised fist shaking in anger at me."

I looked around the mall, and I was mesmerized by its elegance. Dark woods and brass ensconced the five-story structure. The floors were covered in a checkerboard of white and black marble tiles. The elevators were detailed in splendor. There was an ice rink in the middle of the mall, and an enormous skylight over top of it. To keep the direct sunlight out of the mall from the skylight, the architect had erected an enormous sheet of canvass—representing the sails of the cargo ships that had brought wealth, power and prosperity to this city—and the canvas sails revolved around the massive skylight in synchronicity with the sun.

Spooky and I walked the width and breadth of this incredible shopping mall. Most of the stuff we needed we bought at the Carrefour, which is like a French Walmart. But we wanted to see every part of it.

At last I said, "Can you believe this place? There are five Starbucks in this mall—one on every floor."

"Yes," Spooky replied with a professor's weary disappointment. "Five Starbucks, but did you count the number of bookstores?"

"No," I said, upset that, once again, Spooky was one step ahead of me.

Spooky looked hard at me. "There is not one in here. Not one bookstore in this entire mall. Five Starbucks, but not a single bookstore. We are among the believers, now. There is only need for the one book."

I looked at him with disapproval. "You are not being fair in your assessment," I said.

"I have not made an assessment," he replied. "I have only stated observable fact. I would say it was you who are making assessments—both of me, and of the world which you are now in."

"That was a politicized observation of fact," I relied.

"Was it incorrect?"

"It was incomplete." Just then a large group of Arab men came walking in our direction, their light, flowing white robes billowing in the air-conditioned atmosphere. They stared at us with eyes of pure hatred. Some of the men wore the ceremonial daggers famously worn by Qataris. I ran my hand against the grip of my knife taped against my abdomen. We walked by the men, staring hard at them, even as they stared hard at us. The men with daggers touched their hilts even as I drummed my fingers against the steel of my KA-BAR. I felt like a character in West Side Story.

We left the mall laden down with our purchases, and drove into the heart of town, to the Souq Waqik—the ancient market that had made this port into a world-class city. Driving into the roped-off area of rutted, packed sand which served as the parking lot, one quickly sensed that the souq was not the mall. Getting out of the car, we locked the doors, then double-checked that they were locked. "Now, this," Spooky said with triumphant flair, "is where you buy stuff."

"What kind of stuff?" I asked.

"This," he replied, "is the souq. You can buy anything in the souq." The sun was starting to release its grip on the town, and the open-air restaurants were beginning to fill up with customers. Stringed lights came on around the tables and chairs lining the street, and the shopkeepers became fussy about their wares.

"What are you thinking of buying?" I asked.

"I'm definitely getting a rug," replied Spooky, "and I'd like to look at the gold—you can't go wrong buying gold in the souq."

We turned down a narrow street, lined on both sides with the shops of the souq. We walked into a rug store, and the owner immediately stood up from behind the register, and eyed us with an affectionate gaze. He looked us up and down, and knew right away we were American. "Is good," he said, in accented English, stroking the nearest rug. Spooky replied to him in Arabic. Surprised by his Arabic, the shopkeeper replied in the same tongue. Then Spooky said something else in Arabic, and the shopkeeper replied in English. "Yes," he said, "is better talk in English." The two haggled and looked at various rugs, and I wandered around the small shop. Rugs were everywhere, rolled up silk, laid out wool and cashmere rugs, some in brilliant and gaudy colors, others of more muted and subdued hues.

Spooky finally committed to a rug; we had the man's assistant put it in the car, then made our goodbyes, and walked down the street looking into the windows of the shops. They were all very similarly constructed, with a large plate glass window in the center and a small door on the left hand side as you looked at it. Similarly, the shops selling the same type of things were located together. The rug shops were all together, the brass and decorative woodwork shops were together, and the gold jewelry shops were all on the far end of the souq.

As we walked toward the gold shops, we saw a shopkeeper leaning against his door, smiling broadly toward us. He had a warm, friendly smile and bright, intelligent eyes. The man was not Arab in appearance, but looked to be from India or Pakistan. As we approached, he waved to us eagerly. "And what is your good name, sir?" he said to me, in a deep Hindi accent. I couldn't help but smile, listening to his enthusiastic, lyrical voice.

"He's definitely Desi," Spooky said, smiling as well. "They're good business men, know how to make a win-win transaction."

"Call me Jet Set," I said.

"It is very good to meet you, Jet Set-Ji," he replied using the honorific. "My name is Sind."

"Good to meet you Sind-ji," I said.

"You," he said, "must buy something nice for your mother."

"My mother?" I said with surprise. "Why should I buy something for my mother?"

"You are a soldier, are you not?" he replied, surprising me with his frankness. "And you are on your vay to the battle."

170

"Wait, what?"

"And you have neither wife nor girlfriend, and your mother is vecked with vorry."

"How do you know all that?" I said with astonishment.

"It is plain," he replied. "It is on your face like a stamp." Sind-ji laughed. Spooky laughed with him.

I pointed over at Spooky and said, "What about his face? What does his face tell you?" Sind-ji looked at Spooky and instantly lost his smile. "His face is behind a curtain, and I do not vish to pull back that curtain."

"Good call," said Spooky coldly.

Turning back to me, the broad smile once again returning, Sind-ji said, "Vhite gold, is that not vhat is fashionable in America?" I nodded my head, pretending I had any idea of vhat vas fashionable in jewelry back home. "Let me show you some of my sets," Sind-ji continued, as he led us into his shop. The shop was set up in the usual manner, with a glass display counter at the far end of the space, glass display cabinets on the adjoining walls, and the most beautiful objects in the front window. Sind-ji looked at me—looked me directly in the eyes—and I grew uncomfortable with the strength of his gaze. I felt as if he were looking directly into my life, with all its confusion, sin and false bravado. But Sind-ji just continued to smile and said, "Yes, I have just the thing." He walked over to one of the cabinets, opened it up, and pulled out a green case with a collection of jewelry in it. "Everything is in sets," Sind-ji said, "so we sell you the necklace, earrings, bracelet and ring all as one." Sind-ji closed the cover of the case as he spoke. And then he stood as if at attention, in front of me, opened the case and presented it. "The benefit of the set is that you have a unified look. The bracelet matches the ring, matches the earrings, matches the necklace— it is perfect." I looked at the opened case, and was stunned at the simple beauty of it. Sitting in hunter green velvet, the necklace fairly jumped out at me. It was thick and brilliant, but simple—a series of sparse squares encircling the neck, tapering off in size as the necklace walked its way up toward the shoulders. Spare, but elegant, it was a concise statement of beauty that did not need to be elaborated on. The earrings, bracelet and ring were created in a similar manner, and they served to accentuate the centerpiece, the necklace.

"How much is it?" I said, with ill-disguised interest.

"Vell," replied Sind, "let us see." Sind-ji put the case down and walked over to the counter and picked up a set of scales. He then took the items out of the case and put them on the scales.

"Why do you weigh the gold?" I asked.

Sind-ji laughed. "Vhy, to see how much it veighs!"

"You sell your jewelry by weight?" I asked.

"Of course," said Sind-ji, "you're buying gold."

I was curious about this. "But what about the artistry?" I said. "What about the fact that some things must take days to complete and others can be completed in a morning?"

"The artistry," replied Sind-ji, his gaze, once again, burning into me, "is to allure you. The artistry brings you into the shop, but it is the gold you are buying."

Sind-ji and I haggled for a time, both of us enjoying the back and forth. But eventually we struck a deal and I bought the set he recommended. After the transaction was complete, Sind-ji handed me his email address, and told me that he wanted to know how "our mother" liked the jewelry set. He was quite adamant about this, and continually referred to this person he had never met as, "our mother." At the door, as he shook my hand, Sind-ji looked one last time into my eyes, and I got that same feeling that he was seeing deeply into my soul. "You have a mission, that the others do not," he said. "You have to report."

"Report to whom?" I said, trying to laugh, but failing.

"You have to report," he said again, then guided me out the door, closing it directly behind me.

Once in the car, Spooky said, "We need to get something to eat."

"We can eat back at the chow hall," I said.

"No," he said, "we need to eat in town." He was oddly insistent.

"Why?" I said. "It's free on post."

Spooky didn't look at me, all he did was repeat himself. "We need to eat in town."

We pulled into a strip mall off the main road out, and went into an Indian restaurant (Indian restaurants were everywhere). I ordered the Chicken Makhani—like I always do—and Spooky ordered a curry. When the food arrived, Spooky was suddenly not hungry. He picked at his food for a few minutes. Then he said, "I dunno, I guess I'm pretty full. Besides, we really should get back on post."

"Wait, what?" I said. "You were the one who was so adamant about getting something to eat before we got on post."

"Yeah, I know," said Spooky, shrugging his shoulders, "but now I'm not hungry or something." I should have smelled a rat. "Let's wrap this stuff up and go," he said.

Driving back onto post, I saw a significant back-up at the gate. There was an American private pulling guard about 50 meters in front of the gate. I rolled down my window, gave the private my best angry stare and said, "Private, what's going on up there?"

"Searching all vehicles and personnel entering the camp, sergeant," he said, "100 percent shake-down."

"Hoo-ah," I said, feigning enthusiastic support. I then rolled up my window, turned to Spooky in a panic and said, "What the hell! They're going to smoke our asses!"

Spooky just shrugged and said, "Yeah, I was afraid this would happen."

"We got KA-BARS strapped to our balls," I said, "and we're too close to hide them in the trunk. If we get busted, we can kiss Afghanistan good-bye."

Spooky, who had only hours before downplayed the seriousness of our punishment, now changed his tune. "Yeah," he said, "if we get busted, they'll step on our dicks with track shoes."

"Damn it!" I said. "This entire thing was your idea. You had better pull something out of your ass right now or, I swear, I will stab you to death!"

"Don't worry," said Spooky, "I got a plan."

"You got 'a plan'?" I remarked. "What's your genius plan?"

Spooky reached around to the back seat and picked up his to-go box. He opened it and drank down the curry he was so adamant to keep. Then he began chewing the meat violently. "Watch this," he said between chews, and began slowly spitting the curry out of his mouth. "I got food poisoning," Spooky said with a smile, "I'm all fucked up." He then grabbed a bottle of water he had between his feet, and said, "I'm pissin' on myself." He poured the water into his lap. And now it's your turn, intel officer, to sell them on this."

I became extremely angry. I couldn't believe Spooky had gotten me into this. "Alright," I said, skeptically. "Choke yourself."

"What?"

"You heard me, choke yourself. You don't look sick, you look like you just spilled your take-out. Make your face beet red or I ain't going through that gate."

"Oh, you're going through that gate, Jet Set."

"The hell I am. I ain't going through that gate unless you look like you're sicker than death." Spooky looked at me, seeking a sign of fraud, but he could see I meant business—nobody was keeping me from the war.

Spooky slowly raised his hands to his neck, then encircled his fingers and closed them. I would not release my gaze from him, but just kept repeating, "Harder . . . harder."

His face went red . . . then purple. His gags, which were at first perfunctory, grew rapidly more—how do you say—sincere.

I pulled up to the checkpoint, got out of the vehicle flashing my ID card around and barking out orders to the buck sergeant in charge. "I've got a code red," I exclaimed. "Call in to the MED Clinic and tell them there's a master sergeant en route who is code red with food poisoning!"

"Roger that, sergeant!" the young NCO replied. "But I'm gonna at least need to see his—" Spooky—doubled over and moaning with great dramatic flair—somehow managed to shove his ID into the sergeant's face. "Yeah," said the sergeant, "his ID."

"It's kinda disgusting," I stage-whispered to the sergeant, taking him into my confidence. "Guy's pissing and shittin' on himself. Nice guy, but. . . disgusting!"

"I can imagine," said the sergeant, lifting the gate. "I'll call the MED and tell them it's a code red."

The sergeant waved us through, and about 100 meters past, I looked over at Spooky and he looked back at me, and, as if on cue, we started laughing—at first heartily and then hysterically. The more we laughed the funnier it became. "Code Red," Spooky repeated, sternly. "Code Red," he said again. "What the hell is a 'Code Red'?"

"I have no idea," I said, "but they say it a lot on TV."

KANDAHAR

"I don't know what kind of drug deal the captain pulled to get us here, but it worked," I said to Jiggy, as we grabbed our duffel bags and rucksacks, and walked down the tailgate of the aircraft onto Kandahar Air Field.

Spooky, overhearing me, looked at us from over his shoulder. "The captain played his cards very well," he said. "I am impressed with the man."

"Make ya feel bad about what you said back in Qatar?" Jiggy asked.

Spooky's shoulders seized up for a second, and he turned his head forward again, showing us his back. Jiggy and I silently laughed. It was fun getting under Spooky's skin.

We had arrived in Kandahar on the same C-141 that we had left Germany in, which, for some reason, waited three days in Qatar before taking off again. When they lowered the rear gate, that same blast of oven-baked heat and blinding white light hit us again. It was 112 degrees outside in the noonday sun. We helped move the technicals off the aircraft, collected up our personal equipment and made arrangements to have the weapons and team equipment delivered to the company area, which—we were informed—required a special pass, as it was on the Special Operations Compound.

As we were walking down the ramp from the back of the aircraft, we saw a lone soldier standing in front of us, in full battle dress uniform, but with a chauffeur's cap on his head. "Biker Dave," we all shouted to him, glad to see a familiar face. In his hand he carried a placard reading, '20XX, your ride is waiting.' It was good to see a member of our company waiting for us as we arrived. Biker Dave was on the scuba team, and while no one wanted to admit it, the scuba team was the best team in the company.

"When'd you get here?" Dragline shouted.

"About a week ago," Dave said, grinning and looking already at home in-country. Dave's skin was tanned and tight against his cheekbones. His uniform hung loosely around him. In one week he must have lost ten pounds. But his smile was enormous, and it made us all smile.

"We made it to the show!" Crunk said.

"All I'm gonna tell my wife and kids," said Boy Band, "is that I didn't have to fire off an entire magazine disembarking from the aircraft."

I wanted to kiss the ground. We made it, I thought, at least we made it to the war.

Jiggy didn't say anything, but he smiled all the same.

"So," continued Boy Band after a long silence, "you got us a ride, huh?"

"No, dumb ass," Dave replied. "There's no ride. This is Kandahar, not the fuckin' shoppette." Biker Dave jerked his head to his left. "See all them mooks over there layin' out?" We looked over and saw more than 500 soldiers lying around, mostly under ponchos staked up to block the sun. "Those guys have been there for the last four days waiting for transport to take 'em home." Biker Dave folded his placard in half and tore it up. "This ain't Dulles Airport," he said. "When a plane comes in everybody looks at it, guesses how many people can go out on it, then falls back to sleep, hoping that in a couple hours' time they might move up about ten feet in the pile."

Walking over to the temporary trailer used for processing soldiers either in or out, we had to wade through the crowd of soldiers waiting around in the hot sun to exfil. It was funny observing the soldiers, most of them no more than 19 or 20 years old. They were almost all from the 101st Airborne Division, and had done the tough slogging up and down the Tora Bora Mountains. They were greyhound lean, and had that casual cockiness that awakens a sergeant's memories. I was once like that, I thought. I was once a cocky young soldier.

Within 24 hours of arrival I pulled the Humvee up to the gate of Kandahar Airfield. It was 4:00 a.m, and I was the lead vehicle during the eight-day patrol. Riding shotgun was Spooky. He would be the navigator. Spooky had his windshield removed and a mounted 240 Bravo poked through the cab and over the hood of the vehicle. The weapon was on an unusual and complicated swing-arm attached to the door brace, so, theoretically, he could fire to the front, and, bringing it around the door brace, to the side of the vehicle. The sergeant major swore by it, but it seemed a little iffy to me. Sitting in the turret above us with a .50 cal was Crunk. In the vehicle behind us was Jiggy, driving another light-skinned Humvee, with Boy Band sitting in a roof mounted turret with the Mark-19. Next in the parade came Dragline, driving a

Technical, with "Pot Roast" mounting the 240-Bravo in the truck bed. Pot Roast and "Little Spider" had been borrowed for the mission from the scuba team—they were attached to us because we were undermanned for the mission. Guarding our rear was the captain, driving another soft-skin Humvee, with Little Spider riding shotgun, with that same swivel-mounted 240 Bravo that Spooky had.

When we rumbled up to the gate going out of the airfield, the guard came up to me, some wide-eyed PFC with the name "Branson" on his uniform.

"PFC Branson," I said, "good morning." PFC Branson looked to be about 19 years old. His skin was soft and his cheeks were ruddy. He looked like he'd probably played sports in high school, but not particularly well.

"Where you off to, sarge?" he asked.

"Out there," I replied laconically.

The PFC gulped. "Geezus," he said, "there ain't nothin' but Gooks out there." Why he used that particular slur I do not know.

On our sixth day out, we took the A-75 road south about ten miles, passing burned out old wrecks of fuel trucks, Russian tanks and other derelict vehicles. The land was bleached out and desolate all around us, with various small splotches of green, usually surrounding the mud walls of a small village. We pulled off the road into a wadi after about ten miles. There were almost no roads in Afghanistan; A-75 was just about it, and it was so battered that people usually drove alongside it. The wadis—dried riverbeds—served as the roads through most of the country.

By then it was becoming light, and other traffic was beginning to arrive on the road. There were only two types of vehicle outside of Kandahar City: Toyota sedans, and Mercedes "Jingle Trucks." Jingle trucks were flat-faced trucks brightly painted with intricate tribal patterns in brilliant colors. Chains and pendants dangled off the front bumpers and off the sides, making noisy, clattering sounds as the trucks banged their way across the wadis. All the cars were filled to capacity, and most of the Jingle trucks had riders hanging off the sides. Some of the cars carried women, covered in their powder blue burqas, but mostly the road was filled with young men. Some smiled at us, others shook their fists, but all of them drove with wild abandon, swerving in and out as they passed one another, sometimes losing control of the wheel and sliding sideways in the unpaved and rock-strewn wadis.

I was the driver of the first vehicle, but by no means deciding where we were going. That was Spooky's job. He kept his map on his lap, his compass in his hand, and, most importantly, his GPS between his knees—I think the compass and the map were just for show.

"We have to turn right up here, somewhere," Spooky said with shaky self-confidence. "Slow down," he demanded of me at least 15 times, as he stared again at his GPS. "This looks like the place," he advised me on three occasions. And the entire convoy would turn down a wadi that, naturally, would lead nowhere.

After the third time, I noticed a connecting wadi about 500 meters up that three or four cars were turning right into. "See that wadi up there about a half-a-klick?" I said. "The one where all those cars are turning into?"

"Yeah," said Spooky.

"We should probably turn there."

Spooky stared at me. "Well, of course, we're going to turn there," he said.

That wadi got us to Gumbadel by late afternoon. We rolled up on a hill-top overlooking the dusty, mud-walled village, about 500 meters away, but out of sight. Afghani villages are all pretty much the same. People don't live in 'houses,' they live in compounds—usually a main building with multiple outbuildings, all encircled by high, thick mud walls. The various compounds linked together formed a continuous outer wall to the village. The walls, however, were not there for protection from people outside the village. They were there for protection from each other.

Looking down at the village, we suited up for possible combat. The village was much like every other village we had been in, mud walls bleached by the sun, surrounded by a desultory collection of semi-green fields. One field, being by far the greenest, was always the marijuana field. The Afghanis grew poppies for profit, but they grew marijuana for personal use. They grew a surprising amount of marijuana.

I changed out the magazine in my M-4, and chambered a round from the fresh magazine. I then checked my sidearm, working the action, making sure it had a new round in the chamber. None of us wore helmets and only the lightest of body armor—just the vest. I tightened my boots and changed into my blue "Brooklyn" T-shirt—if I was going to die, I wanted to at least look cool.

Captain McMann and Dragline indicated for us to huddle around them. "Okay," said the captain, "you know the drill—we can dial it up and we can dial it down. When we roll into that village, we take absolute control of it. If they want to play nice, then we can chi it up with 'em and all that good stuff."

"But," continued Dragline, "if they want to throw down, we will dominate the egress and the ingress of the village. We will command the best fighting positions, and we will bend them bitches to our will."

Walking back to our vehicles, Jiggy whispered to me, "I think Dragline would make a better motivational speaker than the captain, don't you?" As we pulled out, I felt my heart pounding in my chest. The fact that we didn't really have much of a plan never occurred to me.

We drove quickly past the outer wall of the village, everybody with his weapon at the ready, and we didn't see a soul. We got further in, closer to the town center, and still not one person was on the street. About 200 meters into the heart of the village, I took a sharp right turn and found that I was barreling into the center square. I could see maybe 50 people in and around the central water cistern. When the people saw us they went completely bonkers. They went flying in every direction. There was a little girl, maybe seven years old, barefoot, but dressed in the tribal manner. She took off running in one direction, then deftly made a juke-step left, bent down in full flight, and scooped up her little brother—a toddler about four years old, sitting in the road. She never lost a step, and carried him around the corner of a wall out of sight.

I looked over at Spooky, who was watching her too. "That little girl should play halfback," he said.

We established a perimeter in the village square, and then we waited. After about ten minutes, heads started popping out of doors. After another ten minutes, out came the Chi boys to snoop around.

"Here come the Chi boys," Boy Band said over the radio. "Geezus, they scare me."

"Yeah," replied Spooky. "They send them out first, 'cause nobody gives a shit about 'em."

Chi boys are the open secret of Afghanistan. They are sex slaves, usually about twelve to thirteen years old. They are sold by their parents to men with some money and are trained in singing, dancing, making tea—"chi"—and generally just being effeminate and sexually appealing to the men. They giggle and smile coyly, and often wear women's clothing. They are used by the men for sex until they lose their looks. I don't know what happens to them after that. I doubt many of them live that long.

"God," I said to Spooky as we kept an eye on the Chi boys, "that is such a crime, it makes me sick."

"Yeah," Spooky replied dryly, "I hate thinking about it."

"And there are so many of them," I continued. "Every half-ass town has at least three or four Chi boys. It's a disgrace."

"Agreed," Spooky replied sarcastically. "Good thing the U.S. has nothing like it." I looked back at the two boys, giggling and slowly moving closer to the Humvee. "You know," continued Spooky, "three of them tried to run away from a village up north a month ago."

"What happened?" I asked.

"They killed 'em," Spooky said blankly. "A platoon from the 501st came upon their bodies about half-a-klick outside the ville. The platoon leader asked the elders about the dead bodies, and the elders openly admitted that they were slaves and they ran away. So they killed them."

"Get the hell away from me, you little freak," Boy Band shouted from his vehicle.

"Easy, Boy Band," Dragline said. "We have to make nice with the locals."

"His nails are painted," Boy Band exclaimed, "and he's giggling like a girl—I swear, I'll pepper spray you if you come any closer."

"Negative! Negative! Negative!" replied Dragline. "No es Bueno. We don't pepper spray Chi boys unless they display obvious menace." Dragline was clearly enjoying Boy Band's discomfort.

Once the Chi boys had established that we were not a threat, little girls and boys, all under the age of 10, were slowly pushed out of doors. They came out smiling and nervously laughing. Then adults began to peak their heads out. Eventually an older man came out of a doorway with a teapot in his hand. He smiled at us and shook his tea pot, indicating that things would be alright.

Our interpreter, Amu, got out of Dragline's vehicle. Medium in height and thin, Amu wore the traditional Khet partug—'man pajamas'—and the Parkol—the 'pizza pie' hat. He had been a student in Quetta, before the war. His English was pretty good, and he knew there was money to be made working for the Americans. Amu called out to the old man, knowing that the entire village was listening, and said that we were Americans, and were looking for a good village that needed a water pump.

"He did the water pump bit, didn't he?" I said to Spooky.

"Yeah, probably."

"Gets 'em every time," I said.

There really was a water pump, and we actually were looking for a village that needed one. It was a quid pro quo, but the quo was always bogus. It had happened three times before. We'd come into a village, have tea with the elders, ask about Taliban, and, of course, they'd say, 'none around here.' Then we'd bring up the water pump and—surprisingly enough—they'd remember where the Taliban was. We'd go to the 'Talibani' compound at dawn the next day, kick in the doors, and the guy would always turn out to be some guy who borrowed the informant's shovel and didn't give it back or the cousin of the informer who still owed him two goats and a chicken.

Still, the ruse always seemed to work, and out came a few more village elders, some carrying rugs and pillows, which were thrown down against a wall in the shade. And, all the sudden, it was a party. The street flooded with people. For such a small village, you would be amazed at the number of people it held.

"We need one from each vehicle to party with the locals," Dragline said over the radio.

"Go party," Spooky said to Crunk. "It's important the people see a black guy hanging out with the village elders." Spooky then turned to me, "Jet Set, get on the .50."

I jumped behind the heavy machine gun and pulled back the charging handle, sending the chambered round into the air, as a fresh round loudly chambered. Then, with the muzzle of the weapon aimed into the air, I traversed the weapon completely around the roof mount, showing the village I had a 360 degree range of fire.

"You just lost us a bullet," Crunk said, angry that I was taking command of 'his' gun.

"Dramatic effect," I replied. "Gots to let the locals know we can kill them."

Amu made the introductions and the Chi boys prepared the tea. There were typically two ways in which Afghanis drank their tea, depending on their ethnic group. The Tajiks took a sugar cube and placed it in their mouth. They then drank the tea and let it pour across the sugar cube, thereby sweetening it. The Pashtu, on the other hand, filled the tea glass—they only used glass—one half up with sugar, then filled the rest with tea. The first three glasses were intolerably sweet, the fourth glass was normal, and the last two were bitter.

"These people," I said, "they do the most screwed-up stuff."

"What do you mean?" replied Spooky. "They're just people. People are crazy." Spooky said this like it was a well-established fact that was known by all.

"Okay," I said, "I get that. I get that people are crazy, but some of this stuff just makes no sense."

"What makes no sense?" Spooky said, as we both lazily scanned the sunbaked village, sweating in the heat.

"Well, the tea drinking, what's up with that?" I said. "If you're Tajik, you put the sugar in your mouth, if you're Pashtu you heap it into the glass, then never refill it—it's stupid. It's like wearing your underwear on the outside of your pants."

"Makes sense to me," said Spooky. "The goal is to sweeten your tea. Clearly the goal is achieved. There's more than one way to skin a cat, you know."

"Okay," I said, "what about the way they smoke cigarettes? You got to admit that's just weird."

We were both watching as Dragline gave out a few Marlboros to the village elders. Dragline didn't smoke, but he knew enough to have cigarettes on him when dealing with locals. The men each took a cigarette and placed it between their index and ring fingers, holding on to only the filter. They then interlocked the fingers of their hands and formed a cup with their palms. With their thumbs parallel to each other, they then pressed their lips to their thumbs and inhaled, the smoke passing from the cigarette into the chamber of their cupped hands.

"What the hell?" I said.

"It's a portable hookah," Spooky replied. "Stop thinking about how screwed-up other people are, and—you know—think about how screwed-up you are."

It was more than 100 degrees in the shade, and we were not in the shade. We continued our little back-and-forth listlessly. "Okay," I said, with a lazy indifference, "but you have to admit, a culture that is okay with twelve-year-old boys being raped by grown men is a pretty screwed up culture."

"Whoa," replied Spooky. "They aren't 'okay' with it. They just turn a blind eye to it."

"How is that different?" I said.

"Back home," Spooky said with a wry grin, "we abort over one million babies a year, and no one raises an eyebrow. Life just goes on . . . well, not for the one million babies, but for everyone else." Spooky stared out into the middle distance. "Do you really think we're better than they are?"

After an hour, Crunk wandered away from the meeting with the elders and came over to our vehicle. "It's the same shit as it was yesterday in that other village," he said. "No one knows anything about any Taliban in the area until we mention the water pump, then—what the what—'oh, you mean the Taliban. Yeah, the village that pisses in the river upstream from us is nothin' but Taliban.'"

Crunk looked up at me. "Jet Set, you'll like this: when we told them we could clear away any land mines in the area, they told us there was a minefield the Russians left on the other side of the wadi. It's in the ravine they used to use as a shortcut to their pasture area, but now they can't use that shortcut anymore. Takes them over an hour to get to their best grazing land."

"A minefield?" I said enthusiastically. "We got the equipment, we could definitely do it."

"Yeah," replied Crunk, "that's what they're saying." He looked skeptical. "But when we asked them about it, they told us a child from the village had been killed over there."

"Wow," I said, "that's pretty serious."

"I dunno," said Crunk. "When we asked more questions, the child that was killed miraculously became ten goats that were stolen. And when we tried to clarify, the child and the ten goats somehow became an important government official. I think they just want us to beat up the people in the village upstream who pee in the river while they're bathing."

Just then, the captain and Dragline stood up. They made elaborate gestures to the village elders, and it became apparent the party had ended. They then turned to a much younger man—maybe in his 20s— and through Amu began speaking with him. The younger man spoke earnestly and happily. He looked like someone about to go on a big adventure.

"Mount up!" shouted Dragline, and both he and the captain came walking over to our vehicle. "Supposedly," said Dragline, "there's a minefield on the other side of the wadi." Dragline looked at me skeptically. "So we're going to take this local over there to show us where it is."

The man jumped into the back of Boy Band's vehicle. He was beaming with an enormous smile. We drove slowly through the village, this time with Boy Band leading the way, and my vehicle directly behind him. At the very edge of town, just as Boy Band was passing beyond the village, a compound door opened and an older woman stepped out into the little front stoop. She looked at Boy Band's vehicle and fainted dead away, falling directly backward, her hands clutching her chest like in some silent film.

"Did you see that shit?" Spooky asked.

"Yeah," I replied.

We rumbled on for another 50 meters, then, all of the sudden, Boy Band's vehicle came to a screeching stop. The Afghani man in the back of the vehicle leapt out and took off running back to the village.

Crunk spun the .50 cal on him, as Spooky got a bead on him with his M-4. I slammed on the brakes and put the vehicle into reverse. "I got him!" shouted Crunk over the radio.

"Negative! Negative! Negative!" shouted Boy Band.

"Give me a SITREP!" shouted Dragline.

"Situation normal," replied Boy Band. "All fucked up."

"What's going on, Boy Band?" said the captain.

"Sir," Boy Band replied, "you saw that old lady back in the village, right? The one that fell ass-over-tea-cups when we drove by?"

"Yeah, what about it?"

"That was our guy's mom," replied Boy Band, "and when she saw her son sitting in the back of my military vehicle being led away, she must have lost her shit."

A low rumble of laughter came across the radio, as everyone slowly began to realize what had happened.

"We thought that dude had slit your throat," said Crunk. "I was about to saw him in half."

"Aw," said Boy Band, "you'd do that for me? That's sweet."

"This is no shit," said Dragline, "we almost had a major incident on our hands."

"Listen up," said the captain, "we need to establish some SOPs. There are just too many scenarios that could go to hell in a bucket out here." The whole thing seemed comical to me, but the captain sounded weighted down by it. "We have to communicate a lot better," said the captain. "It's my responsibility first, but I'd like every one of you to assist me. We need to always be mapping things out, always be thinking about the plan, the alternate plan and the contingency plan."

"What the captain is sayin'," continued Dragline, "is that our days of cowboying out here are over."

"I got this, Dragline," the captain broke in sharply. "From now on we follow the field manual. It's all FM 7-8. I take responsibility for this goat screw, and I take responsibility for our future planning. From

184

now on, we do things by the book. Is that clear?"

"Yes, sir." "Yes, sir." "Yes, sir." Yes, sir."

"Uh, sir," Dragline said after a long radio silence. "That doesn't mean that this guy has to know that we almost zipped him up, does it?"

"No," said the captain, "his knowledge of these events would not assist in mission success."

Thirty minutes later, the Afghani man came running back, still with his broad, excited grin, still with infective enthusiasm. He leapt into the back of Boy Band's vehicle and we proceeded on to the 'minefield.'

The 'minefield' was a draw between two steep hills. The draw was rocky and sparsely-vegetated, and the Afghani man kept walking up and down inside the 'minefield' pointing out where the mines were. Usually he was stepping on them as he told us where they were.

I got out the mine sweeper and swept the area—finding about fifteen bullet casings and, for some reason, an old oil filter. By this time, some local men who lived outside the village had assembled. Once they learned that we were looking for 'mines' in the 'minefield' they became greatly interested, and elaborated on the terrible destruction this 'minefield' had caused. They were well-versed in its horrors, and we got to hear again about the child (or the goats) that had been killed, the stolen animals it had taken and even—I think—the many Jinn it had conjured up (the Jinn are ghosts or spirits that roam around causing trouble). Clearly this was one badass minefield.

"There's nothing here," I said to the captain.

"Yeah," said the captain with frustration, "but now, with all these people around, we have to do something."

"Can't you—I don't know—just blow some stuff up?" asked Dragline.

"Of course, team sergeant," I replied. "We can rig-up a series of charges and just blow up a bunch of earth, but—"

"Let's do that," said the captain. "Just blow up the ground a little bit, and we'll tell them we got rid of the minefield."

I brought out the detonation cord—'det cord'—the blasting caps, a crate of C-4 and 3,000 feet of Nonel, then laid out the whole circuit of charges and detonating device. The entire process took about three hours—and—like any good demo man—I refused to let anyone help me. Nonel is thin tubing with a minute amount of high explosives in it. You use it to initiate the explosion from a safe distance away.

The entire time I worked, the Afghanis stood around in one group, pointing vigorously at the explosives, and speaking to each other in very

185

heated terms. Meanwhile, the guys on the team—pulling security—shouted to one another their various complaints and criticisms of my methodology. The entire thing felt like trying to build a back deck on your house, while all your lazy neighbors sit around criticizing your work.

Eventually, I had my chain of demolition constructed, and laid my explosives out in an orderly fashion running up the draw. I moved everybody back, and plugged the Nonel into the clacker.

"Fire in the hole! Fire in the hole! Fire in the hole!" I shouted, then mashed the clacker down. It wasn't yet dark, but the shadows of the hills were long, and you could see the fire in the Nonel surge through the narrow tube en route to the C-4. The draw exploded in spectacular fashion, and both groups of men let out ecstatic cheers. The Afghanis all hugged each other, and bounced around arm-in-arm proclaiming this a wondrous day. The guys on the team smiled and gave me a thumbs-up. I pretended that it was all in a day's work, but silently I gave a sigh of relief. That's the thing about being a demolition man: it's a lot like being a field goal kicker—while you're preparing, everyone doubts you, and wonders if you can do it. All you can do is trust in your skill, in your equipment, and in your calculations. But, until you hear that rumble, and until you see the results of your work, your entire life is one gigantic question mark.

We drove back to the 'minefield', and all the local Afghanis wanted to rush into the blast zone and whoop and dance. Fortunately, our interpreter convinced them that it was not yet safe, that perhaps the Jinn had been awakened. Spooky, Jiggy and I went into the blast area, while the others formed a perimeter around it. There was really not much to see. Although the blast had looked impressive from a distance, it had done very little damage. That's the thing about explosives, they travel in the direction of least resistance, so 90% of the blast flew up into the air.

After we cleared the blast area, we let the locals in, and they pointed at all the small holes where the blocks of C-4 had been laid, and agreed that that was the mine that killed the little boy, or the ten goats or whatever. I gathered up the spent Nonel, and we began piling back into the Humvees. As I was getting into the driver's seat, the man who had volunteered to show us the minefield ran up and made a slight, frantic bow. "You," he said, "eat." He gestured with his hands as if eating, "my house, now." I looked at him quizzically, and he repeated himself, his gestures more imploring. "You eat my house now," he said.

I had no idea what he was saying, so I motioned for Amu to come over. The two exchanged a hurried dialog, and Amu said, "He very proud. You both blew up minefield. He want you for dinner tonight."

"Oh, no," I said, stepping back and shaking my head, "that is completely out of the question."

The man spoke again to Amu, this time with greater animation. Amu turned to me and said, "He saying you bring him great honor if dine with him in his house." I shook my head, and Amu continued, "Today was a great day for him in village. . . If you no dine . . . will be very bad day for him. And, I think, bad day for you too."

I slid into the Humvee and the captain came over to me. "How is the whole team going to eat in this guy's little hooch?" I said.

"The 'whole team' isn't," he replied, "just you—and, I guess, you can bring Jiggy with you to watch your back."

"What the hell, sir?" I said. "I didn't sign up for this."

"Yes, you did," replied Captain McMann. "You're a Green Beret—a triple volunteer—and this is exactly what you signed up for."

Captain McMann was right. I was a triple volunteer. I had volunteered for the Army, for the Paratroopers and for the Special Forces. "But he might poison me," I said. "It might be an ambush."

"Get over yourself, Jet Set," replied the captain. "You're not that big of a deal. This man is showing you respect. You have a duty to respond with equal respect. Don't you see, this is a victory?"

"What victory?" I said. "We blew up a fake minefield."

Captain McMann looked exasperated, but I could see he was controlling his frustration. "Do you see this?" he said, raising his hand to me, with the tip of his thumb and index finger a quarter inch apart.

I looked at him dumbly. "Yes, sir. I see it."

"This is where these people live their lives," he said. "Right here, within this tiny space—inside a village with no running water, no electricity and no work—and, oh yeah, a village in which everybody sort of hates everybody else. The only thing these people have is a piece of good pasture on the other side of those hills." Captain McMann dropped his hand out of awe for the people of the village. "And then a bunch of stuff happened to them—the Russians come, the Taliban come, and now the Americans come." Captain McMann raised his hand again and let me see the tiny space between his thumb and his index finger. "These people couldn't find Russia on a map, they don't know what the Taliban wants. All they know is that bad things happened to them and they can't take the short route to their best pasture anymore."

Captain McMann looked at me, as if trying to articulate some unformed understanding to me. "You saw the men today," he said, "dancing and singing and jumping around with joy. You gave that to them, Jet Set. You gave them back their pasture, so don't say you didn't do anything. You did your duty, and that made all the difference in the world to these people."

Captain McMann stepped away from me, his face a mixture of pride and disgust; he then did an about-face and walked off. He walked six paces, then turned around. "And one other thing," he said, "that man has a name. His name is Dagar. His mother's name is Fatima. He has a son and a daughter, both under seven years old. He also has a wife, but you won't see her."

"Yes, sir," I replied, as I dove into my rucksack, searching for the bar of soap and the disposable razor I hadn't used in the six days I'd been in-country.

It was now fully night and the little village was completely dark, as Jiggy and I inspected each other before approaching the small compound where Dagar lived. We had washed our hands and faces, but decided not to shave our beards. We both had 9 mils strapped to our legs in drop holsters. "Ready for this?" I asked Jiggy.

"What?" he said. "You're just going to go in empty handed, are you?"

I looked at him with confusion. "What?" I said. "You think we should have grenades?"

Jiggy rolled his eyes. "Geez, you single guys. We've been invited to a dinner party—we can't go to a dinner party and not bring something."

It took me a while to get my brain around what he was saying, but then I said, "Oh, I gotcha, I gotcha," and went over to the back of the Humvee, and pulled out a case of water. "How's that?" I asked.

"Jet Set," Jiggy said with a broad smile. "What am I going to do with you?"

We approached the house, stumbling slightly on small stones and ruts in the pathway. As we came upon the door, I was thinking about what I should say to greet Dagar and his family. I wanted to say something cheerful and funny, something a well-loved uncle would say, but I could not come up with anything. Just as I was about to knock, the door swung open and Dagar's bright eyes and brilliant smile lit up the darkness. "Asalam lamakem!" he said warmly.

Without thinking at all, I raised up the case of water to him as an offering and—for some reason—exclaimed, "Opa!" I didn't even know what the word meant, it was just a catchphrase I'd heard in a movie about a big, fat Greek girl who got married or something.

"Opa!" Dagar repeated with pleasure and confusion.

"Opa!" Jiggy said as well, not knowing why.

Dagar ushered us into the house, which was very dark and lit by a single kerosene lantern on a table in the middle of the room. Almost immediately, a small, squat older woman rushed at me, wrapped her arms around me like a wrestler, and squeezed me with delight. I recognized her as the woman we had seen earlier that day fainting as we drove past her. "Maakhaam mo pa kheyr," she said with an enormous, broad smile.

Dagar spoke to us in soft, intimate tones, and encouraged us to sit at the table with the kerosene lantern. Jiggy and I sat down clumsily, our weapons banging and clanging against the pillows and tabletop. Dagar clapped his hands twice, and a small girl, about seven years old, came in with a tea kettle. I recognized her immediately. "You are the girl in the village square who ran away from us today!" I said. She was a beautiful little girl, with enormous almond eyes, and long, black hair. She laughed delightedly, and her broad smile shone in the darkness. She wore the same orange smock and matching orange pants that I'd seen her wearing in the village square. I looked at Dagar. "This one is an athlete," I said. "She will always be your pride and joy!" Dagar beamed with confused pride. The girl, Mina, served us tea, and did so with such an undisturbed continence that I was struck with amazement. She stared at me with supreme self-confidence. Then she curtsied as she left the room.

Dagar laughed at his well-behaved daughter, and said something in Pashtu. "Prencess," he continued in English. "Girl . . . lettle prencess."

Dagar's mother came wheeling into the room carrying a loaf of Afghani bread draped over each arm.

"Doodai!" exclaimed Jiggy with delight.

"Doodai!" repeated Dagar, delighted to hear Jiggy use the Pashto. "Kha ishta walace!"

"Doodai!" repeated Dagar's mother, with delight.

Doodai is a flat bread, but not at all like na'an, or its Pakistani equivalent. Doodai's look is elliptical in shape, and is made from wrapping elongated rolls of dough one around the other—it sort of reminds you of that braided rug your grandparents had in their den when you were a kid. Coming fresh out of the oven, it is the most delicious thing in the world.

Dagar tore off great pieces of Doodai, and handed them to Jiggy and me. We both dipped them in the curry sauce Dagar's mother had laid out on the table, and shoved them hungrily into our mouths.

"Opa!" Jiggy shouted with every mouthful.

"Opa!" Dagar repeated delightedly.

"Opa!" the children squealed with delight.

"Opa!" Dagar's mother shouted with contentment.

"Opa!" I heard from a lilting voice in the next room.

Jiggy and I pretended we had not heard the voice of a proud young mother in the room one over, but it was a little too obvious.

Sensing the awkwardness, Dagar clapped his hands and said something in Pashto. Soon, his mother brought out deep soup bowls of curry, enormous dishes of rice, and other dishes heaped with goat meat. She piled mountains of food on Jiggy's and my plate—"Na, Na," I said.

But she replied, "Hoo, hoo!" Her hands were still shoveling food onto my plate.

It was about five pounds of food, but it was delicious. The yellow curry dish was shot through with flavor. I took a giant slurp from the curry and Mina laughed at me, saying something to her father, which made him, the boy, the mother and that hidden voice in the other room laugh with great warmth.

I looked over at Jiggy, who was laughing right along with them. I felt they might have been making fun of me, so I shot Jiggy a look.

"What?" he said, indifferently. "It's just like when you came to my house for dinner and ate your snap peas with your hands. You're a bachelor and you don't get all the little manners of family life. . . even they can see that."

Once everyone had been served, Dagar's voice took on a reverential tone, and we all bowed our heads and prayed—each in his own manner. At the end of the prayer, I made the sign of the cross, which I thought Dagar may not appreciate. But, instead he just laughed and said something to his mother, and she laughed as well. I don't know what he said, but it wasn't "kafir."

Dagar's mother really liked Jiggy. She would shove him playfully every time she passed by him, and she always laughed when he spoke. He ate about three times more than I did, and she was always quick to refill his bowl. She pinched his cheek from time to time and said things in Pashto that made Dagar, the children, and the voice in the other room laugh.

"Someone has a shine on you," I said to Jiggy.

"She can see that I'm a family man," Jiggy replied proudly.

The evening passed with great warmth. Although half a world away and completely incapable of communicating with our host, I felt like I was home again. When the meal was finished, Dagar clapped his hands and Mina and her younger brother came running in front of him. Dagar began to clap his hands in rhythm and gave the children some words of kind instruction. Soon Mina began clapping her hands as well and bobbing up and down with the most beautiful earnestness. And then she lifted up her voice and began a slow, sweet tune. I had no idea what Mina was singing, but her voice was so pure and the tune so entrancing that I felt as if my heart was melting inside of me—and I missed home. I really missed home.

Then the little boy began, at first hesitantly, but soon he broke out in loud, clamorous harmony with his older sister. Surprisingly, then Dagar, Jiggy and Dagar's mother began singing along too, clapping and laughing with everyone else. Next thing I knew, I was singing and clapping right along with them, as was the voice in the other room.

And there we were, in the baked-clay home of an Afghani farmer, singing, clapping and laughing—a single lantern lighting the room. I could just make out Jiggy's face in the light. He was laughing and grinning, clapping and singing, but his eyes were filled with tears.

THE WRESTLER

"Mount up!" Dragline commanded.

I started up the engine of my Humvee as Spooky and Crunk took their respective positions. Once the entire team was in position and ready, I eased the transmission into drive. We trundled down the road leading out of the village, and waved back at Dagar and his mother, both waving us goodbye as we exited onto the wadi. We headed south along the dried river bed, past the 'minefield,' and then past the neighboring village—the one so hated by the villagers.

We followed the meandering wadi for another 20 klicks—the same desolate, bleached landscape, marked with the occasional green spot surrounding a mud-walled village. In the late morning, the captain came over the radio and told us to pull up just under the ridgeline overlooking the wadi we had been traveling.

"Little Spider," the captain called out to his gunner. "Get 20XX on the radio and coordinate with them on the link-up."

"Roger that, sir," Little Spider replied.

The plan was for us to link-up with the Scuba team and their AMF support—soldiers of the Afghanistan Military Force—working with their team. We were going to execute a raid on a compound in the nearby village in which "good intelligence" said Taliban resided.

Within the hour, 20XX rolled up with four vehicles. The first to pull up was a pick-up truck loaded with about 20 young Afghani soldiers. They came roaring up the ridgeline, then slammed to a halt spewing gravel and dust all around. Behind them came three technicals with the scuba team. The Afghanis all tumbled out of their truck, laughing and waving. They were very young; the oldest could not have been more than seventeen. They were without beards, and wore old woodland-pattern camouflage uniforms. They all carried AK-47s, that, for some reason, had fixed bayonets—but the bayonets were sheathed. From the first technical came the scuba team leader, Captain Hanson, and his team sergeant, Blue Claw.

Captain Hanson was a charismatic man who exuded confidence and daring. His men were devoted to him. He was lean and tall, and always smiling a big, aggressive, challenging smile. He expected to win in everything he did, and when you looked him in the eyes, both of you knew that he would.

Blue Claw, although physically different from his captain, was psychologically similar. Thick, short and somewhat heavy, he was a man incapable of self-doubt. Blue Claw and I had gone to jumpmaster school together, and, of course, he had bested me.

"Fall in!" Captain Hanson commanded. "Come on, Third Commando, fall in!" He was grinning with pride at the AMF forces he commanded forming up in a ragged line in front of him.

"Jala! Jala!" commanded Blue Claw. The rest of the scuba team climbed out of their vehicles and arraigned the AMF in order.

"Captain McMann," Captain Hanson shouted toward us, "my compliments, and may I introduce you to Third Commando!" Upon hearing the words "third commando," the AMF shouted out cheers.

"It is an honor, Captain Hanson," said Captain McMann. "I'm happy to finally get to meet, and to work alongside with, the famed fighters of Third Commando." Upon hearing that phrase, the AMF soldiers again cheered, although I doubt any of them knew why.

"Tell me, sir," said Dragline. "How did they get the name 'Third Commando'?"

Captain Hanson grinned. "I just pulled it out of my ass."

Working with the AMF proved to be a lot of fun. Recruited and paid for by the CIA, they were all enthusiastic smiles and bravado. I had heard stories of stoned, supercilious and indifferent Afghani fighters, but there was none of that here. These boys were a force to be restrained more than anything.

The plan was to roll-up into the compound just before dawn. If we found anything incriminating, we would take the men into custody and take them back to Kandahar Air Field.

Using engineer tape, we made a full sized outline of the compound— the main building and the outbuildings. We marked off the doors and windows, and then did a number of rehearsals, breaking it down into the many small components: the approach, the ladders over the wall, the stack-up at the main gate, the entrance into the compound, clearing the buildings, and finally, the search. Dragline and Captain McMann were in charge of this operation, as Captain Hanson, Blue Claw and most of the scuba team would be in a blocking position at the various approaches to the compound.

We did multiple rehearsals, but there was a lot of down time after the rehearsals. I went over my vehicle two or three times, trying to figure out if everything was in place and in proper order. I field-stripped my weapon and cleaned it, and then I walked over the possibilities of things going wrong and how would I react. I was scared, not about dying, but about screwing-up. Whatever else happens, I thought, I want to do my duty. Please, God, don't let me embarrass myself.

We rolled out of the base camp around 3:00 a.m. and drove slowly with our black-out lights on and NVGs on our heads. From about 300 meters away, we could see the village, and we waited at that point until just before dawn. I was lead vehicle, and when Dragline gave me the command, I eased the vehicle into drive and we made our final approach. We crept into the village, and when we came to the compound, I drove along the wall where we were able to put up the ladders. Then I drove to the main gate and stopped the Humvee 20 feet from the front gate.

Little Spider taught me that one. He told me that on their first raid, they had stacked up the vehicles right at the gate, and when the AMF opened the gate—outward—it hit into the front vehicle. And the front vehicle couldn't back-up, because all the other vehicles were behind it. "So whatcha do?" I asked.

"We had to get out of the vehicles and just run through the gate. But the locals knew we'd screwed up," he said. "There was shooting, and they came running out, and right away saw what had happened. Nice people, the Afghanis, but when they see your ass hanging out, they're gonna laugh at you."

When the gates opened, I gunned the engine, and we poured through the front gate. "JALA! JALA! JALA!" we shouted, banging on doors and punching any piece of steel we could find. "Get up, bitches! Get up!"—we quickly fell back on the English.

An old man staggered into the doorway of the main building. He was alarmed, but clearly overplaying the part. "Get the fuck out of the doorway," Crunk shouted. The guy gave him that confused look one gives when confusion is the best defense. A dog came around the corner at me. I spun in his direction and leveled my weapon at him and glared. He stopped, intimidated, three feet away and began barking. I looked at him, seeing that he was afraid. "Afraid to bite me?" I said. "What a pussy. You're a girl."

Two women came out of an outbuilding yelling and gesturing excitedly as Dragline, Crunk and Spooky stacked up against the door of the main building. Dragline brought the shotgun around to blow the handle off the door, and just as he did, the door swung open, and a very

large man—at least six feet five inches, and weighing over 270 lbs—
stepped sleepily into the door frame. He was unarmed, and didn't
appear to be menacing, so Dragline kind of hooked his tricep with the
stock of the shotgun and spun him aside as the three entered the room,
sweeping to the right and left.

"Four of 'em ran out the back," shouted Dragline. "Get the AMF
after them!" Amu shouted something to the AMF and they all took off
running, their faces beaming with teenaged delight, joyful in the
prospect of actually shooting someone.

Children came streaming out of the main building, followed by six
men and three women. We herded them together as best we could, and
the eldest of the men began loudly protesting.

"What is he saying?" I asked Amu.

"He is saying that it is outrageous that foreigners" (I recognized the
word kafir) "should enter his house and look with dishonor on his
women. . . . He is calling me a traitor."

Yeah, I thought, I can see that. "Tell the good sir, we are not here to
bring dishonor to his house," I said, "only to keep the village safe from
the Taliban."

Amu spoke to the man, who responded. "He is saying," Amu said,
"no Talibani here."

"Yeah," I said, "there never are . . . let me guess, they're all up-
stream from the village, and they piss in the river while these people are
bathing."

Amu laughed as the man pointed up-stream and said something
about Talibani.

The women were shouting and throwing their hands in the air, some
of the children were crying, but others were curious and found the event
festive.

The man spoke again, this time with less emotion.

"He says it is not right that the women should be put to shame like
this," Amu repeated.

Captain McMann spoke up. "Tell the elder that once we clear all the
outbuildings, we can put the women in one of those buildings, and he
can stand guard over it." Captain McMann seemed to be finished, but
then looked up at the elder and said, "Tell him one other thing—
everybody in this compound is getting their photo taken, and their
fingers printed."

Amu spoke to the elder, who once again flew into outrage. "He says
it is harram—forbidden by Allah—for us to take uncovered pictures of

the women's faces."

Just then Dragline came out of the main building. "Harram is it?" he said, walking directly toward the elder. "Then what the fuck do you call these, baseball cards?" Dragline had found the identification cards for the entire family. All the women were photographed with uncovered faces. "They have Taliban markings too," Dragline said, showing the elder the Taliban symbol on each of the cards.

"Having Taliban ID cards," said the captain, by way of calming down Dragline, "doesn't mean they are Taliban, or even sympathizers—everybody had to get Talibani IDs."

"Roger, sir," said Dragline, "but the fact that the Taliban made them show their faces for ID cards proves that it is not harram for them to do so." Dragline glared at the elder, who simply shrugged his shoulders as if to say, "Okay, you got me on that." Casting about for something to say, the elder pointed to the enormous man who had earlier been standing in the doorway. The elder said something to Amu in a manner that suggested he was just giving him facts, not pleading for anything.

Amu studied the man and seemed impressed. As he did, the man jutted out his chest. "This man," said Amu, "is the champion wrestler in all of Kandahar province."

We all looked at him a second time. Although he had a large gut and fleshy face, his chest was tremendous in size, maybe 56 inches, and his shoulders and his triceps stuck out even under his loose-fitting man-pajamas, as if a steel cable ran from one arm, across his shoulders to the other.

Once we had the outbuildings cleared, we hustled the women into one of the buildings and had the men moved over some distance away. "Guard the men," Dragline ordered me, as he, the captain, Amu and the elder walked to an open area, away from, but with a good view of the women's outbuilding.

"Sit down, Hulk Hogan!" I commanded, raising my weapon up slightly—not aiming it, just reminding him of its presence. He gave me a look of confusion—the same look I had been seeing from everybody who didn't want to do what I told them to do since I got here. All the other men were sitting. He knew what I wanted him to do, he just didn't want to do it.

"Sit. The fuck. Down," I said again, walking toward the wrestler, my weapon now pointed at him.

He gave me that same stare. I was about three feet away, and I barked at him a third time, talking to him with the angry, pleading tone of a parent. "Everybody else is sitting down!" I said. "Why can't you sit on your enormous fat ass?" He stared at me the way a hog stares at a wristwatch.

I drew closer to him—this was becoming a problem—now my authority was being questioned, and, of course, that was the point of his "confusion." "You need to sit," I said, the muzzle of my weapon eight inches from his chest. The man pushed the muzzle aside, and for a second I thought about shooting him. Things were now completely out of control. I could not allow him to continue to stand in direct defiance of me, but if I acted excessively to get him to sit, that would cause an incredible uproar in the village—destroying whatever goodwill we had with these people, and destroying any possibility of intel gathering. The shoe was now on the other foot, and the wrestler could see it.

He dropped his look of confusion, and suddenly smiled, taking a step toward me and grabbing at the muzzle of my rifle. For a split-second I froze, not sure what to do. Then the training took over, and I took a step at him. Putting my right hand on the handguard, I grabbed the stock of my weapon with my left hand, and I swung that machined steel collapsible rifle butt up against the temple of his head. "I'm the one with the weapon, bitch!" I shouted, as blood spurted from his head and he fell to the ground.

"Damn, Jet Set!" shouted Boy Band, as we loaded back up into the vehicles. "You fuckin cold-cocked that big boy!" Boy Band chuckled, but he wasn't recounting my 'act of valor,' he was setting me up. He was continuing to talk about what had happened so that it could not be swept under the rug. "Hell," he continued, "what'd he get, ten, fifteen stitches?"

"Let's roll out," commanded Dragline, a note of simmering fury in his voice.

When I struck the village champion, knocking him down and opening a large gash in his head, I had completely sunk the mission. The other men all jumped up and started shouting and lunging at me (you know, the old hold-me-back routine). The women burst from their chamber wailing and cussing us out. Whatever intel the captain hoped to get from the village elder went to hell in a bucket. Dragline was furious, and the captain called it a 'leadership failure'—the worst term of criticism he reserves for anyone.

As I put my hands on the steering wheel, I saw that they were shaking wildly. And sitting in the seat, my legs couldn't stay still. I kept thinking about what happened. He knew what I wanted him to do, I thought. All the other men did it. I gave him the chance to correct himself, but instead he invaded my space, and he went for my weapon. I could have justifiably killed him. Instead I knocked him down—you're welcome.

"We'll get out of this place," said the captain, "find a rally point a couple klicks down the wadi and have an AAR [After Action Review]."

"That doesn't sound good," I said.

"Don't worry about it," Crunk said. "Dragline and the captain should never have put you in that position." I felt better hearing that, but then I noticed Crunk wouldn't look at me when he said it.

Spooky jumped into his seat with a broad smile. "Popped your cherry today, huh!" he said.

"I guess so," I replied in a dejected manner.

"Don't be like that, you did the right thing."

"You think so?" I said. "I sort of messed up the whole mission."

"Bullshit," he said. "What mission? We had some bogus intel from some sorry-ass CIA chick. The guy was trying to punk you out and you whipped his ass. Good on you."

"What about the operation?" I said.

"Don't you get it?" said Spooky. "That was the operation. The point of the operation was to fuck with the locals and let them know we mean business. We stormed a compound and what'd we find? Six AKs and a couple keys of opium—what is that?" Spooky shrugged. "What we did was we let these people know that we know who they are, and we can reach out and touch them when we want—that's what the mission was."

"But Dragline said—"

"Dragline doesn't give a shit," Spooky interrupted. "He's proud you took a stand. He's just keeping up appearances."

"I don't know," I said. "What's gonna happen at the After Action Review?

"I can tell you one thing that's going to happen," said Spooky. "If no one else brings it up, I'm going to ask why you were left alone to guard that mountain of a man and three others. Especially when the captain didn't need Dragline with him. Dragline should have been there with you."

There was a stilted silence. It was awkward to hear such criticism of the team sergeant, especially from his closest friend on the team. Spooky stared at the terrain in front of us and shook his head. "But that was one big son of a bitch, wasn't he?"

I laughed, and shook my head in astonishment. "You should have seen him up close. I was almost afraid my rifle butt wouldn't reach up to his head."

"Yeah," said Spooky with admiration, "but you dropped him like a bad habit."

The AAR was not as bad as I was afraid it would be. The captain walked us through the events leading up to what we were now calling The Wrestling Match, and Dragline took over from there. "I think Jet Set got himself into a bad situation because he dialed it up too fast—what are we always training on, dialing it up, and dialing it back down. Jet Set dialed it up too much, and he put himself into a position he could not retreat from." Dragline looked directly at me. "Still, he didn't retreat—he fuckin' advanced—and for that we have to give him some credit." Dragline swatted me on the shoulder, then cleared his voice. "Jet Set wasn't the only one who could have done things differently," he continued. "I might . . . uh, shouldn't have left him there alone to guard those men—to guard that man."

After the AAR, Captain McMann came up to me in private and said, "Jet Set, if there was any leadership failure, it was on my part." It made me feel a lot better to hear that from him. Captain McMann is not a man you ever wanted to let down.

We got back into the vehicles and headed down the wadi for the long trek back to the airfield. By the time we arrived in Kandahar, we had been eight days without showers or razors. We were covered in dust, sweat and muck. We all were wearing turbans and tribal hats. Manning the gate again was PFC Branson, who had checked us out of the Air Field over a week before. When he saw us, he was wide-eyed. "Where ya been, sergeant?" he asked.

"Out there," I said.

He lifted up the gate and stared at us with open admiration. I never felt so cool in my life.

I REMEMBER, I REMEMBER

The boys were drinking.

Coming toward the team hooch from the darkness of the compound gate, I could see their faces lit up by the klieg lights in front of the hooch, but they could not see me in the darkness just beyond the arc of light. Boy Band was master of ceremonies, and Crunk was right beside him, alternately agreeing with or criticizing Boy Band's running commentary. Jiggy was sitting in a folding chair not far away, chewing on sunflower seeds, as he did not drink. Sitting on a long picnic table were Dragline and Spooky. Dragline was sipping his drink and smoking one of the Cuban cigars we had picked up for him in Qatar. Spooky had his drink resting between his legs. He had one ear bud from an iPod propped in an ear, the other dangling loosely down.

Boy Band wasn't a big drinker, but he liked to think of himself as a man who liked to get his drink on. For Boy Band, drinking wasn't so much about getting drunk as it was an opportunity for him to display his magnanimity. It was about him letting you know he was happy with the world and happy with you. You put a glass in his hand and he only wanted to put a glass in yours, a natural bartender.

Crunk liked to drink a little bit more, but he wasn't married to it either. When Crunk drank, he had a habit of interrogating you—not in an aggressive manner, more in an oblique fashion, the way "good cops" do. He'd usually start by asking you, casually, some 'values questions.' And when you'd answered him, he'd look out to space, pause, and say, 'Well, how does that square with what you just said about [insert your answer to an earlier question].' A regular Socrates he was when he'd had a few.

Spooky would usually get calmer when he drank—and that deeper calm only made you more uncomfortable around him.

Dragline liked to drink quite a bit, but as he aged, he seemed to enjoy his cigars more than his bourbon.

Army General Order Number One stated that soldiers in-country were not allowed the use of alcohol. Whether for a year or for a day, drinking in the Army while deployed was verboten. Falling under the Special Operations Command as we did, however, put us on a

200

compound within the compound—with German Special Forces, Dutch Royal Marines, the French Foreign Legion and British Special Forces, all of whom were allowed—even encouraged—to drink. And it didn't take too much horse trading to get a bottle or two of whiskey or a case of beer.

"Hey, Crunk," said Boy Band, popping open a beer.

"Yeah," Crunk replied.

"Ever had an Irish seven-course meal?"

"What's an Irish seven-course meal?"

Boy Band looked up with a smile. "A potato and a six-pack."

I stood for a time just outside of the team's vision, watching them. I wanted to join in, but not just yet. I kept thinking about that big wrestler earlier in the morning. I kept seeing the blood spurt from the side of his head, and how he collapsed to the ground. We busted into the guy's home, I thought to myself. We barged in and started rifling through their effects, and for what? Because some other guy from another village told some CIA agent that his hated rival was Taliban? They all say that. I stared down silently at my boots. Is this what we're doing, I thought, just rousting people?

I looked back again at the team. "You know," said Dragline, holding his Cohiba out in front of him, looking at it with admiration, "smoking a good cigar is like being in a good marriage." He looked around at the team, letting them know that it was time to pay attention to him, that he was about to impart some wisdom. "In the beginning," he continued, "your cigar is flavorful and unique. That's when you tell your buddies about how it has a 'roasted essence' or an 'earthy quality,' and, of course, you always have to say something about 'cedar variations.'"

Dragline then bit down hard on his cigar, and continued, "but about half-way through, you realize this cigar wants to kick your ass. It ain't about flavors and cedars and roasted seasonings, it's about domination." Dragline pulled the cigar out of his mouth and stared at it respectfully. "And it just keeps coming at you. I mean, a good cigar, like a good wife, is relentless." Dragline put the cigar back into his mouth, but this time with more caution. "Then your 'good cigar' becomes a constant struggle. Two-thirds of the way through that cigar, all the 'cedar qualities' and 'roasted seasonings' are gone. The only thing left is you and that burning, angry, suffocating cigar—which you hate . . . and which you love. It becomes the only thing that matters to you anymore." Dragline looked around at the guys, intent on telling them something of worth. "Think about it," he said. "You've got this burning ember inches from your face that just wants to kill you... Who else cares about you that much?" Dragline fell silent for the longest time as he stared half-drunkenly at the last embers of his cigar. Finally, he tossed the small stub on the ground, stepped on it triumphantly and said: "I'ma gonna go call my wife. I think I'ma gonna call my wife."

Watching Dragline walk off, I thought about maybe calling someone back home, but I couldn't think of anybody I wanted to talk to about what had happened. I couldn't call my folks. They'd never forget it, and constantly remind me of the time I called them in a 'state of PTSD'. Then I remembered the chaplain's office. The chaplain, I knew, was a Catholic priest. I had not met him yet, but I figured now would be a good time to see him.

The chaplain's tent shared a common area with the Judge Advocate's tent. It sat across from the chow hall, and I had noticed that the two offices, which had separate entrances, were connected. It was about 8:00 p.m. when I arrived at the chaplain's tent. I tried to listen at the door to hear what was going on, but the hum of the generators washed out all other sound. I opened the door, and there in the middle of the common space, I saw a clean-cut, middle-aged man wearing cut-off BDUs, a civilian T-shirt and a pair of leather sandals. He was sitting in a chair with a twelve-string guitar cradled in his arms. Next to him sat an attractive female Air Force captain, who looked to be in her early 30s. She was in desert uniform, and she had a six-string guitar cradled in her arms.

Although my body was lit up by the lantern lighting the room, my face was shielded from them by a low hanging beam that blocked off the light, so they did not see me roll my eyes as I stared at the two. Oh, geez, I thought, if it isn't Father Feel Good, come to sing Kumbaya to the fighting men of the Special Forces.

The chaplain looked up smiling and waved me in. "Come on in, boyo," he said in a thick Irish Brogue, "Sergeant . . . Redmond—ah, a boy after me own heart." He stood up and walked toward me. He was about six feet tall and of slightly heavy build. Under his thick glasses, he had bright, piercing blue eyes. "My name's Fath—Major McFarland. This is Captain Paloma, from the JAG Corps."

Captain Paloma gave me a sincere, eager smile, but did not get up— showing the appropriate degree of formality an officer should use with a sergeant when sitting in the Chaplain's office holding a guitar while in uniform (although I doubt there is a regulation speaking to the situation).

"Yes, Father," I said. "I was hoping to take confession from you tonight."

"Oh, to be sure, to be sure," he said. "Are you in a hurry? We could do it right now."

"No hurry, Father," I said. "You look like you are about to play. I can wait."

Father McFarland smiled and so did Captain Paloma. Then they picked up their guitars and worked into sync. I was expecting to hear some tired old folk song or some lamentable Peter, Paul and Mary dirge. Instead, I heard a few plaintive notes from Father McFarland's 12-string, then an ethereal and delicate response from Captain Paloma. And presently, the two guitars took off together, both playing slight variations of the same tune, which they seemed to weave in and out of each other with poetic precision, setting a mood of heartfelt remembrance. Father McFarland's ethereal voice leapt into the melody like a child leaps into a game of Double-Dutch:

Sister Clarissa could have been on the stage
But Jesus came over, and told her
He'd rather she taught the fifth grade.

Sister Clarissa is engaged to Our Lord
He has promised to take her to heaven.
He never goes back on His word.

Sister Clarissa is eleven feet tall
Her rosary hangs, and it clatters and it clangs
When she moves down the hall.

She writes 'Sister Clarissa' up high on the board
The chalk won't dare squeak
The children sit meekly without a word.
Somehow you know summer's over.

Who made me?
God made me
To know Him
To love Him
To serve Him in this world

And to be happy with Him forever.

Sister Clarissa believes in free will
The communion of saints
The forgiveness of sins
And a quiet fire drill.

And when she hugs you
She hugs you too tight
And she gives you a star on your forehead
For spelling 'Connecticut' right.

Who made me?
God made me
To know Him
To love Him
To serve Him in this world
And to be happy with Him forever.

Many years later, on a memory walk
Through the old wooden doors
Down the same corridors
Dusted with years of chalk

You see Sister Clarissa
And she looks just the same
And the sound of her rosary still brings a chill
And she remembers your name.

And the years disappear
As though they've never been.
And you hear yourself saying
'Yes, Sister'
'No, Sister'
Like you were ten.

And you're so glad to see
That she's still the same way
And to tell her you love her
Before she goes over to

Her Fiancé.

Who made me?
God made me
To know Him
To love Him
To serve Him in this world
And to be happy with Him forever.

As the chords of the guitars died away, I felt my heart pounding inside of me. I looked at the two with wonderment, and I stood up and involuntarily began to clap. That one simple song had transported me into another time and place I thought I had forgotten. And my mind was flooded with distant memories from long ago.

Father McFarland and Captain Paloma quietly put their guitars away. For the longest moment I didn't know where I was, then I heard Father McFarland say, "I will have to go into my office to prepare for the confession. Captain, sergeant, make yourselves at home." He then walked briskly away, and the female captain and I were standing alone together in the large open area.

I looked over at Captain Paloma. She was in her early 30s, very physically fit, with blue eyes and long auburn hair pinned up in a French braid. Although she wore an Air Force uniform, she had Jumpmaster wings above her left breast pocket—and I immediately deciphered her career. "So, ma'am," I said, with a subtle smile, "glad to see a paratrooper in the Air Force JAG Corps."

She looked at my Special Forces tab, and laughed nostalgically. "And I can see you know your way around Fort Bragg, as well."

"I've run down Ardennes more times than I care to remember," I said. "And you? I'm guessing you've risen up through the ranks."

"Oh really, sergeant," the Captain replied challengingly, "you know my career path?"

"It's written on your uniform," I replied.

Captain Paloma stared at me curiously. She then smiled and said, "Tell me what my uniform tells you."

I looked her up and down. "Well," I said, "I know you're a JAG, so you went to law school . . . and, of course, undergraduate. You're a captain, but . . ." I hesitated and looked away.

"You were going to say that I'm old for a captain," she said with a coy smile.

"I was going to say that you . . . have not followed a traditional career path," I replied, laughingly.

"Come on, then," the captain continued flirtatiously, "tell me more about . . . me—or what you think is me."

"You want me to do this?"

"Absolutely. Show me what you got."

"Okay," I said, looking straight into her eyes. "You did more than one tour as an enlisted. I'd say you did six years, from right out of high school, until about 24, 25. Then you finished up college. I'm going to guess you took some classes at night while you were in. You graduated, went on to law school, sat for the bar and took a direct commission into the JAG Corps. Only this time you were smart, and you chose the Air Force over the Army—good call, by the way."

Captain Paloma's eyes grew wide. "That's incredible," she said. "You just told me my life story." She looked away and shook her head. Then she smirked cynically, "What kind of voodoo mind-games do they teach you in the Special Forces?"

"They just teach us situational awareness," I said. She looked back up at me with a little too much admiration, and I looked down at my boots. "The only reason I knew your story," I said, "is because it's so close to my own."

"How's that?" she asked.

"I went to college, too," I said. "I wasn't finding any success after college, so I enlisted into the paratroopers." I shrugged my shoulders, as if to say, 'whatcha gonna do?' "I went into the Special Forces, did about five years total active time, then got out. I used my GI Bill to go through law school, and the whole time I stayed in with the National Guard, keeping my costs to a minimum."

"You're an attorney?" Captain Paloma said, with surprise. "Why aren't you a JAG officer?"

"Because I'm a Green Beret," I replied coldly.

She smiled. "Yeah, you guys are weird about that."

The door to the tent was opening up, and Father McFarland was noisily entering the room, so the captain stepped away from me. "You should come by and see us once in a while," she said. "The chaplain is usually in his office and he always has terrific iced tea."

"I'll think about it," I said.

"If you come visit," Captain Paloma whispered to me playfully, "I'll let you call me by my first name."

"What is it?"

"You'll have to come visit to find out won't ya?" She picked up her guitar and a small camouflaged backpack and began walking happily toward Father McFarland and the open door. Father McFarland turned to the wall to put something away, and she spun around and in a stage whisper said, "Call me Linda."

"Ahem," Father McFarland said, clearly uncomfortable. "I'm ready for your confession."

We walked over to the 'confessional,' which was just a corner of the tent with a small screen alongside a chair. Rather than kneeling behind the screen, I sat down in a chair opposite Father McFarland. Before taking my confession, Father McFarland had a short conversation with me. "Timmy," he asked, "do you understand the purpose of Confession?"

"To give me absolution of my sins," I replied.

"It is true," he said, "but it is more than that. The absolution of sins is the outward sign of an inward grace. The purpose of forgiveness of sins is the reconciling of man to God." Father McFarland touched his finger tips to his cassock. He looked me in the eyes, as if to show me that he wanted me to understand why we do what we do. "When we sin," he continued, "we deprive ourselves of God's grace. And by doing so, we make it even easier to sin again. It is a downward cycle that leads to complete separation from God—it leads a soul to Hell. The only way out of this spiral is to acknowledge our sins, to repent of them, and to ask God's forgiveness. Then, in the sacrament of Confession, grace can be restored to our souls, and we can once again resist sin."

I nodded my head. I was feeling things and thinking about things I had long ago forgotten. "What is required of me?" I asked.

Father McFarland laughed. "Come on, Timmy, you are a Catholic man, confirmed in your faith by the Bishop himself, are you not?"

"I am."

"You are a soldier of the Church, are you not? Then, you tell me, what is required?"

This caught me off guard, but I thought about my Catholic education, and I thought about the priest's commission. "Three things are required," I said, my catechism coming back to me in a torrent of memories. "To receive the sacrament worthily, the penitent must be contrite—that is to say, he must be sincerely sorry for his sins; he must confess those sins fully, in kind and in number; and he must be willing to do penance and to make amends for his sins."

Father McFarland smiled, and slapped me on the arm. "You make your mother proud, boyo," he said. And then we both settled into our chairs, we made the sign of the cross, and we began the formulaic rubric of the sacrament: "Forgive me, Father, for I have sinned . . ."

Father McFarland then walked with me through my conscience, teasing out where I was at fault, through my thoughts and my deeds, in what I had done, and what I had failed to do. It was not a therapy session, but an examination. Father McFarland was not light with the penitents either, but loaded me up heavily.

The night was densely black as I left the chaplain's tent. I had not brought a flashlight with me, and as I made my way cautiously back to the team hooch, my thoughts continually fell back upon my First Holy Communion. I was only a kid—in second grade—but I remembered how the night before I prayed that I would grow to become always good—a good son, a good brother, a good boy and a good man. I remembered my First Communion—our class proceeding down the aisle toward the altar, the smoke of the incense wafting through the church, as families gathered around us and cameras clicked. And I remembered how much I wanted to be exactly as God wanted me to be, and how it all seemed to be so obvious. I remembered praying at the altar, and I remembered how seriously I took everything that day. I remembered my starched white shirt, my red tie and my dark suit. I remembered how sure I was of myself, always to be a good boy, a good man and a good Catholic. I remembered, I remembered.

Then, I thought about my life since that day, the myriad regrets and mistakes I had made in life—through my fault, through my fault, through my most grievous fault. And far more than that, I thought about the malicious things I had done. Not out of ignorance or confusion, but out of selfishness. Things I had done knowingly, with wanton disregard. Scenes of my life flashed before me that covered me with shame. And as each scene, each event, came before me, I found myself involuntarily—accusingly—saying, "I remember . . . I remember." And I recalled a poem I had learned long ago in school. It was a poem about a world-weary man, looking back on his young innocence and feeling only regret. Returning to the hooch, in the darkness of the Kandahar night, the poem came back to me with absolute clarity. And I found myself speaking the last stanza out loud:

I remember, I remember
The fir-trees dark and high;

I used to think their slender tops
Were close against the sky:
It was a childish ignorance,
But now 'tis little joy
To know I'm farther off from Heaven
Than when I was a boy.

THE ASSAULT

I looked up at Chief Warrant Officer Brad Freman—'The Chief'—as he stepped in front of the white board we were all staring at from our seats in the TOC—Tactical Operations Center. He wore his uniform 'sterile,' that is, without name tag, unit patch or any other identifying devices. In his late 30s, the Chief was tall and broad shouldered. He smiled a lot and liked to tell jokes, but when he stopped smiling, his eyes became small and hard, and all of the sudden things weren't so funny anymore.

The Chief was a living legend in the company. Most of the guys were cops in their regular line of work, but few of them had ever actually shot anyone. The Chief had not only shot at people, he had two kills—both of them clean, gun-fight kills. That had to be respected.

The Chief's expertise was intelligence. Although not the intel officer for the company—we didn't have one—he sort of took over the slot. His intel was extraordinary, and while he could not technically plan an operation, he was so well trusted that he, in fact, often actually planned operations.

The Chief smiled and said in a manner that told us to listen, "Alright . . . I'm in charge now—I'm the boss with the apple sauce." He then nodded to the staff sergeant operating the laptop, and on the white board a satellite picture of a medium sized village came up. "This here is the village of Deh Chopan," he said, "about 150 klicks north of Kandahar." The Chief circled the area of the village with his laser pointer. "The Marines went in here a couple weeks ago, and found—you know—the usual stuff: a bomb-making factory, couple hundred cell phones, some RPGs. They estimate about 60 fighters in the region."

"Did they find anything else?" Sergeant 'Marky-Mark' Simpson asked.

"They did. They found a laptop and some interesting video tapes." The Chief paused just a second and smiled. "Your mom has some explaining to do." Quiet laughter roiled the room. "But seriously," he continued, "the videos and the laptop were an intel goldmine." The Chief motioned to the staff sergeant to go to the next page, and up came a video. The video was of some makeshift parade, four silver Toyotas ambling slowly down the road toward the camera with masked jihadis sitting on the roof and hanging out the windows, jostling their AKs and RPGs up and down in the air. "Take a good look at those vehicles," the Chief said, "because when we go in there, we will—I'm sure—find at least one of them. And anyone we find in or around those cars is definitely a bad guy." The staff sergeant handed out photos of the cars, with the men hanging out of them. "And take good note of the guys, too," the Chief said. "I know they have their heads covered, but these guys don't change their clothes all that often, so if you can mark the clothing, you can mark the man."

The Chief walked us through a very thorough look of the vehicles and personnel in the pictures, noting dents in the cars, missing hubcaps, the shoes, the pants and the shirts of the men. After about ten minutes of observing the pictures, we continued to watch the video. Soon we saw the people from the houses come out and wave to the Talibani. The room erupted with laughter. "I know," said the Chief, laughing, "when we roll down that same road, they'll all come out and wave to us as well."

The video went dark, then opened up again on three well-armed youths—boys in their teens—standing in the open, looking down a street, mud buildings on either side of them for easy cover. "Now, watch this shit," the Chief said. "These are the knuckleheads who've been giving our convoys fits. This is an 'ambush.'" He made the "air quote" sign with his hands.

Of the three youths, one had an AK, one an RPG, and the last a PKM—a medium machine gun similar to our 240 Bravo. After the requisite 'Allahu Akbars' the guy with the AK ran forward and, without aiming, fired a twenty-round burst down the street beyond the picture frame. Then the guy with the RPG ran forward, and, with minimal aiming, fired his rocket. Lastly, the guy with the PKM fumbled forward, barely able to keep his weapon straight, and, firing from the hip, shot off a fifty-round burst, the last five rounds striking the wall around him, as he peeled away with his finger still mashed on the trigger.

The Chief signaled to stop the video. "So," he said, "that was their 'ambush'—which they proudly videoed. What do you guys think?" The room became loud with derision.

"Amateurs."

"Hacks."

"Call that an ambush?"

The Chief smiled. "Let me ask y'all a question, how do you counter an ambush?"

Almost in unison we yelled back, "Fire and maneuver!"

"Exactly," he said. "It's right in the 7-dash-8. But what does an 88 Mike do when receiving harassing fire?" (An 88 Mike is a truck driver.)

"They haul ass!" someone shouted to loud approval.

"Exactly," Chief replied. "They just maneuver, and give these Talibani something to 'ulu' about. But tomorrow, we're going in," Chief clapped his hands together, "and we're going in with guns blazing!" The room cheered.

Our plan was very simple. We would convoy down the road that passed the village, drawing an ambush upon ourselves. We would then assault through the ambush, pull into the village square and command it with fire superiority, then dismount and clear out the buildings from north to south. "It's got ingress and egress avenues here and here," Chief said, as he pointed his laser-pointer to the map. The staff sergeant passed around copies of the picture we were seeing on the screen. "If we can command that battle space," Chief said, "they will come out and fight . . . . and we will kill every one of them." The room was now buzzing with excitement.

"There is one last thing I want you to see," the Chief said. "It may have limited intelligence value, but it is highly motivational." We all fell silent, wondering what he was talking about. "Staff sergeant," he said, "play it." The video came back on, showing, once again, the open space strewn with rubble, surrounded by the baked, dung-colored buildings of the village, shimmering from the heat of the mid-day. The camera was stationary—probably on a tripod—and we watched as two of the silver Toyotas approached it. The drivers and all the passengers were masked, but they were young-looking, no more than nineteen years of age. They pulled the cars to a stop in front of the camera, and the drivers and all the passengers got out.

The driver of the first car ran around to the trunk of the car and opened it. Inside was a young kid, no more than twelve years old, his hands and feet were bound and his head was covered with a scarf. He was crying and scared—he had wet himself. Then, we saw the driver of the second car get out and pull another young boy from the trunk of his car. That boy, too, was bound and his head was covered. Both boys were dragged in front of the camera, and both clung to their captors, crying and begging.

The driver of the first car said something in Pashtu, then pushed the first boy down to the ground. He pulled out a Glock pistol and, shouting Allahu Akbar, waved the gun around, then turned to the first boy and put the gun close to his head. I drew in an enormous breath, realizing I had stopped breathing since the video began. We all watched in stunned silence, hoping this was just a scare tactic.

The driver played around with the boy a little bit, shouting "Bang!" and pushing the muzzle of the gun into his head. The boy whimpered. Someone barked an order and the driver shrugged his shoulders, then pulled the trigger twice. The boy jerked into the air convulsively, then crumpled to the ground, a plume of dust rising with his fall.

The second boy was now in a complete frenzy. Although his hands and feet were bound, he hopped around on his knees crying and begging. The kid with the Glock shoved him to the ground. He then laughed and said something in Pashtu. He looked back at the camera, and smiled—he had the eyes of a boy at play—then, with the pistol two feet away, shot the kid four times, twice in the head, twice in the chest.

A shout of Allahu Akbar went up, and the killer—now ecstatic in his joy—jumped up and down, ran over to the first dead boy, placed the pistol to his head and shot him a third time. By now the killer was literally bouncing around in ecstasy. He shouted out another 'Allahu Akbar!' and leapt to the other boy lying dead on the ground and squeezed off another round into his head. Then he turned to the camera, his full body in view.

"Freeze it," the Chief said. The room was absolutely silent. The Chief lifted his head and his gaze seemed to stare right into all of us. "Take a good look at this guy," he said, "notice the shoes that he's wearing, notice that sweater he has on—light brown, with a diamond pattern—remember that Glock, not a lot of Glocks in Afghanistan." The Chief cleared his throat—he had a boy of his own back at home, about the same age as these two dead kids.

"This guy is asking us to kill him," he said, a cold severity in his voice. "He wants us to kill him—he knows it, and so do we." The Chief looked out over our heads, at something we didn't see. "And it's only fair," he said, "that he should die. Kids don't deserve to be killed. Not here, not anywhere. He knows it, and so do we. The world can't operate like that, there has to be justice. He knows we're coming for him. And when we kill him, we'll be doing him a favor. He knows it, and so do we."

"Full battle-rattle!" the team sergeant said. "We scrounged up enough helmets and body armor for all the AMF, so everyone's protected. No one hits the target without Kevlar and protective vest."

"You don't have to tell me twice," Jiggy whispered to me, a tight smile on his face.

"No question," I said, letting out a nervous laugh.

"Jet Set," said Dragline, "you're driving for the Chief today, you'll be on point. Crunk is going with you, he'll be on the .50."

I'd never driven an up-armor before, but I had become a pretty good driver. "Roger that, team sergeant," I said. This is an honor, I thought. I would be driving the Chief into battle. I imagined that he had specifically asked for me and Crunk—that I had impressed him in some way.

Before I went over to the Chief's vehicle, Dragline inspected me, wanting to make sure I had the proper ammo load, and to see that all my equipment was as per SOP.

The 'basic load' of ammunition for an infantryman is 210 rounds—one 30 round magazine in the weapon, and six more in your load-bearing vest. But nobody carries the basic load. First off, you don't put 30 rounds in your '30 round magazine'—it'll jam the weapon. You load 29 or 28 rounds in a magazine. 210 rounds sounds like a lot, but if things go wrong, you can eat that up very quickly. Better to carry a double load—one magazine in your weapon, six in your load-bearing vest, and another seven in your butt pack. And you'd better have additional ammo cans in the vehicle for reloading. Of course, you don't want to have to reload your magazines in the middle of a firefight—it would be awkward stopping everything and calling 'time out.' Not sure where the enemy would land on the 'time out' issue.

The problem with wearing full armor and a basic load—or double load—is that you almost cannot fit into the vehicle. And once in, you can't move around very well. When shit happens, it happens, like, right now, and your lumbering, slow-motion ass cannot make those dashing, heroic gestures you picture yourself making.

As we prepared to mount up, the Chief came over to me. "Jet Set," he said, "you ever driven an up-armor?"

"No, Chief, but I always wanted to."

"Well, these things get a little tricky," he said. Pot Roast came walking toward us. "Pot Roast," Chief said, "you've had a lot of experience driving up-armors, haven't you?"

"Practically all I've driven," said Pot Roast.

"How's it compare to driving a regular Humvee?" said the Chief.

214

"Well," said Pot Roast, pausing to think about it in a way that seemed a little staged, "they flip a hell of a lot easier than issue Humvees. And when that weight flips, it'll likely kill everybody inside—the gunner is definitely finished," Pot Roast said, staring up at Crunk.

The Chief was trying to be deferential, but I could see what was happening. He doesn't trust me, I thought. Chief doesn't want me on his team. I went red with shame. The Chief just looked at me, and his cold blue eyes—for the first time that I can ever remember—seemed sympathetic and embarrassed. But still determined.

"But, I—" I said, "I want to be on point. I . . . I can do this."

"We got four guys in this vehicle," he said. "We're going into the shit, and I can't—I won't—put that into the hands of an untested man."

I felt like crying. It wasn't just that he didn't believe in me, it was that he was right. He was right not to believe in me. "Well," I said, feebly, "I want to go with you, Chief. I want to be in the lead vehicle. You can't," I sputtered, "you can't just throw me away in front of everyone." I felt I would rather die than be humiliated in front of the company.

Chief's eyes lightened, and he smiled. "Oh," he said, "you're not going anywhere. I need every swinging dick I can get. Your ass is going to be in that lead vehicle, and your gun better be at the ready."

I looked down. I could feel all their eyes on me, and at once I realized that they had all conspired in this removal. I knew I didn't have a choice, everything was already set in stone. The only thing I could do was accept my position and show enthusiasm for the mission. I kicked a small rock on the ground. "Alright," I said, "then let's go kill us some Talibani bitches!"

"Mount up!" the Chief shouted.

They wouldn't be expecting us in the middle of the day—that was the plan—so they wouldn't have time to bury IEDs. We left out of the TOC around 3:00 a.m. and drove by NVGs through the wadis until dawn. Around 11:00 a.m. we were within two klicks of the village and we found a lonely hillside to serve as our mission support site. From there, we restated the mission and did a few rehearsals. We then checked our equipment one more time, girded ourselves for war, and pulled out from the hillside and into the wadi which led directly to the village.

Once in the wadi, Pot Roast punched the gas, and we took off at a rapid clip. At about 800 meters the village came into view—low mud walls arising slightly from the lighter brown of the surrounding terrain.

At 200 meters out we slowed down a bit and got into convoy formation, hoping to look like just another convoy coming through.

As we came upon the village, Chief said, "We're coming up on their favorite ambush site." And immediately we started taking rounds—BANG! BANG! BANG! The driver's side of the vehicle took three rounds—it sounded like someone was hitting us with a sledgehammer. "Turn left! Turn left! Turn left!" Chief shouted into the microphone, and Pot Roast turned down the narrow road that we watched the three young jihadis firing down in the video. We were driving right at a group of men—one holding an RPG—I was afraid he would suddenly take his work seriously. To my right, I heard automatic weapons fire, but didn't see anything. We were coming up on the open area, where the walls on the left side of the road ended. As we cleared the wall, I saw five or six men running hurriedly away—we had caught them unprepared. The last two men were carrying a PKN, and as I saw them, Crunk's .50 lit them up—erupting mini explosions into the mud wall. I didn't see that the first of the two men was hit, but I saw the wall all around him blowing up, and something shoved him hard to the ground. Crunk turned the .50 onto the second man, and his body bounced against the wall in grotesque contortions.

Crunk then turned the weapons on the fleeing others, who were running wildly to get through a doorway on the far side of the wall. I didn't see any direct hits, but I saw a lot of really frightened men clawing at each other to be the next one to safety.

We continued to move forward through the open space, and came to a stop about two-thirds of the way from the northern exit—we would wait there for the rest of the convoy to come on line with us. As we lumbered to a stop all hell broke loose. The windshield erupted in front of me as rounds smashed against the windows. From every doorway and cut-out a furious barrage of fire poured out. The 'bulletproof' glass windows were starting to sag inward, like they were being beaten by mallets.

"Drive through! Drive through!" Chief shouted over the roar of the gunfire. Meanwhile, Crunk opened up with the .50, hot brass falling down into the cab and all over us.

We drove forward about 30 feet, bullets banging into us from three sides. The armor and the windows seemed to be holding, but it was touch and go. I looked up at Crunk: he was hunkered down on that .50, brass casings flying out of the weapon and onto the floor.

Pot Roast jerked up in his seat. "Chief, I'm hit!" he shouted.

I leaned forward. "Where you hit?" I shouted.

"Inner thigh! Hurts real bad!"

"Jet Set, you're in charge of him," said Chief. "Now, where the fuck are the others?" Chief looked around and saw the AMF's truck stopped just behind the walls, unwilling to move forward into the open space. I took Pot Roast's pressure bandage from his vest, as I heard Crunk pull back the charging handle on the .50, reloading. Just then two enemy troops came out from a doorway, one with an RPG. "Bullshit!" Chief shouted, opening his door and getting out. Chief raised his rifle, paused to aim—bullets flying all around him like confetti—then fired two rounds at the man with the RPG who fell in a heap. The Chief shifted his aim, fired two more rounds and the second man went down.

Pot Roast was bleeding in powerful rivulets, and I was stretching across the inside of the vehicle trying to administer aid. And with the bullets banging all around the vehicle, I realized two things: number one, that if I did not get out of that vehicle, open his door, and treat him from the outside, Pot Roast was going to bleed to death; number two, that there was no way in hell I was going to do that.

"Jet Set," Chief said, in a calm, even voice.

"Yeah, Chief?" I yelled back.

"I think you're going to have to come out and work on Pot Roast from outside the vehicle." He spoke with such confidence and in such a reasoned tone, that I knew there was nothing I could do but go out there. And before I knew what I was doing, I opened my door and stepped out into the open. I was shaking, but I knew what I had to do, and I knew I wasn't getting out of there until I did it. I ran to the other side of the vehicle, opened Pot Roast's door, took out my knife and cut away his pants' leg. I was bent over Pot Roast, my armor vest riding up over my back, and I knew, I knew, I would be shot—I only hoped it wouldn't be in the spine. Pot Roast had taken a round in the thigh—the bullet must have pierced a spot where the vehicle's armor did not meet up. The bullet was close to the artery, but the bleeding, while heavy, was not spurting or following the beat of his heart. "How ya doin?" I asked.

"Not too fuckin' good, as you can see," he replied, trying to give me a smile, but failing.

I could hear the rhythmic thumping of the .50 over my head, and that calmed me down a bit. I took the rubber elastic band from my load-bearing vest and fed it from my right hand to my left hand around his thigh, about four inches above his wound.

"I'm going to put a tourniquet on your leg," I said.

"No," he said, trying to push away the rubber band. "I'm keeping my leg!"

"Tourniquet doesn't mean losing your leg anymore," I said. "That's old school. I'll put it on loose and pin a note to your uniform—you'll be okay," I said. "I'll stay with you until we get to the helicopter, then tell them you have it on."

"Damn it, Jet Set," Pot Roast said, "don't screw me on this." I put the tourniquet on with a little play in it, then took his pressure bandage and tied it tightly around his leg. There was a large puddle of blood in the driver's seat between Pot Roast's legs. I dipped my thumb into the blood and marked his forehead with a "T". I kept thinking, I was supposed to be the driver, Jesus, this could have been me.

The Chief was shouting at the AMF, "Get the fuck out here! Get the fuck out here!"

Crunk was reloading the .50 up again. I turned around and saw that the AMF was not moving forward. Dragline was trying to drive around their truck, but they were parked in the very center of the road.

Just then, an enemy came out of a doorway with an RPG, went down on one knee, aimed directly at the Chief and fired. The rocket streaked out furiously. Chief was about 20 feet in front of the vehicle. The concussion of the explosion rocked the up-armor. I didn't see where the rocket had hit, but when I lifted my head again, Chief was gone.

I had Pot Roast's leg in my arm, blood pouring onto my vest and uniform. "Chief!" Crunk shouted, "Chief!" There came no reply.

"This is bad!" Crunk yelled out. We were alone in the open, our leader gone, our driver immobile, and we couldn't get him out of the driver's seat to drive the vehicle. I couldn't move him alone, and Crunk couldn't leave the .50 to help.

"We're going to make it!" I said, but I didn't believe it at all.

I turned to look behind, and saw Dragline pushing the AMF's vehicle out into the open space. The AMF vehicle had their brakes on and Dragline's vehicle was on their rear bumper pushing it forward. The two vehicles were fighting with each other like a pair of rams—but Dragline was winning.

Just then I heard Crunk shout, "Chief!" his voice filled with amazement. I looked over and saw the Chief staggering up, wobbling around disoriented. He picked up his rifle and fired a few rounds into the doorway to his front, just to let them know he was still alive.

"Guy's an animal!" I shouted. Crunk laughed in agreement.

Chief came over to Pot Roast and me, and made a quick assessment. "Pot Roast," he said, "we're going to have to get you out of there. How is your wound?"

"Not great," said Pot Roast. "It's bleeding a lot."

Chief looked at me. "Yeah," I said, "he's losing blood. We got to get him out of here."

Dragline's vehicle had now broken through, and the captain's vehicle was also in, and they were both laying down a good volume of fire—even the AMF were doing their part. Now that they were in, they were in. With all our guns in play, the return fire had dwindled to sporadic at best.

The Chief went around to the back of the Humvee and opened up the rear hatch. He threw out some water cans and a box of MREs and made room for Pot Roast. Then he came back around and we slowly lifted Pot Roast's legs out of the vehicle.

Although the firing from the buildings had slowed down, it was now more well-placed—a bullet hit the windshield beside my head and splattered me with shards of plastic. At one point I bumped Pot Roast's leg on the doorframe and he gasped, looking at me angrily. Jiggy and the captain came running toward us. They came over and positioned themselves on either side of Pot Roast, and helped us lift him into the back of the vehicle. I was glad to see Jiggy, and when I looked over at him, he was laughing, a nervous but excited laugh. "What's so funny?" I said with amazement.

He couldn't stop laughing as he raised his rifle and fired two rounds in the direction of a muzzle flash. "We're here, man," he said. "We finally made it."

This got me to laughing as well. "Yeah," I said, "we're finally in the shit." Jiggy climbed up into the back of the Humvee to continue Pot Roast's first aid. "He's got a tourniquet," I shouted to Jiggy, then I ran over and climbed into the driver's seat. Chief climbed into the passenger seat next to me, and I looked at him quickly and said, "Looks like I'm driving after all." I tried to sound triumphant about it, but I could feel Pot Roast's warm blood rising up through my pants.

"Yeah, y'are," said Chief, his eyes blazing with excited energy. "You're the boss with the apple sauce!"

Our convoy of vehicles lurched slowly out of the open space. I had to drive around the bodies of the two men Chief had killed. One was lying on his back with his arms and legs akimbo. It looked like he'd been splattered with a big ball of blood and dirt. His eyes were open, but they had no life in them—like the eyes of a fish you see at the market. The other was lying face down, with a part of his skull blasted away. His hair was matted with blood and he looked more like a pile of clothes than a body.

As we pulled out, the firing died away. That would have been the best time to hit us, with only our rear gun capable of firing. I think they let us go because they didn't want to give us a reason to come back.

"Jiggy," Chief said, "how's he doing back there?"

"He's lost a lot of blood," said Jiggy, "but the bullet missed the artery. I'm just keeping him stable right now. I really don't want to go into his thigh in the back of a Humvee."

Pot Roast let out a groan, and the Chief said, "Pot Roast, how you holding up, buddy?"

"I'm okay, Chief," Pot Roast replied, but his voice cracked in the middle of his response.

We traveled about 100 meters, me looking to the front and to my left, Chief looking to the right. "You see that shit?" he said. "Stop the vehicle!"

I slammed on the brakes, and we all lurched forward. "Watch what yer doin'!" Jiggy shouted angrily. "We got wounded!"

I looked over to where the Chief was pointing, and saw a silver Toyota sedan sitting between two parallel support walls that were holding up a house. The structure formed something of a carport for the car.

"That's one of theirs!" I exclaimed.

"You're damn skippy it is," Chief said. "And I bet at least one of them fuckers lives in that house above it." Chief opened his door and jumped out. "Crunk," he said, "keep me covered." He approached the car, one hand holding his rifle, the other digging into his cargo pocket. He pulled out a red thermite grenade, and fired two rounds into the front windshield. Coming up to the car, he thrust the butt of his rifle two or three times into the shattered windshield, breaking a large hole in it. Pulling the pin on the thermite grenade, he let the small sputtering flame grow in intensity for a few seconds, then dropped it through the hole onto the driver's seat. He turned around and ran back to the vehicle, and as he climbed in I saw that he was laughing like a truant teenager.

Captain McMann called the dust-off, and by the time we got to the Landing Zone, we could see the UH-60 en route. Jiggy pulled out a poncho from his medical bag and covered Pot Roast with it to shield him from the prop blast. As the big chopper came clumsily down, Jiggy and I cinched the poncho close around Pot Roast. Jiggy, the captain, one of the AMF soldiers and I carried Pot Roast onto the deck of the aircraft. Jiggy had given him a dose of morphine, so Pot Roast wasn't feeling the pain too much. "Jesus," he said, as the shot went in, "it's like some dark cloud just came up and grabbed me."

As we transferred Pot Roast to the flight surgeon, I shouted to the guy, "He's got a tourniquet!"

"What?" he shouted back.

"He's got a tourniquet!" I repeated.

"What?" he said again.

I grabbed the guy by his harness, almost pulling him off the chopper, and shouted into his ear, "He's. Got. A tourniquet!"

"Get the fu—," he shouted, pushing me off him, then grew silent. "Roger," he shouted, "good copy." And he gave me the thumbs up as the helicopter lifted off.

As soon as the dust-off cleared the airspace, Captain McMann and the Chief huddled around Jiggy. "Is he really going to make it, Jiggy?" the captain said.

"I think so, sir," Jiggy responded. "There was a lot of blood loss, but it was a good, clean wound, didn't hit any vitals, and—thank God—missed his artery. . . we can probably find the bullet somewhere in the vehicle."

Upon hearing this, the Chief broke out in an enormous smile. "Hot damn!" he shouted. "Four kills and only one wounded! That's a beating! That's a beating!" He spun around in his excitement and jumped up on the hood of the up-armor, then threw himself at Crunk sitting in the cupola, and hugged him broadly. "Damn it, Crunk!" he shouted, "that was some shootin'! That was some shootin'!"

Crunk laughed embarrassedly. "What can I say . . . there they was!"

It felt invigorating to hear the Chief so happy about the outcome of the engagement, and I tried to think about how he was wrong for being happy. We had killed, and we had a wounded man. But he was not wrong. We beat the hell out of them, and that was all that mattered—Don't over think it, I thought. It's you versus them—just like football, but with guns.

The captain, the Chief, Dragline and Spooky huddled together over a map and a radio for about an hour as we all pulled perimeter security.

The entire time they consulted, we watched the town, as the plume of black smoke from the thermite grenade grew in size and intensity. "They couldn't push the car out from under the house," Boy Band said with a laugh. "They couldn't get into the cab and put the car in neutral."

"Yeah," I agreed. It was funny, because just from looking at the smoke we knew that the car had caught the house on fire, and now they were both burnt to cinders. It felt good to know that we had fucked that village up. That we had rolled into that shithole, killed four men and set a house on fire. It was definitely a good feeling.

Just then, the Chief came back. "That captain of yours is brilliant!" he said.

"What's the plan?" Crunk asked.

Unfolding a map on the ground, the Chief said, "The village we just hit is here." The Chief used a twig to point to the village on the map. "And for the last three months, IED attacks have happened along this wadi here, here, here, here and here."

"Okay," I said, "but that's at least six klicks away from the village—and most of these guys don't like straying too far from the ville."

"Right," he said. "But Captain McMann pointed something out to me. While it's six klicks away from the ville, and only four klicks away from a closer ville, that ville is over these mountains, and this ville is on a more or less direct line down the wadi."

He was right. We had crossed those hills about a month before, and they were brutal—even in our all-terrain vehicles.

"Moreover," said the Chief, "this wadi is a high traffic area, and, if you look closely at the map, at that bend where everyone is getting hit, it is the one spot where the wadi becomes the narrowest in the entire district."

"These guys are smart," Crunk said.

"I think so," replied Chief. "They may be young, but I think they're smarter than the average bear—keep the attacks away from the ville, and you get better support."

"Makes sense," Crunk said. "So, what's the plan?"

"Simple. We pull a checkpoint tonight."

"You really think they'll go out tonight," I said, "after the beating we just gave them?"

"I'd almost guarantee it," said Chief. "They got something to prove now."

After midnight we set up on a narrow, flat stretch of the wadi, about 400 meters south of a sharp bend in the contour of the land. There were numerous tire tracks in the area to let us know that this was a main path. My up-armor was in the center, the captain's Humvee was on my right, and the AMF's technical was on our left. Behind us, and covering our rear, was Dragline's technical.

"Um, Dragline," said the captain, over the radio, "I'd really like for us to practice a few 'what-if-we-need-all-guns-to-the-front' scenarios with you, you know, so I don't get my head shot off when you turn your weapon around."

"Don't you trust me, sir?" Dragline said dryly. Going through those rehearsals, I realized how right the captain was.

A hasty checkpoint is not the same as an ambush, but the rules of ambush still apply—surprise, speed and violence of action. By the time we set-up and ran a few rehearsals, it was about 1:00 a.m. We were still jacked up from the earlier fight and feeling triumphant. By 3:00 a.m. we were starting to flag, and by 4:30 most of us were beginning to lose interest. It had been a long couple of days and I was beginning to feel the wear. My NVGs were strapped to my helmet, but I hadn't looked through them in at least an hour.

Then, over the radio I heard a double click—the warning that something was up. I bolted upright and lowered my NVGs. Directly to our front, less than 200 meters away, I could make out two small sedans, seemingly loaded with people. They were driving directly toward us, moving about 20 miles an hour, with no lights on. I looked over at the Chief, and he too was just waking up from a confused state.

"Look at that front car," he said, "can't make out the color, but that's a Toyota sedan, the one behind him is . . . similar in appearance."

"I don't think we can engage them," I said, "until they show hostile intent."

"No," Chief said with a smile, "but the AMF can." He got on the radio, "Amu," he said, "are you seeing what I'm seeing?"

"Roger, my Chief," Amu said. "About 150 meters to our front . . . and the boys are good to go."

"Keep discipline," Chief replied. "They should all fire at your—I mean, at the lieutenant's order" (the AMF had an Afghani officer with them who was nominally in charge).

"Yes, my Chief," Amu replied.

Twenty seconds later, Amu got back on the radio. "My Chief," he said, "they are ready . . . NOW!" The vehicles were about 30 meters to our front when the night around the AMF's vehicle became ablaze with gunfire. They opened up with a furious barrage, tracer rounds flying around like hornets, but mostly too high. The two vehicles stopped immediately, and very quickly returning fire could be seen coming from them—again, most of it too high.

The command of "FIRE!" came over the radio from Captain McMann, and a withering hail of gunfire erupted from our line. Crunk's .50 and Boy Band's Mark 19 both opened up almost immediately, and I saw the first vehicle as it seemed to melt into nothingness. Four men leapt from that vehicle, all with weapons. One stood in the middle of the road, firing his weapon from the hip—his tracer rounds flying high into the air. Crunk and Boy Band both turned on him and cut him in half. The other three ran to the left, looking for cover—but we had picked this spot specifically because it lacked such cover. Running around they drew our attention, and all our fire. They stumbled to the ground individually, and all were killed within a minute.

The men in the second vehicle all jumped out, took prone or kneeling positions, and brought a steady rate of fire on our position. Two bullets slammed into my windshield directly in front of my face, and that completely enraged me. I leapt out of the vehicle, threw the door forward to use as a shield, and fired directly at the muzzle blasts coming in my direction. Two bullets bounced off the door. The more they fired the angrier I became—This is our victory, I thought. You're just here to die.

They didn't see it that way. An RPG round streaked at us, rising slightly higher as it roared forward, and I remember wondering if it would lift above the vehicle before it made contact or if it would slam into us. It was like a math problem I wanted to solve before the answer killed me, but when the missile screamed past us by a hair, the blast of the propellant knocked me down. Lying in the prone position, I continued to fire at every muzzle blast I saw. Just then a machine gun opened up 50 meters to my front. Looking through my NVGs, I could see two men also lying prone, one firing a PKN, the other feeding him the linked rounds. They were walking their fire right toward me, and I realized that I had been picked out to kill. The bullets began to turn up the ground around me. I felt surprisingly calm as I watched the tracer rounds hitting all around me. I put the infrared point of light on the gunner's elongated torso, took a breath and slowly squeezed the trigger. The gunner jerked back slightly, raised his head as if confused, and I put the light on his open mouth and squeezed the trigger a second time. He tumbled back dead. I shifted immediately to the assistant gunner. For a moment he stared down at the gunner with shocked amazement, but in an instant he leaped up and began running away. I brought my point of light onto his back, but could not keep it on him as he ran away in panic. Still, I had a good idea of where he was. I took a shot and saw the outline of a figure spin around and fall to the ground, but just as quickly he was up again and running. I put the point of light on where I thought he was, and fired again. I could just barely see a figure fall down.

Knowing I had killed the machine gunner, and likely the assistant gunner, I turned over on my back and began to breathe excitedly. "I won," I said out loud, "I won." I covered my face with my hands and forced myself to re-breathe my exhale. I am alive! I thought, I am still among the living! I lay there on the ground in the middle of this gunfight reveling in my existence. Then I heard two rounds bounce off the vehicle, and saw Crunk swing the big .50 over my head, as he began to thump some enemy position.

I was embarrassed—here I was, in the midst of a fight, thinking of myself. I spun back over, grabbed my weapon and searched for a target. The fighting had greatly diminished, and only sporadic gunfire continued to come from two separate positions. The AMF began shouting out to the isolated survivors in a manner that was alternatively inviting and taunting.

The Chief and Captain McMann were standing behind the open door of the captain's vehicle when Amu came running up to them. "My good sirs," he said excitedly, "there are only two rebels left, we have made offer of quarter, but they have not given us answer."

"Then kill them both," said the captain. "They've been given terms and have not responded. . . Wait," he continued, "give them an ultimatum first. They have two minutes to surrender. Tell them that."

Amu ran forward and shouted out something in Pashtu. It may have been the two-minute warning the captain required, it may have been a cruel taunt—who could tell. But both men responded with a grunting understanding.

The night went silent, and I flipped up my NVGs, trying to get a better perspective of the look of the battle space. All I saw was the consuming darkness. Forward of our position I knew was nothing but dead bodies and the last remains of a doomed ragtag force—but overwhelming all that was the incredible enormity of the darkness. I flipped down my NVGs and got into the driver's seat—Pot Roast's still-wet blood soaked through.

"Roll forward online," Captain McCann said, and the other vehicles spread out and came parallel with me.

We rolled forward slowly with our NVGs on, knowing where they were, and them not exactly sure where we were. It wasn't fair, but who would want it to be? A shot was fired at us from behind a small berm to our right. I could see a rifle barrel protruding up above the beaten down grass. Crunk turned his .50 on it, and I saw a pair of feet lift up into the air, then roll lifelessly down the slight decline.

Something was shouted out to us in Pashtu from the brush. "He wants to surrender! He's a pussy and a homosexual," Amu said, spitting on the ground. "And now he wants to surrender?—kill him!" It was nice to know Amu was on our side.

"Tell him to put down his weapon and come out," Captain McMann said.

Amu said something to the fighter, and he rose up from behind a well-fortified position and began walking toward us, rifle in hand.

"I said," Captain McMann continued, "for him to put down his weapon."

Amu shouted for the guy to put down his weapon—even I knew that much Pashtu—but he seemed not to acknowledge it.

"Put down the weapon!" commanded the captain, and Amu shouted the same again in Pashtu. Still, the fighter, his eyes glassy, continued to approach with an AK-47 in one hand, waving the other with a big grin on his face.

"Drop the weapon!" Captain McMann shouted, "Or we will kill you!"

The fighter seemed to be in a daze as he continued to walk forward. At 15 meters, Captain McMann called into his microphone, "Light'em up!" The entire line opened fire on the lone Talibani, and he disintegrated.

"Boy Band," shouted Dragline, "get the camera. Spooky, have the AMF set up a wide perimeter. Jiggy, Jet Set, get your note pads and start itemizing enemy weapons—Crunk, you stay on the .50. This is a crime scene and we're going to secure the shit out of it." Whether it was a crime scene or not, Dragline was right to immediately establish a chain of evidence. We had killed a lot of people, and we would have to account for that.

Captain McMann and Dragline drove their vehicles into the middle of the perimeter, and Captain McMann called over to the Chief. "Chief," he said, "this is good work. From the planning to the execution you showed real professionalism."

Chief looked at his rifle. "Well, sir," he said, "this ambush was your idea. But we got some bad guys, anyway. I just hope we got our bad guys."

I searched the dead even while I could hear the captain calling in the body count over the radio: "Roger, Alpha One, I count six enemy KIA in or around the two vehicles."

"That's a good copy, Delta Two. Carry on," came the indifferent reply.

"Alpha One, I've got two enemy KIA 20 meters to the north of the vehicles."

"I read you Lima Charlie," came the now more interested response.

"Alpha One, I count three dead in a wide quadrant 30 meters west of the vehicles—how copy?"

"I copy three dead 30 meters west of the vehicles," came the now excited response of another voice—probably the Battle Captain of the night shift. "Delta Two," he continued, "are there no enemy wounded?"

"Negative," the captain replied, ".50 cals are funny like that."

We had eleven confirmed dead, and we hadn't lost a soldier. Adrenaline pumped through the entire unit. The AMF, positioned out on the perimeter, began a song of triumphant and mocking defiance.

"They're giving away our position," I said to the captain.

"Jet Set," he replied, "don't you think the three to five thousand rounds we just shot might have already done that? This is a victory, drink it up."

Jiggy was over by the first car in the ambush, and I saw him looking into the driver's window. "Hey, sir," he said, "you might want to see this." He then turned to the Chief and said, "You called it right, Chief!"

The Chief, Captain McMann and I walked over to the silver Toyota sedan. In the driver's seat slumped a dead man. He wore a red and white checked scarf around his head, and he had on a light brown sweater with diamond patterns. In his hand was a Glock pistol.

"That's our guy," said Jiggy. "That's our guy."

Captain McMann looked through the window at the dead man and said, "Yeah, that's definitely him."

The Chief looked into the cab, delighted. "I just had a feeling we would get him," he said. "I just knew it."

Captain McMann looked at the Chief with admiration. "You did it!" he said. "You did it! You said we'd get this guy, and we did!" Captain McMann wiped the sweat away from his forehead.

"We got him," was all the Chief said in response.

"You did me a damn good turn," Captain McMann said, "and now I'm going to do you a damned bad one. I'm putting you in for a Distinguished Service Cross!"

Chief went suddenly flush. "Oh no, sir," he said, "Crunk and Boy Band did most of the work."

"They almost had us back in the village," Captain McMann said. "We were this close to getting wiped out, but thank God you stepped out of that vehicle and neutralized their assault. You survived an RPG attack, and without your input I would never have figured out that these were the guys laying all these IEDs so far from their homes. Whether you want it or not, you're getting a DSC."

FOR VALOR

"Move the machine gun, I'm trying to vacuum," said Boy Band.

Jiggy was sitting on his cot, using a wire brush to scrub the mud off his boots. I was ironing my fatigues, trying to put a sharp crease into the trousers. The radio droned on softly in the background. The Dixie Chicks were singing Landslide exactly the way Stevie Nicks had done it more than a quarter century before.

"I feel like a private again," I said with a laugh.

Jiggy grinned and nodded his head. "Some of the best times in my life, no responsibilities, no pressures—just a 19 year old kid with money and a car." I went back to my ironing, and Jiggy went back to brushing his boots. I sprinkled some more starch-water on my trousers and worked on that crease. Today would be nothing but drill and ceremony—Battalion Day—medals were to be awarded.

Boy Band put down the vacuum and walked over to Crunk, slapping him on the back with a camaraderie the two usually kept concealed, and said, "I want to see the look on the command sergeant major's face when they pin that Bronze Star on you—"

"With 'V' Device!" Jiggy and I interrupted in unison (the "V" stands for valor).

"And I want to see the battalion commander's face," continued Crunk, "when they pin that Silver Star onto the Chief."

We all snorted cynically. Captain McMann had put in the Chief for a Distinguished Service Cross—the second highest medal for valor in the military—and Crunk had been put in for a Silver Star. The company commander endorsed the submission, but the battalion commander—without bothering to make an inquiry—had reduced the award to a Silver Star for Chief and a Bronze Star for Crunk. When the news came down to the team that the battalion commander had reduced the awards, Captain McMann was incensed, and he resubmitted the awards, claiming additional information. This he did against the expressed request of the Chief and with the strong misgivings of the company commander. When the BC saw the new requests, he lost his mind.

Spooky was in the TOC the morning the whole thing erupted. "So then the BC stands up in front of the entire TOC and tells everyone in the place that Captain McMann was disloyal," Spooky told us, "and that he should have expected such unprofessionalism from National Guard soldiers."

"No shit?" exclaimed Boy Band.

"Well," continued Spooky, "the captain wasn't about to take that crap. He jumped up and said to the BC, 'Sir, it is because of my duty, and because of my loyalty to my men, that I resubmitted those awards.' And then," Spooky continued, "the captain took it over the edge. He said, 'Loyalty, sir, goes both up and down the chain of command. And loyalty, sir, would best be exemplified by making an inquiry into the facts of the action before belittling the gallantry and valor of the men whose courage shone through during that action.'"

"What happened next?" I asked.

"The BC demanded a court martial of Captain McMann," Spooky said.

"No shit?"

"No shit," replied Spooky. "And it was all the company commander could do to keep Captain McMann from resigning his commission."

"No shit?"

"No shit."

But that was some weeks ago, and things seemed to have settled since then. So much so that the other officers in the company started calling Captain McMann 'Demi'. They came up with this name from a scene in the movie, A Few Good Men, where Demi Moore stood up in court and said, "Your honor, I object!" And the judge overruled her objection, and so she said, "But I strenuously object!" Because that's a thing.

For a short time, Captain McMann was called 'Strenuous Objection' McMann, but that quickly morphed into 'GI Jane,' and, ultimately, into just plain 'Demi.'

"Battalion!" shouted the command sergeant major, giving the preparatory command. "Atten—tion!"

The battalion moved with proud precision from parade rest to the position of attention. It was the first time the battalion had held a formation since Delta Company had become attached—a slight that had not gone unnoticed within the company.

The battalion commander took the sergeant major's place at the head of the formation, the command sergeant major standing to his left. "It is an honor," began the BC, beaming with pride, "to be—uh . . . honoring you men today." He wasn't the greatest public speaker, but he was trying. "Today, it is my privilege to award the Silver Star to Chief Warrant Officer Brad Freman for his acts of heroism and intrepidity in the actions of 23-24 June, 2002. Additionally, it is both a privilege and an honor to be able to award Sergeant First Class Clinton Stitch the Bronze Star for valor for his actions during that same engagement." The entire battalion erupted in cheering, and I was beginning to think our company's feelings of exclusion were overblown. "Lastly," the BC continued, "today is a special day in the gallant history of 2nd Battalion, 3rd Special Forces Group, because today each of you will be awarded the Combat Infantryman's Badge— an honor reserved only for Infantrymen and Special Forces soldiers who close with the enemy." This time the cheering was louder and more thunderous, especially from me, because this was the day I was being awarded the Combat Infantryman's Badge.

The BC called for the Chief and Crunk to 'post', and they each stepped backward from their rank, made a left-facing movement, and double-timed to the left of the formation. They faced the front, presented themselves to the commander, came to attention and saluted. The BC received their salutes, and put them at ease. He then grew a little casual and began to speak in a more relaxed manner, "Before these orders are read," he said, "I want to say a little something about Delta Company." The BC looked down and kicked some imaginary dust off his boots. "There is in Delta Company a fierce loyalty among the men. It is a quality I had not expected from National Guard soldiers. It begins with the officers, and echoes through right down the line." The BC looked over at Captain McMann, and gave him a slight nod, which was noticed by all of us. "I don't think the battalion has properly welcomed Delta Company into our family—I'll take the heat-round on that." The BC began to slowly pace across the width of the formation, reflecting on his words. "I'd like this ceremony to be our belated welcome to Delta. They are good men," he said, looking up at the other companies. "In many ways they have more to teach us than we have to teach them. For example, I mentioned that today I have the privilege to award you all the CIB—but that is not exactly correct. Two men from our battalion have already been awarded the CIB. Today they will be honored with their second award of this prestigious badge." The BC paused. "Both of these men are in Delta Company."

Cheering and clapping came from the battalion. I looked over to Spooky, and then to the sergeant major. They were both looking down, slightly smiling. They were the only two men in the battalion who would be receiving their second award.

After pinning the medals to the two men, the BC asked them to say a few words. Crunk looked down shyly and said, "This is a great honor, sir, a great honor."

He asked the Chief to say something, and he didn't want to, either. But the BC wasn't going to let them go. "Chief," he said, "this is a big event, Stars and Stripes is here. I'm not going to order you, but I'd like you to say something."

The Chief nodded his head, stepped forward, looked up at us and said, "I never felt at home before I came to the Army. I never felt like I belonged. Things I thought were important in life, nobody else thought were important in life. Things I could do well, nobody else much cared about." Chief looked down at his boots. "But when I came to the Army, things made a lot more sense. I was a good soldier and I moved up—that only makes sense. I was encouraged to try out for the Special Forces—and that made sense, too. I finished close to the top of my class in the Q, so I was encouraged to take on greater responsibility. And now we're at war, we're told to kill the enemy, so we think about how best to do that—and we execute. That only seems reasonable, right?"

Chief paused, then looked the entire battalion up and down. "And now I receive an award from my comrades-in-arms for my actions. And that seems strange to me, because I'm just glad to be among people who believe in the same things that I do. Who care about things like honor, and valor, and duty." Chief wiped something out of his eye. "It isn't the fact that I was awarded this medal that makes me happy. It's the fact that I belong to an organization that has such awards, that counts these things as valuable." Chief lifted up his set of orders. "I have an official Army document that has the words written on it, 'for valor.' And all I can say is that I'm proud to belong to an organization that weights and measures and esteems such things. Who am I? I'm just a soldier, but I have in my hands and on my chest proof that this country cares about things like duty, honor and country. I have proof that this country cares about itself, and about the people who protect it."

THE NEAR OCCASION OF SIN

"The Body of Christ."

"Amen."

"The Body of Christ."

"Amen."

"The Body of Christ."

"Amen."

As I made my way down the communion line, Father McFarland's brogue became more distinct. In his liturgical vestment for the Feast of the Assumption, he held the cup of hosts before the communicants. "The Body of Christ, Timothy," said Father McFarland, a smile of satisfaction on his face, which turned immediately into a frown when he saw Captain Paloma behind me. When Mass was let out and Linda and I began to file out of the tent, Father McFarland tapped me on the shoulder. "Can I have a word with ya, boyo?" he asked. Then, nodding over to Linda, he said, "Linda, me luhv, Timothy and I will leave you to your duties."

"Yes, Major McFarland," said Linda.

"Walk with me, Tim," Father McFarland said, moving back up to the altar, where the chaplain's assistant was blowing out the candles and putting away the Cruets. "Linda, she's a nice girl, don't ya think?" he asked.

"Captain Paloma? Yes, she is," I said, knowing where this was heading.

"You spend a lot of time with her?"

"She's helping me put my JAG packet together," I said.

"Is she now?" said Father McFarland, raising his eyes ironically. "Because, what I see is a male sergeant spending an inordinate amount of time with a female captain."

"Our relationship is"— I hunted for the word, "chaste," I said at last.

Father McFarland laughed, "Tim," he said, "you make that sound like an accomplishment." That hit home. Who is this man, I thought, who intrudes on my inner-most thoughts? Father McFarland looked over at me as if he knew what I was thinking. "I am your priest and your confessor," he said. "Tell me, Timothy, are ya savin' room for the

233

Holy Ghost?"

I decided to hit the note of indignation: "You are my confessor," I said, with, uh . . . indignation. "And you just administered to me the Blessed Sacrament. Are you now accusing me of compounding one mortal sin upon another?"

Father McFarland laughed. "Where there's smoke there's fire, boyo. Wouldn't I be remiss if I didn't send up a warning?"

The guy was running circles around me. "I respect Lin—Captain Paloma—and would do nothing to hurt her."

"Hurt?" he replied, with actual indignation. "It would ruin her." Father McFarland looked across the room, making sure we were alone. "Tim," he said, "she's a darlin' girl. But if the two of you slipped, it would be more than a sin, it would be a blunder." Father McFarland leaned into me. "She's got a good future in the Air Force, and you're setting her up for court martial." He straightened up in his chair and said, "And you might as well throw your JAG packet out the window."

"We will be careful, Father."

"Tim," he said, "The Act of Contrition is three sentences. Repeat for me the second sentence."

I sifted through the Act, repeating the second line, "I firmly resolve with the help of Jesus, to sin no more and to avoid the near occasion of sin."

"The near occasion of sin, Tim," he said, "not just sin, but the near occasion of sin."

"I will be more careful," I said.

"See that ya do, Tim, see that ya do."

I began to walk toward the door, feeling a little dejected.

"Where do ya tink, you're goin'?"

"I was gonna go back to the hooch," I said.

"No, ya don't, boyo," said the Father. "Today is Sunday—a day of rest—and you're gonna talk with me a spell." Father McFarland had a sly smile on his face, and he pulled out a handle of Jameson's whiskey. We sat down together in Father McFarland's office.

"You're not going to get in trouble for having contraband—and sharing it with an enlisted soldier, are you?" I said.

"Psst," he replied, "what are they gonna do to me, bend me dog tags, and send me to Fort Bragg?"

"That's the oldest joke in the Army," I said.

"Well, I'm in the Army, in a manner of speaking."

"What is your deal?" I asked. "How does an Irish priest get a chaplain's commission in the Army?"

"Oh, I'm American born," Father replied. "Me folks came over in the 50s, after the war, but when I was two years old me da inherited a dry goods store in Limerick."

"A regular Frankie McCourt," I said.

Father McFarland's eyes lit up. "Oh," he said, "I knew the McCourts. Good family. Me brother went to school with Malachy McCourt. Frankie is a good writer, but," Father McFarland paused. "Family honor," he said. "It's a sin to tell such stories just to sell a few books. Besides, a lot of that stuff was made up."

"How do you know?"

"Well," said the Father with a laugh. "Either he made it up, or he had an incredible memory for a three year old." We both laughed out loud. "So what's Brooklyn like these days?" Father said, changing the subject.

"Still there," I replied.

"You know," said Father McFarland, "it was in New York where I took me vows."

"Tell me about it."

"Well, just before me consecration Mass, when we were in the sacristy, his Excellency looks at me and says, 'You're a fine one, ya are. You should become a chaplain in the Armed Forces.'"

"Wait," I said, "you're saying that Cardinal Archbishop O'Connor recruited you into the Army?"

"Himself."

This sounds like BS, I thought. "Doubt it," I said.

"To be sure, it was himself. And I said, 'But I'm with the Dominicans, they'd never release me from me duties.'"

"And what'd he say?"

"'The ting to do is to join the Reserves,' says he. 'And from there ya sort of engineer your way into active duty.'"

"And that worked?" I said.

"Well," said Father McFarland with a snort, "I got me commission, didn't I?"

"What was it like?" I asked.

"The Chaplaincy School? 'Twas a breeze."

"No," I said, "the Mass of your consecration."

"Oh, Tim, it was a wonderful ting," he replied, "and wasn't it me-self who carried the thurible down the nave and onto the altar, incense billowing up, filling all of Saint Patrick's with that magnificent

235

fragrance. Me mother and da in the first row, crying and praying for me." Father McFarland took a big swig of his drink and stood up, deep in the memory of that day. "With the thurible noisily clacking against its chain. And I didn't just flop it around like some of these priests," he used the term contemptuously. "The way they swish it around, like they're shakin' a thermometer. No, boyo, you should have seen me." Father McFarland made a few slow deliberate paces through his office, swinging his right hand back and forth. "I had that thurible scrapin' the floor, Tim, swinging it out at least five feet, and back again another five feet. . . that incense was billowin', Tim, just a-billowin." Father McFarland stopped, his face alight with nostalgic admiration. "You should have seen me that day, Timothy—I was grand, oh, but I was grand."

BLIND HOGS

"Hey, Crunk," said Boy Band, with laughter. "What do you want people to say about you when you're dead?" You never think about death—that's bad juju. The one thing you never do is think about death. But as we sat in some forsaken village somewhere in Afghanistan, Boy Band had asked Crunk about the one thing you never mention.

"Easy, Boy Band, that's bad juju," Dragline said.

"Let's not lose focus," the captain said.

"I don't think about it," Crunk said.

"C'mon," replied Boy Band. "What do you want people to say about you after you're dead?"

"Easy, Boy Band," Dragline said.

"Just sayin'," replied Boy Band. "When I die, I think I want people to say . . . 'Wow, that guy . . . he sure owed me a lot of money.'"

I had hoped Boy Band wouldn't make me laugh. In this heat laughing was almost like work, but I laughed all the same. And, of course, that put Boy Band into a talkative mood. "Hey, Jet Set," he continued, "you still helpin' out that priest down at the chaplain's office?"

"I think he's helping out that JAG captain," Jiggy replied.

"Yeah," said Crunk, "those two are definitely dancing too close."

"Hey," I said, "there is nothing going on between Captain Paloma and me. It's entirely professional. She's just helping me out with my JAG packet."

"Oh," said Boy Band, "so that's what we're calling it now—the 'JAG packet?' I can't keep up with the code words anymore."

"You want to get out of the SF?" Jiggy said, an edge of hostility in his voice.

"I want a commission," I replied. "I want to be a JAG and to move up."

"You could be a sergeant major, and never leave the Special Forces," said Crunk, obviously angry that I would leave the Special Forces.

"You want to leave the SF?" Jiggy said again, with some hostility.

It was Boy Band who eased the tension. "He's not married to the SF the way we are," he said. "Jet Set has options." I looked over at

Boy Band, thinking he was leading up to a joke. But his eyes were fixed on the ground, like he was staring at the very word 'options', realizing what that was. "It must be," he said, "liberating to go from grinding it out as a sergeant, hoping to make, like, master sergeant. And one day you realize there's a path open for you, that you could be a lieutenant colonel or even a full bird colonel. Must feel like when you're in a big game, and you break through the line and see nothing but open field in front of you."

"It is," I said. "It feels exactly like that."

We were sitting in some ville, over-watching, as some white-bearded man appeared at the far end of the village, coming up the road that I had overwatch on. "What's that?" I said.

"What's what?" Jiggy asked. Everyone looked over to see the older man walking slowly up the road smiling to us and waving with his free hand, while in his other hand he carried a tea pot. Directly behind him was what looked like an enormous bundle of sticks, and it seemed to sway from side to side behind the man's back.

"I don't know," I said, "but I don't like it."

"That doesn't look cool," Spooky said. "Let's tighten up this perimeter; Jet Set, put your weapon on him." I drew down on the old man and ran my finger lightly around the trigger well.

The grinning old man and that enormous bundle of sticks kept coming at us, and at about 50 meters I yelled out to him, "*Wodariga!*" He ignored me and continued to walk forward, grinning and waving. "*Laasuna portakra!*" I commanded. "Put your hands up!" I stood up so he could see I was aiming at him, but he just kept coming.

"Do 'em!" said Boy Band.

"Take him out," said Crunk.

I put my finger on the trigger, and began to breathe out, preparing to fire. Just then the man turned to his right, to a door to a house. And I saw that behind him was an old woman, probably his wife, bent beneath the weight of that massive bundle of sticks she was carrying. The old man opened the door and the old woman carried her burden inside. The old man waved to us with his free hand. He couldn't wave with the other, of course, because it had the tea kettle in it. I nervously lowered my weapon. "These people," I said out loud. "I really hate them."

"I like it," Dragline said, coming toward us at an excited pace, the captain and Spooky right along with him.

"Yes," said Captain McMann, "this is the best intel we've received since we got here."

"Saddle'em up!" shouted Dragline. "We got some hot work ahead of us."

We left the village and circled the vehicles up on a military ridge line about three kilometers away. The captain called us all in, and huddled over a map of our area of operation, the southern region of Kandahar Province.

The captain began, "About two weeks ago, the commander of the Afghan National Police Force in Spin Boldak got his head cut off."

We all murmured. "Sir, we're not six klicks away from there right now," I said.

"That's right," Captain McMann replied, pointing at Spin Boldak with a twig, "about six klicks." The captain put down his stick and looked at us. "But we received some very good intel from the CIA that the killer was a Talibani chieftain who lives in this village . . . here." Captain McMann picked up his twig and pointed it at a village with a name I have already forgotten. "The thing is, this guy is, as I said, a chieftain and he has some connections with the Afghan government. Probably has a cousin married to the cousin, or some nonsense like that." Captain McMann stood up and looked around at us.

"Anyway," he continued. "We can't just jack him and carry him away. We're going to need to get evidence, and to do that we're going to need to get inside his house and search it."

"Sir," said Dragline, with unusual earnestness, "we've been dick-dancing around with these villages for a while now, and it never gets us anywhere."

"Team sergeant," said the captain, "this intel is excellent."

"I know, sir . . . I've been in on the same briefings as you. What I'm saying is that I have a plan."

Captain McMann straightened himself, relieved that he was being supported. "What kind of plan?"

"Well, sir," Dragline continued, "we've been coming into these villages, guns at the ready, freaking everybody out, and— surprisingly—no one wants to play with us. Sir, we should play this like we were cops," Dragline said. "You want to shake a guy down— search through his stuff—you don't yell at him and push him around. You low-ball him. Tell him some bullshit about how you pulled him over because you're both Redskin fans or some shit: 'Hey, saw your bumper sticker, we goin' to the Super Bowl this year or what?'" Dragline cocked his head sideways, as if he was just curious. "'Crap!

You know what?'" he continued, "'The desk sergeant just drove by, I need to look busy. Be okay if I just take a peek into your glove compartment?'"

"This works?" Captain McMann said, looking astonished.

"All the time."

Captain McMann was silent for a good minute, processing everything he'd just heard. "So, anyway," he finally said, "back to the plan."

"Well, sir," continued Dragline without skipping a beat, "we have that old tea kettle Amu keeps. I say when we enter the village, we go in low profile. Instead of rolling through into the square, we put the guys in good but less-threatening positions. Then, you, me and Amu walk into the central square with only our side arms. I'll bring the tea kettle, and—you know—wave it around a bunch, and smile and stuff. I'm sure we'll find the chieftain lying about on his mat or whatever, and we just start talking to him. We hang out, we drink some tea, I'll give him the old 'how 'bout those Redskins' bit, and we'll see if we can't get him to invite us into his compound." Dragline looked first at the captain, then at all of us. Triumph was in his eyes. "And once we're in, we can accidentally find whatever it is we need to find to make an arrest."

Captain McMann thought about it for a moment. "But you're not actually going to ask him about the Redskins are you?" he said.

"No, sir," replied the team sergeant, as if speaking with a child. "I figure I'll keep the conversation more . . . mission-oriented."

"Makes sense to me, team sergeant," said Captain McMann. An hour later we were rolling into the village, but we peeled off before we reached the village square. I took up a position against a wall that pointlessly jutted out into the open square for no apparent reason. And this pointless wall had a pointless window in it. And as I squatted against it, doing my 360 degree recon, I looked up and noticed that the header-brace for the 'window' was an automobile crank shaft. There was no reason for the wall, and there was no reason for the 'window' in the wall. But I had to be impressed by the ingenuity of these people who used an old crank shaft as a bracer for the window in the wall that did not make sense in the first place.

Dragline, Captain McMann and Amu walked into the village square, Dragline dramatically waving the tea kettle around. They looked like a traveling minstrel troop, and I figured the people would see right through the ruse—but I was wrong. The people came out in droves.

You cannot imagine how large Afghan families are, children piled up all around them. Then, of course, out came the village elder, and with him his eldest son. The people parted in a wave, and the village elder welcomed Dragline, the captain and Amu forward. Carpets and pillows appeared, and were placed in the shade of the only tree in the square. Dragline was really hamming it up and seemed to be doing a Santa Claus impersonation. He bent down and patted a boy on the side of the head, then—astonishing everyone—found a quarter behind the boy's ear. The crowd swooned with amazement, and the small boy beamed with delight as Dragline gave him the quarter.

Dragline then walked over to the carpets, circled three times around the biggest pillow, then plopped himself down in a noisy huff.

The captain and Amu made the introductions with the elder, his son, and about eight other men. They all wore the Khet Partug, but with turbans. All were bearded and thin, and they appreciated the cigarettes given out by Dragline. All then sat down together and the tea was put on the boil.

I sat at my corner overlooking the square, but at least 100 meters away. Crunk and the vehicle, with its .50 cal machine gun, was on a ridge about 200 meters from me and facing into another funneling street. I didn't like being so far away from the heavy weapons. We were all looking back every few seconds at the tea party in the village square, and making comments on the various people assembled. "Look at that dude," said Boy Band, "the one with the fresh white headdress."

"The dude over there, next to the captain?" Jiggy asked.

"No, the one next to Amu," replied Boy Band. "The one pimpin' that pretty white turban-of-love to all the Chi boys to see." I looked over and noticed the guy next to Amu did have a brilliant white turban, which he wore tight against his eyebrows, with at least 18 inches of extra wrap dangling off the back.

"Yeah," said Jiggy, "he's straight pimpin'."

One of the games we played while sitting around in a village was 'Name That Headdress'. "What would you call that look, Crunk?" asked Boy Band.

"That?" said Crunk, as he paused to contemplate the look. "That's what I'd call a 'Low-Rider with a Popped Trunk'."

"Guy looks Talibani to me," I said.

"Definitely," said Crunk. "Look how cocky he is."

"That guy's Talibani for sure," said Spooky. "But whatcha gonna do? A Talibani guy in the village is like a gay guy at the office—you

241

know what he's about, and he knows you know, and you know that he knows. But you gotta keep up appearances, so all you end up doing is talking about the weather."

The captain, Dragline and Amu spent a long time drinking tea with the village elders. But eventually, they started drifting away, until it was only the Chieftain and his son. Dragline began speaking earnestly with the chief elder, through Amu. Dragline laughed a lot and so did the elder. Two or three times I saw Dragline point to the chief's compound, and the elder smiled and shook his head. Finally, Dragline got up and rotated his hips around and walked a few steps with an exaggerated limp.

"What's he doing?" Jiggy said.

"He's acting like he's injured," Spooky replied. "I think it's on."

The elder also stood up and led Dragline toward his compound.

"Yeah, it's on," said Spooky.

Dragline stumbled a bit, and Captain McMann and Amu ran over and steadied him, letting him lean on them as they assisted him into the compound.

Twenty minutes later we heard the captain over the radio. "One at a time, pull into the compound. No one pulls in until the other is established outside the compound walls—and be real cool about it."

Spooky moved first, waving and smiling and moving back, setting up in a good oversight position right alongside the compound walls. "Boy Band, you're next," he said. "Just act like there's nothing to see here."

Boy Band moved his vehicle back, establishing himself at a nice intersection 20 meters from the compound. "Jiggy," Spooky said, "fall back." Jiggy lowered his weapon and meandered his way back to just outside the compound. "Now you, Jet Set," Spooky said, "nice and slow." I stood up, made a display of shaking the dust off my uniform, and casually walked back to a partially concealed position 25 meters from the compound door, the whole time whispering to myself in an Irish accent, "Nuttin' tah see here, folks. Nuttin' tah see here."

"Crunk," said Spooky, "put her in reverse and slide her back this way." Crunk slid the vehicle backward, and I could see his M-4 sticking out of the side of his Humvee.

"One at a time," said Captain McMann. "Come inside and look at the evidence. Then go back to your stations."

When it was my turn to peel-off, I came into the main building and, as always, was completely blind from leaving the brilliant light into the darkened room. Once my eyes adjusted, I saw Amu holding a large scroll of butcher block paper. It had beautifully written Arabic letters on it, embossed on both sides by hand-painted AK-47s.

"It's a Taliban graduation certificate," said Dragline. "Dumb ass had it hanging over his fireplace."

"Anyway," Captain McMann continued, "when we saw it we felt it gave us probable cause—"

"Which we didn't need," Dragline interjected.

"To search his possessions," continued Captain McMann, looking sharply at Dragline. "And we found this." Captain McMann held up what looked like a ledger.

"It's a set of orders," Amu said, "and it is ordering him to kill the police chief of Spin Boldak."

"Who got his head cut off two weeks ago," I said, finishing the thought.

"Exactly," said the captain. "So, we're going to take both him and his son in."

"The orders are actually written to both him and his son," Amu volunteered.

Dragline nodded his head to the corner of the room, where the village elder and his son were squatting silently, duct tape wrapped around their eyes and mouths, and zip-ties binding their hands. Then over to the kitchen area, where four women were in that transition zone between crying and screaming. "Speak very calmly," said Dragline, "these bitches is gettin' truculent."

Truculent, I thought, I always liked that word.

When we got the two men out of the compound and into the vehicle, we raced out of town—no security, no order of march, we just hauled ass. About two klicks out, we pulled a perimeter, checked out our High Value Targets and congratulated ourselves on the victory. Dragline was beaming with delight, and imitating himself, oafishly sitting down, and pretending to have an injured leg. "I ought to win a damn Oscar for that!" he exclaimed.

"You were brilliant," agreed the captain.

Dragline grew more serious. "But it does prove one thing," he said to the captain. "After all our running around out here just bothering people and racing into towns, getting these guys proves one thing."

"What's that?" said the captain.

"Even a blind hog finds a chestnut now and again."

THE QUICK AND THE DEAD

"Toe-Poppers, right?" Boy Band said. "That's what you got to worry about when you're sweepin' for mines. They'll take your lower leg off, and the mission stalls because it takes four of us to medivac your ass out."

"Jesus, Boy Band," I said. "Do you mind?"

"Oh, I'm sorry," said Boy Band. "Italian Toe-Poppers. What are they, like, a Tupperware cup of C-4, a plastic lid and a little wooden plunging device. Only thing metal on them is the blasting cap. Almost undetectable with a mine sweeper."

"Stop!" I shouted. "I can't concentrate with his ass talkin' shit!"

"Cut it out, Boy Band," said Dragline, "bad juju to talk like that."

"Boy Band," said Spooky, "you're gettin' reckless. You been askin' the gods to notice you for the last two patrols. You know what they say, 'the nail that's sticking up gets hammered down'."

"I can't help it," said Boy Band. "I been having dreams."

"What kind of dreams?" said the captain.

"I don't know. I guess they're bad dreams, but they don't seem all that bad." Boy Band stared down at his rifle. "It's like real silent, you know, real, real silent. Like when you're a kid at the pool, and everybody's screaming and running around, and you jump into the deep end and suddenly it's all gone. All that noise, all that commotion vanishes, and it's just . . . silent. But you kind of like it."

Dragline stared at Boy Band for a moment, his eyes almost sympathetic. Then he spit tobacco juice on the ground. "You stay focused, Jet Set," he said. "We have to clear a path to the cache before dark." We were in the middle of nowhere—the entire team in line behind me, as I cleared a small pass toward the jumble of mortar, artillery and RPG rounds strewn across the bed of some nondescript wadi. Two days earlier, the captain had been handed an aerial photograph, given a grid coordinate and a mission—we were to blow up a weapons cache that had miraculously appeared directly beneath the flight path of the daily mail chopper. I was the engineer sergeant, so I would take the lead.

"I don't like this shit, sir," I had said when this mission came down. "How is it that the every-day mail runner flies this route, um, every day, and then—OMG—one day there's this enormous stockpile of high explosives just sitting out in the open directly under its route?"

"Yeah, it's hinky," he agreed, "but look at what they got lying around—count the RPG rounds." I counted. There were at least 90. "You know as well as I do," continued the captain, "that every swingin' Richard in the Stan has a rocket launcher, but none of them have rounds for it." He was right, RPG rounds in the Stan were like cigarettes in jail. "Look at that cache," he continued. "Do you know how many wives a haji could buy with that many RPG rounds?"

I knew the captain was right on an intellectual level—but I would be the one blowing it up, and I would be the one cutting a path to that cache, so, on a gut level, I didn't like it. But here I was, 48 hours later, testing the ground with my mine sweeper, laying out engineer tape, and gingerly placing one foot in front of the other.

We got to the weapons cache about 6:00 p.m., and I scoured it looking for possible booby traps. It was clean. And upon examining the ammo dump, I came to understand why it had all of the sudden been revealed—and as I examined it, I could see inside the mind of the man who placed it here. The cache had been stored in a hollowed out section of the wadi, where the seasonal rains had cut away underneath the bank, but not collapsed the surface. The ammunition was stacked up inside this cavernous area, but instead of covering it up, or collapsing the wadi bank on top of the ammunition, the architect of this goat-screw had simply piled up a wall of rocks concealing it—like a wall of rocks, holing up the side of a dried river bank in the middle of nowhere, wouldn't invite curiosity. It was clear that something shook the stacked ammunition loose—maybe the helicopter running down the wadi—and it finally collapsed against the wall, spilling out into the wadi.

"Geez," I said, "these freakin' people."

"What do you mean?" said Spooky with a smile, wanting to hear me say what he already knew I would say.

"First off," I said, "it's a frickin' wadi—it was made by the river that runs through here when it rains. What does this guy think? That it will never rain in Afghanistan again? Secondly, instead of burying and hiding the cache, this guy just put rocks around it, like, 'whatever ya do, don't look behind that wall of rocks that's sitting out here in the middle of nowhere for no reason.' And lastly . . . well, what the hell, there is no lastly. Lastly is firstly and secondly combined into one gigantic what-the-hell!"

Spooky laughed. "Oh, so you've never done anything half-ass in your life?"

"Have I ever taken 2,000 rounds of high explosives and walled them up along a dried river bank? No, I can say without equivocation that I have not done that."

"Well," replied Spooky, "let me give you a scenario, and tell me if it hits closer to home." Spooky started unrolling the det cord and unpacking the C-4 from its crate. "You're the village elder, and you've had this stack of ammunition in the compound since the Russians were here. Look at this mortar round, those are Czech markings aren't they?" He was right. The mortar rounds were Czech.

"Yeah," I said, "the mortar rounds are Czech, the RPGs are Chi-Com, and the tank rounds are actually Austrian."

"So one day the village elder's seventh son by his third wife says he wants to get married. And now the elder needs to build a new hooch in his compound. 'I got to get this crap out of my compound,' he says. He looks around to figure out who is the lowest man on the totem pole, and he sees his youngest son's youngest son, Raza-with-the-lazy-eye. 'Raza,' he says, 'take this large and very heavy pile of crap out into the wilderness and bury it somewhere we can get to later.' Raza-with-the-lazy-eye starts hauling this stuff out of the compound, and nobody's helping him. He goes about a mile and a half down the wadi and says, 'Screw this,' and stashes it right here." Spooky looked at me with dismissiveness. "And now Raza-with-the-lazy-eye has to explain himself to you, because you've never done a half-ass thing in your life?"

I started to reply, but suddenly realized how incredibly important and meaningful my duties were. "I don't have time for this conversation," I said, "because—you know—my work is too important, and stuff."

The ammunition wired to explode, we pulled back about 1,200 meters, me walking backward the entire way, unrolling the nonel across the vast, flat, empty expanse of the Helmand valley. At approximately that distance, we found a small berm to park the vehicles behind and to stand upon to view the tiny spot that was our demolition point. "We far enough back, ya think?" asked the captain.

"Yes, sir," I replied. "We're totally safe."

"Crunk, radio this in," said the captain. "I'll sweep the area one more time with the binos." Crunk called in the imminent explosion and Captain McMann viewed the site with his binoculars one last time. Lowering the binos from his eyes, he looked at me and said, "Call it."

Dusk was settling in on the vast valley floor, as I shouted out, "Fire in the hole! Fire in the hole! Fire in the hole!" and mashed the firing device. A thin streak of fire raced across the valley floor like a tiny bolt of lightning, then an enormous, silent eruption rose up from the site as a great ball of brown dirt, black smoke and brilliant fire ascended upward—followed a moment later by the deep rumbling, cracking sound of the explosion. A low 'aww' rose up from the team, first from the sight, then from the sound of the demolition. We watched first one then multiple RPG rounds rise up from the fireball, zig-zagging across the sky like crazed fireflies.

Then a single RPG let loose upwards in a wide arch, aimed directly toward us. "Um . . . Jet Set," said the team sergeant, "you're sure we're safe, right?"

"Completely," I said, although the round was definitely coming our way with no sign of stopping.

"Sure, sure?" said Boy Band.

"Yes, we're way beyond range." I knew I was right . . . but that thing kept coming.

"Well," said the captain, "we should at least get off this berm."

"Sir," I said, my eyes glued on the RPG arching ever closer, "it can't get even near us."

"Well," said the captain, "it's not that I don't believe you, it's just that—" At that exact moment the RPG began to sputter. Losing its trail of fire, it spiraled to the ground, exploding on impact about 100 meters away. No one said a word for the longest time. Then Boy Band said what we were all thinking: "That was awesome."

It was now night. I combed the demo-site using my Surefire light to make sure everything was expended, then we policed up the exploded det cord and the nonel, and drove out to an isolated spot a few klicks away from the demo site, pulled a perimeter and posted guards. After getting some chow, we bedded down.

"Stand To! Stand To! Stand To!" Dragline said, shaking us up. I was already awake, but the early morning shaking still irritated me. I stood up, cleared my weapon, put a new round in the chamber and faced out, searching for a possible enemy. It was no less dark that it had been when I went to sleep, but in the east the dirty light of dawn was beginning to appear. I'm not a big fan of dawn. People always make the dawn sound like it's breathtakingly beautiful and profoundly original, but when you have to live out in the elements, you lose interest. When you see a lot of dawns, you realize that the earth wakes up much the way you do.

We had a team meeting after Stand To. "Listen up," said the captain, "we got a FRAGO. We're going into Lashkar Gah, on a direct action mission. I expect it to get hairy."

"What can we expect?" said Crunk, looking down, as if disinterested.

"Not terrible," Captain McMann said. "Lots of activity, but no reports of artillery."

"Mortars?" Jiggy asked.

"Sixty millimeter, maybe some eighty-ones, but no one-twenties."

"Machine guns?"

"Dushkas," the captain replied coldly, as a low moan let out from the team. "At least two." The DShK, Dushka—the word means 'little darling'—was the Russian made heavy machine gun, similar to our .50 cal. If their Dushkas were already emplaced and had proper range cards, we wouldn't have a chance. We'd get mauled. "If those Dushkas are sandbaggd in, they're going to be some mean sons-of-a-bitches," Boy Band said, kicking the toe of his boot into the ground. "I don't like it."

"You ain't got to like it," said Dragline, "you just gotta do it."

"Oh, I'll do it," replied Boy Band, "but that doesn't mean I gotta like it."

"Anyway," continued Captain McMann, "there are definitely about 20 to 30 Taliban in two villages outside Lashkar Gah, and we're going to smoke 'em out. Spooky is making the sand table now. He'll give y'all the full intel briefing at 0900." Captain McMann had slipped into a familiar tone with us, and we all noticed—he was scared.

An uneasy silence came over us. At last Dragline broke the awkward quiet. "We don't know the value of this intel. The Taliban may be long gone by the time we get there." We looked at the captain, expecting to see him concur with Dragline, but his face remained blank.

At 9:00 a.m. we filed into the tent Spooky had constructed with a couple of ponchos and some bungee cord. Hanging from the bungee cord were photographs of the villages and the area around them that must have been faxed to the captain during the night. In the short time since Stand To, Spooky had built a remarkable sand table. It showed the Helmand River, the mountains surrounding the valley and, with great specificity, the two villages where we could expect to find our targets. The first village was on the south side of the river, a river that was only about 30 feet across and ankle deep this time of year. Spooky's sand table showed the villages as small, walled-encased affairs, with the usual fields of poppy, grain and marijuana surrounding them. The plan was to take the first village by storm —roll in hot, establish a perimeter, and hopefully kill or capture all the Taliban. It was not the most impressive of plans. If the Taliban were not in the first village—or if they fell back into the next village—our surprise would be blown, but the mission would continue, and we would just drive on into the next village, 300 meters away and across the small river.

"That's the plan?" Crunk said. "Just roll on in, guns blazing, hoping we catch 'em? And if we don't, we just keep rolling into the next village—Dushkas and fuckin' mortars lighting us up all around? That's some plan!"

"There should be air support," Dragline said hesitantly.

"Should be?" Jiggy replied.

"We got gunships from the 2/24th laid-on in support of our attack," Dragline said defensively.

"Yeah," I said, "and what level of priority are we?"

"We have ourselves and we have our training," said the captain. "And whatever else happens," he continued, "we will take these towns." We all fell silent.

"It just feels hinky," said Boy Band. "It just feels like we're biting off more than we can chew."

"We are the available asset, and this is our mission," the captain replied.

"Yes, sir," said Boy Band, nodding his head in resolute agreement. "It is our mission and we will accomplish it." He then bobbed his head up and down. "We'll need to rehearse," he continued, speaking to no one in particular. "We really are going to need to rehearse our movements . . . " His voice trailed off, and he looked a little bit lost.

We did about two hours of rehearsing various scenarios. Then we drove six klicks down the wadi, the long, flat and dusty landscape spread out on either side. On the bleak horizon I saw the outline of a small dirty village—the low walls, with the brilliant, vibrant greenery rising up from the deadened earth surrounding it. Just then the captain ordered us to pull behind a slight rise. We formed a tight 360 perimeter, and Dragline came over the radio telling us all to 'suit-up'. I pulled on my armor vest and my helmet, as did the others, and soon Dragline came to inspect us. He was unusually quiet, and not a little pissed-off: "Button your chin-strap, Crunk—and get your head out of your ass! Jet Set, you better keep your mouth shut and your shit wired tight!"

When the inspection was complete, I got back behind the wheel of my vehicle, took out my wallet, and pulled out my holy cards. Laying them in front of me, I looked at my cards of the Blessed Virgin Mary, Saint Joseph, and Saint Michael. I picked up Saint Michael's card and read the prayer on the back. In a whisper I said, "St. Michael the Archangel, defend us in battle. Be our defense against the wickedness and snares of the Devil. May God rebuke him, we humbly pray, . . ." Having completed my prayer, I picked up the holy cards and tried to put them back into my wallet, but my hands were shaking too much. I looked over at Spooky, who was conspicuously looking the other way, then up at Crunk, who turned his head as soon as I looked at him. I tried to put the cards back into my wallet, but it became the most difficult task in the world, and almost impossible to put my wallet into my back pocket. Finally, I just stuffed the wallet down the front of my shirt.

"Move out!" Dragline shouted from his vehicle idling to our right. And when the others were looking away from me, I made the sign of the cross, and punched the accelerator. We drove up hard onto the first village, but a warning shot went up while we were still 300 meters outside the wall.

"That's not good," said Jiggy over the radio.

"Radio silence!" shouted Dragline.

The village was about 30 meters away from the wadi, and I hit the dried river bed hard, jarring Crunk in the cupola—"Damn it, Jet Set!" Fuck-it, I didn't care, we were getting into the village, like, right now!

I barreled through the front gate, and straight down the road—lined and created by the mud houses built up alongside it. A door flew open directly at my ten o'clock, and I saw the barrel of an AK 47 stick out as I drove by it, not two feet away from my head. I heard shots behind me, but knew the man had hit nothing. "Dragline, one of them fuckers is in the doorway I just passed. Can you get a gun on 'em?"

"Rog," said Dragline, and I heard his 240 Bravo opening up behind me. If that guy ain't dead, I thought, he's shitting all over himself.

"We got more open doors coming up," said Spooky. I reached down with my right hand and pulled out my 9mm, just as some dude stepped halfway out of the next doorway, pulling back the charger on his AK. As I drove past him, he looked at me, and I fired two rounds into his chest. His eyes went from that sinister squint, so common among Afghanis, into a wide-eyed look of awe and surprise—almost like he was impressed.

"Good shot!" said Spooky. "Damn good shot."

We got into the center of the ville, and this time no one was around. "To our direct Front!" shouted Crunk, and I looked up and saw about five guys running through the back gate, trying to get out of town. Crunk opened up the .50 on them, but I don't think he hit anyone. I hit the accelerator and we lurched forward, but just then Captain McMann shouted, "Rally! Rally! Rally!"

"But, sir," I shouted into the radio, "we got 'em runnin'!"

"I'm not gonna walk into an ambush!" Captain McMann replied icily. "Pull a 360 right here and we will assess."

I pulled the vehicle around and we established a perimeter. "'But, sir, we got 'em runnin'," mimicked Spooky. "Who are you, Johnny Reb?"

"First thing we gotta do is clear this ville," said the captain. "Jiggy, Jet Set and Boy Band, patrol the hell out of this place. Anyone messes with you, zip tie 'em—leave the women and children, but screw with every man in this village." The village was small, no more than 500 people. We found a noticeable lack of military aged men.

"Ain't nothin' here, sir," Jiggy reported. "They all got to be dug-in up at the next ville."

The village was secured. Jiggy and I went back and found the two men we'd shot on our way in. The first guy was hit with Jiggy's 240 Bravo. He was gone. But the guy I shot in the chest was still breathing. I looked at him. He looked like your average nondescript Afghani—skinny, wearing man-pajamas and a beard. Looked to be about 40, but was probably closer to 30. I felt like I should have felt something, but I didn't. When he saw me, he looked away embarrassed. That didn't surprise me. He wasn't going to make it, and he knew it, but he was still among the living, and so it embarrassed him that I had won. Jiggy put two pressure bandages around his chest, sealed both sides (front and back) with plastic wrap, and turned him on his side. "Need ya back," said the captain over the radio. "Gonna need every rifle we can muster to take that next village."

"Sir," replied Jiggy, "I've got a downed man."

"We'll come back for him after we clear that ville."

The captain huddled us up and we walked through the plan very quickly: speed was security; we would come out of the village gate and tear-ass toward the next village, coming on line as we moved through the open ground between the two walled enclosures. "I figure when they see us coming," the captain instructed us, "they'll probably make an effort to close that gate—that's why I want us all on line. I need you

251

two," he was looking at Crunk and Boy Band, "pouring everything you've got on that gate. If they get the gate closed we'll have to blast right through it." The captain spit on the ground and rubbed it in with the heel of his boot. "It's real simple: we breach that gate, then we cut 'em wide open."

"What do you think we should do about them Dushkas, sir?" Spooky asked, in a manner that seemed to say "Let's not forget about them Dushkas, sir."

"Right," replied Captain McMann, "the Dushkas are going to be Crunk and Boy Band's primary objectives. If they open up with Dushkas, you two need to take them out."

"Primary along with the gate . . . which is primary?" Spooky said.

The captain and Dragline glared at Spooky. "The primary objective is to take that village," the captain said through clenched teeth. "Getting to that village is a lesser included task. Breaching that gate is also a lesser included task. Being a Green Beret and having the ability to think on your feet is a given prerequisite for being in this planning circle right now. Do I make myself clear, master sergeant?"

"Yes, sir," replied Spooky, looking down ashamed.

"Good. When we get in, your orders are to tear that place up. I mean, be indiscreet." All eyes turned toward the captain, and he corrected himself. "That does not mean commit war crimes. You all know the rules of engagement; if you violate them, you will be charged—but be aggressive. That's what the Army pays you for."

We formed the vehicles in a column, just inside the outer wall of the ville, but we pretty much knew someone was calling in our position, so we moved as quickly as we could. As soon as we were in order, I punched the gas pedal and we headed out. Just as we did, mortar rounds began screaming in.

There was a well-beaten track running in a meandering line between our position and the front gate of the other village. Speed was everything. If we didn't strike the second village right away, they'd have time to place IEDs on our route, and they'd get their guns in place. As it was, a Dushka opened up on us immediately. Fortunately it hadn't been sighted-in yet, and the rounds were hitting all over. It started kicking up all kinds of rocks and dust all around us. First it came in to our right, then the gunner overcompensated and it started hitting wide to our left—but from there it started to zero in. I looked up at the village gate we were racing toward, and—just as the captain had said—three men were trying to close it.

"Get that Mark 19 on the gate!" shouted Dragline.

"Got it," replied Boy Band, and I saw the gate disintegrate into a cloud of gray explosions.

"Kill that Dushka, Crunk!" shouted Captain McMann, and I immediately saw where the Dushka was positioned vaporize into angry brown dust, and the Dushka fell temporarily silent.

There was a low retaining wall made of mud brick about 70 meters outside the village, and as we closed in on it, the other vehicles fell in line behind me, as I was on the pathway to the village. They had to slow down to do this, but I didn't slow down at all. The gate was a sheet metal and soldered iron affair. It was unlocked and the two doors of the gate rested still open about three feet apart from each other. "Get down!" I shouted to Crunk, although he was already ducking, and we hit that gate at 35 miles and hour, smashing the doors apart—the right door coming completely off its moorings. Crunk stood back up in the cupola, and I noticed Spooky was cradling his M-4 across his chest with one hand, the other on the 240 Bravo to his front.

Breaching the gate, I continued deep into the ville, not wanting to cause a pile-up at the entrance—the fatal funnel as it is called. I continued to drive about 70 meters into the ville, Crunk and Spooky searching for targets, and generally firing at the rooftops. Then I pulled the brake and we came to a stop. I turned around expecting to find the rest of the team spaced out behind me, but they were just driving through the open gate, at a very slow speed. Crunk and Spooky must have looked back at the same time.

"This ain't good," Crunk said.

"No es bueno," replied Spooky.

The problem was that we were way in front of the rest of the force— basically alone—and we couldn't back-up because the team would think we were retreating, and might back up as well. That would be a total goat-screw. We had to stay where we were, and pretend this was part of the plan. And, sitting there in the calm before the storm, all I could think to say was, "I meant to do that."

Almost immediately, a door to our direct front burst open and two men swung out half-way into the street with AK-47s firing, one from a kneel, one standing. Crunk spun his weapon around, but it was Spooky who got them, and he did it right. He crawled up into that machine gun, his whole body forward, crouching over it. His cheek was so close to the charging handle you would think the recoil was hitting him. He fired a short 6 to 10 round burst at each man, killing them both.

Just then, a grenade came lofting forward from a rooftop to the right of us.

"Grenade!" we all shouted in unison. The grenade rolled under our vehicle—which would have been a mess if it had exploded—but then it continued to roll around the rear right tire and away from us. It blew up with an enormous clatter, but without injuring anyone. I popped my head up, just to see if I was still alive, and I looked over at Spooky who was popping his head up too. "Fuckin' grenades," he said. Just then another grenade came launching over from the same rooftop area and landed on the hood of the Humvee.

"Grenade!" I ducked down under the dashboard, and looked over toward Spooky, expecting to see him hiding under the dashboard, too. Instead I saw only his legs. I popped my head up slightly, and saw Spooky stretched-out the length of the hood, knocking the grenade onto the ground. The grenade was lodged in the brush guard. To my way of thinking, that was totally cool. The engine block would take the brunt of the explosion, and we could hide behind the metal dashboard. Spooky didn't see it that way.

I thought for sure the top of his head would come off, but a moment later, he pulled himself back into the vehicle, and said, "Make sure we don't roll over it." Just then the grenade went off, directly in front of the vehicle. My ears began to bleed.

"So maybe you guys want to come forward," I said, trying to sound cool, but feeling a small amount of crap leaking onto my underwear.

"We're through," was all Dragline said in reply, and I looked back and saw the rest of the team coming forward. I waited until the first vehicle was 20 meters behind, then I put the vehicle in drive and began to lurch forward.

Knowing that we were now once again an armed column, Crunk opened up with the .50 on the point of the roof where the grenades had come down, and as we passed that point I saw a man emerge from the rooftop with an RPG on his shoulder. Crunk spun his weapon around to try and engage him, but by then Jiggy was already on him with the 240 Bravo. His first rounds hit too low, exploding against the mud wall of the edifice he was standing upon, then a little high, as he tried to adjust fire in the moving vehicle. The guy retreated behind the safety of the mud wall, and we knew we would see him again. I drove another 50 meters, and came to the open area of the village center.

"The Dushka's to the right," Spooky yelled. I looked up to our 2 o'clock and saw a man sitting behind the giant gun, spinning it into place. He opened up on us and it was like a bunch of bombs were exploding all around us. I felt the right front tire give out, and the Humvee listed right, as it kept rolling on the 'run-flat' inner rim. A round hit the front hood where it met the front light, and blew the light off and took a chunk out of the hood. Crunk, Boy Band and Spooky all turned their weapons onto the Dushka, but as we were continuing to move into the center of town, they all missed. It was Jiggy who took out the weapon. He leapt out of his vehicle, ran forward, knelt down and aimed his M-4 at the man who was frantically trying to train that terrible weapon on us, and fired two rounds at the guy, killing him instantly. It was like something you'd see in a movie, and now we owned the center of the village.

We had won, even before we knew it. "Dominate your terrain," was all the captain said. I was looking at him as he spoke, and I saw him look down from his position, and I could see that he thought he was no longer on the mic when he looked over and said, "It looks like we captured this ville easier than expected. . . . It's looking pretty sweet." I grunted my agreement, as did others. Then, directly to our front, about 30 meters from us and 30 meters from the back gate leading out of the village, a door to one mud-built house along the road opened, and I saw the barrel of an AK protrude. All our guns trained on that door . . . and then we watched as five children, no more than seven years old, were pushed out into the street, the door closing tight behind them.

Three of the children were boys and two were girls. The boys were wearing the loose, off-white "man-dresses" of the Afghanis, as well as the "pill-box" hats typical of boys and young men. The girls were wearing the bright, lavender, heavily-embroidered dresses that were the mark of unmarried Afghani girls, along with the elaborate headdresses of their tribe. I remember thinking that the little girls were overly-dressed, like they were on display for a husband when they should have been going to kindergarten. But that moment of insight was quickly lost in the screaming and crying of the children. They ran around frantically for a few moments, then ran back to the door that had just been closed on them, and began pounding their little fists on it. I heard rifle fire, and the children jumped back from the door as the ground around their feet exploded angrily.

Boy Band came over the radio. "They're shooting at 'em!" he said, in a voice of surprise, shock and intense hostility. "They're shooting at their own children!" Boy Band's voice cracked as he spoke.

"Yeah," said Dragline. "They're going to make a break for it, using those kids for cover." Dragline said it so matter-of-factly that I was startled. It was weird, but it wasn't weird. On the one hand, these men were the rulers and the protectors of this village—how could they do this to their own children? But on the other hand they were trapped like rats. They were going to do what people always do when trapped—they were going to prey upon the weak.

The door opened again, and a man came tentatively out, then another man. The children tried to run back inside, but the men pushed them away from the open door. The men were armed with AKs, and they looked at us with that smile that isn't a smile. And then they looked back at the open doorway, signaling to the others.

Seven men came out of the doorway; one of them was the one with the RPG we'd seen earlier on the roof. Another had an RPK, but the others all had AKs. They began walking backward, away from us, dragging the children with them. "Boy Band, Spooky," said Dragline, "get your sniper rifles out."

"Negative," said Captain McMann flatly. "We're not going to shoot 'em with all those kids around. This isn't the movies." The men edged backward, slowly at first, but then more frantically, so that by the time they made it to the gate, they were stumbling and tripping all over themselves.

"They're nervous," said Spooky. "They maybe ain't got the stomach for this kind of operation."

"They don't seem to be losing any sleep about it," said the captain.

The first man opened the gate and was through. Then the second man.

"Sir," replied Spooky, "they know they can't just run out and get away. We'll catch 'em in the open."

"So what are you saying, Spooky?" replied the captain. More men had gotten out the gate, and now there were just two men left.

"They're going to have to cause a diversion—they're going to have to detain us for a bit."

"What do you mean?" said the captain.

"They're gonna kill those kids," said Spooky dryly. Another man got out; now there was only one man left.

"Oh shit," said Captain McMann. It was the only time I ever heard him cuss.

"They're gonna do it!" shouted Boy Band, as he leapt down from his cupola and took off running directly at the gate.

"Richie, no!" shouted Crunk, as he in turn jumped down from his gun position. But Crunk landed hard, and fell sprawled out on the ground. He recovered immediately, but Boy Band had a big lead on him.

Boy Band ran like I'd never seen him run before—running like the young tailback he'd been in high school. The man at the gate reached into his satchel and pulled out a grenade. As he lifted it up, he saw Boy Band racing down upon him, and his eyes grew wide. He grabbed at the grenade pin and yanked at it. The pin did not come out, and the man looked up to see Boy Band closing in fast. He pressed the grenade to his thigh and bent down to pull it again, but again he could not get the pin out. Boy Band was less than 10 meters away now. The man pulled a second time, and I saw the pin and the spoon jettison away. He held the grenade up with both hands, smiling triumphantly, just as Boy Band slammed violently into him, clasping his hands around the Talibani's hands. The two fell down together, gear and equipment clattering loudly around them. The Talibani at first tried to tear himself away, tried to release himself from the grenade. He bucked and he even bridged up high on his back, but Boy Band was like a fury, pressing the grenade down into his chest, as if to say, 'Whatever else happens, you will be killed by this grenade.' The struggle must have been brief, but it didn't feel that way. In the last instant, the Talibani relaxed and looked up at Boy Band smiling, as if to say, 'And so will you.'

Grenades don't explode like in the movies, with fireballs and drama. When a grenade goes off, it's just hell in a very small place. Boy Band's body jumped up a few inches, then it collapsed back down motionless. The Talibani simply crumpled in place, and we knew he was instantly dead by the fact that he seemed to take up less space than he did seconds before. As Crunk arrived all the children began to scatter. "Richie! Richie!" Crunk shouted. I put the vehicle in drive and we all raced to the scene. When we got there, we jumped out of the vehicles and surrounded Boy Band as Crunk cradled him in his arms. Boy Band's armor had stopped any torso wounds, but his neck was completely gone, and blood was pumping into the air, falling onto Crunk's uniform. His jaw was sideways and flapping uselessly, and both his hands were severed at the wrist. He made a futile effort to talk, but then lay back and died.

"Set up a perimeter," Captain McMann said coldly. "Jiggy, go out that gate and kill anything that moves. I don't care if it's a cow, a goat or a UN representative. You kill it." We called the KIA report in to Headquarters. Ten minutes later Spooky came up to me and said, "Go relieve Jiggy. And if you don't see anything in the first three minutes, empty a magazine into something."

"Empty a magazine?" I said. "Why?"

Spooky turned on me with eyes like murder. "Why?" he said. "Because an American soldier died here today. His name was Richard Gennaro, and he served his country with honor." I went out the gate and put my hand on Jiggy's shoulder. "Go back inside," I said. Ten minutes later, I fired off my magazine into a hillside 100 meters away.

"Put him on your vehicle," Dragline said. Jiggy got out a collapsible stretcher and we lifted Richie onto it, then carried him into the back of my vehicle, covering him with a poncho. Crunk got into the back with him and squatted down on one of the rear wheel hubs. There he sat overwatching the body.

"Crunk," said Dragline quietly after a few minutes, "I need you on that .50."

"I can get to it if we need it," said Crunk.

"Crunk," said the captain softly. "The team needs you on that .50. Spooky, get on the MK-19." Crunk tucked the poncho tightly under Richie's head, crawled into the cupola, and I pulled the vehicle around.

We drove back through the village, exactly as we had entered it—completely disregarding a basic rule of movement. Re-entering the first village, Captain McMann said, "Let's check out our enemy KIAs and WIAs." Jiggy and I dismounted, and we went back to the place where we first made contact with the enemy. Both men were gone, which we expected. But at least we could say we looked.

Driving out of the village, I hit the wadi and started to pick up speed ... then more speed ... then more. I just wanted to be back at Kandahar Air Field. I just wanted to be away from this place. I was running with one tire on run-flats, and I knew that I was speeding. I knew I was acting strangely, but I really didn't care. I wanted to be back at the base. Finally, it was Crunk who spoke up. "Jet Set," he said in a calm, even voice, "we're not in a hurry. Richie is dead."

"The captain radioed in our status report," Dragline said, "so expect Kandahar to be buzzing with rubberneckers." About two miles outside the wire, a UH 60 helicopter flew past us, then circled back, coming in low. I saw the door gunner's head pop out with an expression of curiosity, and it enraged me. I hammered my foot to the floor, hoping to get out of sight of the gawkers, but the helicopter simply moved forward along with us.

The prop-blast from the helicopter was furious, threatening to tear off the poncho that covered Richie. Crunk spun his weapon around and pointed that big .50 cal directly up at the hovering aircraft. The door gunner, resting his arm on his own .50 cal, fell back in amazement. He shouted something into his microphone, and the chopper banked away sharply.

As I pulled the vehicle onto the road toward the airfield gate, I saw PFC Branson burst out of the guardhouse at full speed. He ran over to the gate and lifted it up without a word. He slung his weapon over his right shoulder, came to attention, and, as we slowly rumbled by, he shouted out the command, "Pre-sent ARMS!" He brought his left hand across his chest and took hold of the rifle sling; then with his right hand, he formed a salute, holding the salute until we had driven by. We made our way slowly past PFC Branson, and as we did, I saw that he was crying.

Once inside Kandahar Air Field, people stopped what they were doing and looked at us. Some Navy lieutenant commander walked alongside the vehicle and asked if we needed help. "No, sir" I said, "we just got to get to the—" I paused. The morgue was right next to the Medical Treatment Facility. "Aid Station," I said.

The lieutenant commander looked perplexed. "But why would you—" he started to say, then stopped himself. Lowering his head, he said, "I'm sorry."

As we approached the morgue, I saw Linda running in our direction, her face stricken with worry and concern. She ran up to me as I was getting out of the vehicle, and wrapped her arms around me. "They didn't say who it was," she said, "they just said a sergeant on your team. I thought—" Too distracted to say anything to her, I just walked through her embrace, climbed into the back of the vehicle and took a handle of the collapsible stretcher.

We were delicate with Richie, but his lifeless body was difficult to maneuver. Some of the soldiers came out of the Aid Station with a gurney, and we placed him on it. I was exhausted and disoriented, and I looked inside the back of the vehicle and saw Richie's blood-soaked load-bearing equipment, helmet and rifle. "We'd better clean this off," I said to Crunk, "so Richie will ha—" I looked over and watched the soldiers wheel Richie Gennaro away, not really understanding I would never see him again.

Spooky and I climbed back into the vehicle, but Crunk shook his head, took his weapon and said that he would stay behind.

"What's he doin'?" I asked.

"Pullin' guard," was all Spooky said in response.

Just because a man dies does not mean the world stops turning. We had completed a mission; now we needed to be debriefed. After Action Reviews needed to be done, and those weapons and vehicles were not going to clean themselves. Around 8:00 p.m. we finally piled back into the team hooch and began cleaning our rifles. We worked in utter silence for an hour. The weapons were already clean, but we just didn't want to acknowledge that. Around 9:00 p.m. I put my weapon away and went out to get some air. It was dark in the way only the desert can be dark—the stars were brilliant, and the world was covered in a sable blackness. A quarter moon hung over the crystal clear night, and the winds coming off the desolate planes of Kandahar beat against our tent. I walked slowly, my flashlight in front of me, toward the chaplain's office. I didn't bother knocking but simply pushed at the always-open door. It was locked, and I knocked hesitantly, wondering why Father had locked his door.

After a time, the door opened and a young, bright-faced captain greeted me. "How can I help you, Sergeant?" he said. The captain was about twenty-five years old, and his pale cheeks were ruddy, although his brown hair was already beginning to recede. He was clearly confused with my presence at his door.

"Is Father McFarland here, sir?" I asked.

The captain looked at me strangely for a moment, as if trying to understand. Then his eyes lit up and he said, "Oh, Major McFarland, Major McFarland. 'Fraid not, 'fraid not. He got orders two days ago. Up in Bagram for two weeks, then back home." The captain looked down at the ground wistfully, lost in his own thoughts. Then he remembered himself and said, "But I'm the new chaplain. Can I help?"

"Can you take confession, sir?" I asked.

For a second he looked at me like I had committed a crime, like he was going to have to arrest me. Then I saw the gears turning, and again he brightened up. "Oh, like a priest—no, no, can't 'take' 'confession.'" He actually air-quoted with his fingers for both words. Separately.

"Then no," I said.

"Did something happen, Sergeant?" he said. "Do you want to talk?"

"No," I said, in a matter of fact way, "not really."

The captain, at that point, took a look at me, trying to place me in the universe of the military. He looked over at the left arm sleeve of my shoulder and saw my Special Forces tab and patch and paused a beat. "Was that your team that came in today?"

"Yes, sir."

"I was in the morgue soon after you left," he said. "I said a prayer."

"Thank you, sir."

"There will be a service tomorrow."

"That's nice, sir."

"Sergeant Gennaro was your friend, wasn't he?" the captain asked.

"Yes, sir."

"What was he like?" the chaplain asked. "I mean, I have to talk about him, and I'd like to know special things about him."

I knew the captain was going to have to speak about Richie in the morning, and I wanted to help him out, to tell him all about the man who had died. But I was caught off guard. Until that very moment, I had never thought about what Boy Band was like—he was just Boy Band. I didn't know what to say. I wished Father McFarland was still here: he would have gotten the words out of me. What would Father McFarland have said, I thought. And I smiled just thinking about it. "What was Boy Band like?" I said at last, "Oh, but he was grand. . . . He was grand."

When I left the chaplain's office, I began walking back to the team hooch. The darkness was consuming, but I stumbled a few feet down the pathway between the tents, and I heard the gravel kick around in the darkness. "Timmy," she said, "is that you?"

"Linda?" was all I could say in response. I turned off my flashlight and ran to her, my entire body suddenly on fire. Linda had been waiting for me, and now we were together in the darkness of the Kandahar night, staring at each other, our faces inches apart.

"Are you okay?" Linda asked, her upper lip quivering. My hands were shaking, but I grabbed her up into my arms, and she placed the palms of her hands on my chest, letting her hands lie there, feeling the heaving of my body as my torso rose and fell with each breath. Her face was no more than inches from my own, and we stared at each other for the longest time, our bodies pressing against each other willfully. I leaned forward to kiss her even as she rose up toward me. The evening was hot, and I tasted the sweat on her upper lip. The taste of her salt was like a charge of electricity running through my body. Linda pressed herself against me, her hands searching down my lower back and slipping under my belt, her nails digging into me. I brushed back her hair and began kissing her neck and her ears. From deep in my stomach I let out a low groan, and Linda responded with a moaning "yes."

She was completely wrapped in my arms, and I lowered my hands down to her hips and tightened my grip, as if I were choking her torso. She arched her back, exposing her neckline and shoulders, and I buried my face in between the buttons on her uniform, leaving a trail of saliva on her neck and shoulders. I wanted her completely, and opened my mouth to encompass her neck and shoulders in my teeth, clamping down powerfully. Then Linda tore herself away from me, and I could see her face, intoxicated with desire. "Wait," she said, "in my room." Linda took my hand and practically marched me back to her tent.

She pulled me through her door, and I spun her around into my arms. We kissed again briefly, then pulled away and began unbuttoning our clothes. I took off my uniform top and T-shirt, and Linda took off her boots and her uniform pants. Uninterested in continuing to be apart, we embraced again. Linda wrestled with my belt and fly buttons, as I grabbed her uniform shirt and T-shirt at the small of her back and pulled them over her head and off, like a brawling hockey player. My pants dropped to the floor, and Linda licked the palm of her hand with her tongue and reached down for me. She held me fiercely, almost violently, and stared into my eyes, as if daring me to match her intensity. I tore off her bra with a single motion and buried my head in her breasts. In the soft light of a glowing computer, I could see her breasts, pert and round, the nipples jutting up excitedly.

Linda's cot was on the far side of the room, and I scooped her up in my arms and carried her to it like a newlywed carries his bride across the threshold. We collapsed in a tangle, not bothering to stop kissing, sucking or grasping at each other. There was a reading light left on by the bed, and I saw Linda's naked body. She took her fitness seriously, and it showed. She caught me looking at her and said, "Do you like it?"

"Very much."

Linda was silent, her hand caressed my face, and in an instant I saw hope, fear, and tremendous excitement flash in her eyes. "Take it," she said. "Take it all."

My mouth ran down from her neck to her breasts, zig zagging from left to right, like a doting father who was afraid one child would feel less appreciated than the other—and then I was on that tummy, hard and flat. And then beyond.

Linda moaned softly at first, then her moans grew deeper, and her hips began to rhythmically push forward. I reached up and grabbed her hair at the back of her head. She liked that and stared down hard at me. "Give me that," she said. I stood up, and she wrapped her mouth around me, gliding her lips up and down like a piston driven machine. That awoke the animal-like desire in me, and with one hand holding her hair tight in my hand, I cupped the other under her jaw and worked her pouty lips back and forth on me, sliding deeper and deeper into her.

After a time, Linda pulled me on top of her, wrapping her legs around my torso, and guiding me inside of her. I could feel Linda shudder as I drove further. She stared up at me, with a look that was actually hostile, like she wanted to beat me, to devour me, to consume me. I stared back at her—even as our bodies thrust forcefully against each other—unblinkingly. "Yes!" she shouted. "Take it all." We were one.

As Linda and I joined, we tumbled out of the cot and onto the floor. I put a pillow on the ground and told her to get on her hands and knees. "Put your face on that pillow," I said, "and arch that back up into the air." Linda did what I told her to. "Good girl," I said, then entered her from behind, encircling the small of her waist with my hands, holding her still as I pounded away inside of her. Even as my body was consumed in the actions of love, my mind raced away, and I found myself thinking about my rifle, the way it fired the bullet forward, then slammed back, fired forward, then slammed back. I loved the working of my rifle, I loved the firing and I loved the recoil. It was a perfect motion, and it felt like it could go on forever. Linda began to buck and to shutter, her moans becoming deeper and more guttural. I put my fingers in her mouth. "Bite down," I told her, and she did with a moan. I bit her shoulder and then the nape of her neck. "Are you mine?" I said.

"I am all yours," she replied. "I am your woman."

I was on the verge of climax, and Linda could sense it. I began to break away, but Linda held me in place. "No," she said. "Stay inside of me. I want you. I want all of you." I climaxed inside of her, and we collapsed together, still as one, in a spasm of delirious passion.

LOOK HOMEWARD ANGEL

"We absolutely cannot eat chow together," Linda said to me as I left that first night together. "And we can't be seen even walking to the chow hall together. "

I was surprised by how much Linda had already mapped this out. "Look," she said, "I have done more than my share of fraternization cases since coming here, and the thing is, everybody thinks no one notices. But everyone notices."

That was two weeks earlier. Four days earlier the orders came down that the company was going home. After that, all the company did was go to "Return Briefings'" or, as we liked to call them, "Don't kill yourself when ya get back" briefings. Linda was miserable. When we made love she cried, and her tears fell on my skin. I felt each one, and they burned. We tried to be discreet, but everyone on my team knew— even the captain. The new chaplain knew as well. He kept trying to rope Linda into a conversation about fraternization, but she always begged off. He tried to corner me the last time I came around too, but I feigned some other duties.

Jiggy didn't like it. He never said anything directly to me, but he was always talking about 'people.' "People," he'd say, "very often lose their soul even as they find their soulmate—it's a real problem in this modern world. All the courtship rituals have been destroyed, and now one of the most important things in life is left in complete chaos." I didn't disagree with Jiggy, but I thought only of Linda, and no matter what I swore to myself, every night I'd find myself walking the same path to her door.

The captain didn't like it either. At first he had the team sergeant come around and talk to me, but—let's be honest—Dragline really didn't care. In fact, I got the feeling that if I told him about Linda and me, he'd punch me in the arm and put me in for a medal. After that, the captain made a point of talking to me about good order and proper discipline. Again, I couldn't disagree with him, but . . . every night I was walking that path.

Still, Linda had another 10 months in-country, and I was waiting on a flight out. It was difficult, because we never knew when it was to be our last night together. We would go through this routine where I would say, "maybe tomorrow", and she would cry. Then I'd say, "maybe not"—but it was coming down to the wire, and we had so many feelings for each other that we couldn't explain and weren't even sure were really there. Never start a relationship when at war. It will destroy you.

The day I left was heart-wrenching. Linda had a hearing in the morning, so she didn't get my message until lunchtime, and by then I was in the sealed-off holding area, where we could see each other from a distance of about 70 meters, but she couldn't come in, and I couldn't get out. We waved to each other about 45 times, and mouthed to each other words of affection, but the whole effect was ruinous, not least because it was all done in the open with everybody watching.

The Team flew into Rhein Main, same place we'd come from a year before. And again we had a six hour wait. We walked over to the enormous lobby with the giant television screen in the distance. And once again they were playing a romantic comedy that we couldn't hear. But this time, without saying a word, we took the seats directly across from the seats we had taken last year, our backs to the movie. No one said a single word the entire time, and no one even acknowledged the movie we were refusing to notice.

AS YOU WERE

The formation ran in lock-step as Dragline called cadence and we all sang back in perfect reply. And for a brief moment we forgot. It was as if nothing had ever happened.

Momma told Sally not to go downtown,
There were too many Green Berets around.

Sally got mad and she went anyway,
Out the window in a black negligee.

Three months later all was well,
Six months later you could start to tell.

Nine months later out he came,
A bow-legged paratrooper swinging a chain.

We began the run at the usual "Airborne-shuffle" pace—a 10-minute-mile. But at the major's nod, the pace continually picked up, and staying in formation became more difficult. First he dropped it to a 9.5-minute-mile, then a 9-minute-mile, then an 8.5-minute mile.

And that's when we began to lose troops—first one, then another fell out. "Sergeant major," Major Brenner shouted, "take charge of the fall-outs." The sergeant major peeled off and organized those unable to keep up, and ran them at a slower pace.

I would have thought the major would leave it at that, but I would have been wrong. We dropped to an 8-minute mile—and lost some. At that point we went to a 7.5 minute mile, and then a 7 minute mile. There were no more fall-outs—those who were left were determined to stay up even if it killed them. The cadence calling had stopped, and so had the synchronized foot falls. Now we were just running, jockeying with each other, and pushing one another forward, as if to let the major know that if he killed us he would die too.

I looked over at Dragline—already past his fiftieth birthday—and saw his face contorted in pain, but his eyes were ablaze, unwilling to give an inch. We turned the last corner and could see the finish line less than 400 meters away. At that point, all hell broke loose. The younger soldiers took off like horses to the barn, while those of us who were older took off in a manner that—if plotted on a graph—would perfectly indicate our exact age. The major looked every bit as exhausted as Dragline, as he shouted, "Pull it back in! We finish together!" This got a grim laugh. The major was admitting that he couldn't keep up.

"Son of a bitch!" I shouted, back in the hooch, pulling off my sweat-soaked shirt. "Does the major want to kill us now that we've gotten back home?"

"The major knows what he's doin'," said Spooky.

"Smokin' us like that?" I said. "We came back from Afghanistan two months ago, and the first time we're together, he runs us almost to death—what's that all about?"

"Suicide prevention," replied Spooky. "He doesn't want anybody cappin' themselves."

"So, he's going to smoke us to death?" I said.

Spooky looked at me like he was Father Flanagan and I was some troubled kid from Boys Town. "Guys are coming home and cappin' themselves," he replied. "3rd Group guy and a dude in the 82nd capped themselves and their wives just this year. The Army is spending millions to 'get to the root' of the problem—but everybody already knows what the problem is. It's too much free time, too much time to think. Major doesn't want anybody thinking too much; it gets them into weird places." Spooky looked over at me like it was all so obvious. "When a guy comes home from war, you have to keep him with the group, and it only helps to sweat him—keeps 'em out of the dark places."

"Well," I replied, "I wish the major would stop being so good to me."

As the helicopter approached the parade ground, the children in the trailer park ran out into the prop-blast, laughing and dancing. The MPs ran after them—against their better judgment—and tried to shoo them away. But the kids squirmed out of their grasp and sprinted around in the wash of the rotors. They loved it when the helicopters came in—it was the only time anyone paid attention to them.

We stood in formation, chuckling to ourselves, and watched as the helicopter landed. Before the blades had come to a stop, the door to the

UH-60 opened and the governor jumped out and—almost ignoring us—bounded swiftly to the podium. I say he "almost ignored us," because he did give us something of a salute, one of those I-have-no-idea-what-I'm-doing salutes, where he throws up his right hand, and lowers his head to it.

The governor stood behind the lectern, directly to our front. On the sides and to our rear were aluminum bleachers, packed with family, friends and loved ones. Flanking the governor were his chief aides. He threw up his hands, beamed the crowd a big smile and waved triumphantly. It was cool.

After what was deemed an appropriate amount of time, the governor pushed down his arms as if he were closing a suitcase, and his face grew grave and solemn. "Soldiers, families, friends and loved ones," he began, "I want to say how proud I am, as governor of the State of Virginia, of you. The people of Virginia, the Army and your country are very proud of you, and our prayers will be with you as you perform your duties in Afghanistan." There was some confusion among the families, and even some of the guys in formation were looking perplexed—"We're going back?" someone whispered.

"You leave," he continued, "everything you know and everyone you love back here, to go and defend our freedoms in a foreign land." The governor paused to let the weight of his words sink in. He gripped tightly the lectern with both hands, and hung down his head with gravity. "Some of you may not make it home."

That got our attention.

"But, know this, as Governor—" An aide in a charcoal gray suit leapt up and whispered excitedly into the governor's ear. The governor turned around to consult with the aide, on his face a look of befuddlement. After an awkward moment of silence, the governor turned back toward us, paused for a moment, then broke out an enormous smile, threw his arms up and said, "Welcome home, boys!"

The crowd came to a standing ovation. But in the formation we began laughing loudly, pointing at the governor and giving each other high-fives. It was a bit chaotic, and when it didn't end in the appropriate time, the governor began his arms-closing-the-suitcase bit—which didn't work at all. Then the aides came and did the same move, and everybody laughed at them even more. We were on the verge of mockery, when the sergeant major stepped up to the lectern, nudged the governor out of the way, grabbed the microphone and said, "As you were! . . . As. You. Were!"

We immediately went silent. The people in the bleachers, seeing us standing silently at parade rest, also went silent. The governor, looking at the sergeant major with astonishment, said, timidly, "Thank you for your service," as the sergeant major stepped away from the microphone and back into the head of the formation.

The governor turned out to be a really great guy. After the speech, he came down and hung out with us for a good 30 minutes. There was coffee and doughnuts, and he and I split a glazed. The sergeant major came over to take a picture with the governor and shake his hand. And while they were standing there smiling for the camera, the governor asked the sergeant major, "Sergeant, what was it you said to the men on the podium today when the troops were getting rowdy?"

"Oh," said the sergeant major, "I just said, 'As you were.'"

"Yes," replied the governor. "'As you were.' What does that mean?"

The sergeant major laughed. "Boys," he said, "what does 'as you were' mean?"

"It means, forget everything you just saw," said Spooky.

"Ignore everything you just heard," said Crunk.

"Nothing just happened," said Jiggy.

"It's not a request," I said. "It's an order."

Later in the day, back at the team hooch, Captain McMann and Dragline sort of arranged things so that the team would end up needing to eat lunch in the hooch with the door locked to outsiders. "So, how are you guys finding re-entry into civilian life?" The captain asked. His tone was light, but he had a notebook with him.

No one said anything at first, but then Jiggy—the most guileless man on Earth—spoke up. "Sir, it's really much more difficult than I thought it would be."

"Tell us about it," said Dragline, in about the most scripted manner I've ever heard.

"Well, you know," began Jiggy, twisting one hand around the other as he spoke, "I'd been deployed on other missions, so I assumed coming home this time would be about the same. But after what we went through, I find the little things in life really difficult. And I know it's me. I know I'm the one reading in too much, but I can't help it."

"Well, what are we talking about," said the captain.

"I find it hard not to see right through people anymore," Jiggy replied. "I mean, used to be, if someone said something, I just believed

269

it. But now, if someone says something to me, I—like—see right through to their intentions. It's not even a thing I think about, I just see right through them. I think, what's causing this? What's motivating this conversation? What does this guy want from me and why? I don't believe anyone and I don't trust anyone. Everybody seems like an agent to me trying to use me for their own end—even with my kids I'm like, what's behind this? What are they scamming for? I'll be honest, it kind of helps me out in normal business dealings, I've saved at least $500.00 just because I didn't believe my mechanic . . . and I've known him for 25 years. Only thing is, it makes me hate everybody. I get tired from hating everybody all the time. I get tired, but I can't sleep nights. I just lay in bed and think about all the people trying to get over on me all the time."

After a time, Dragline said, "Um, thank you for sharing, Jiggy." He looked around the room. "How about the rest of you? Anybody else have any re-entry stories? It's good to share them." Dragline then looked at us with a twinkle in his eyes. "Just make 'em funny—even if they weren't at the time."

"Well," said Crunk, who hadn't said more than two words since Richie's death, "I can't stand not having a weapon with me at all times."

This got Captain McMann's attention. "What do you mean?" he asked.

"Well, sir," said Crunk, "I just can't stand the idea of not being prepared for an attack. I mean, it seems reckless not to have a gun with you at all times. And it pisses me off how slack and ill-equipped people are for, like, a home invasion or a carjacking." Crunk looked down at his hands. "I was at my uncle's house for a party, you know, the whole family, just relaxing and enjoying ourselves. And then the doorbell rings, and my Uncle just gets up and opens the door! Crazy, right? I mean, everyone he loves in the whole world is in that little confined space and he doesn't have a club, doesn't have a gun. No challenge and password, he just opens the door. It was criminal. I just had to get my kids out of there."

"Who was at the door?" Dragline asked.

"Oh, it was Cousin Jane—but it just as easily could have been Khalid Sheik Mohammed for all my uncle cared."

The Captain looked over at his notebook, wondering if he should write this down. "What about the rest of you?" he asked. "Do you all do that?"

"I keep a baseball bat by the door," said Spooky.

"Me, too," said Jiggy.

"Me too," I said.

"And I keep a gun on the nightstand," said Crunk.

The captain reached for the notebook.

"Me too," said Spooky.

"Me too," said Jiggy.

"Me too," I said. The captain picked up his notebook.

"Me too," said Dragline. The captain closed the notebook back up again and set it down. "Yeah," he said, "so do I."

"I constantly touch my chest with my trigger finger," I said. "You know, I touch exactly where my rifle hung for the last year. I'll be in a meeting, and I'm touching my rifle with my trigger finger, just to make sure everything is always ready to go."

"Yeah, I do that too," said Spooky, as everyone else nodded their heads.

We were starting to compare notes.

"Do you guys have nightmares?" I asked.

"'Course." "Obviously." "Is there another type of dream?"

"What do you guys have nightmares over?" I asked.

"Not having my weapon." "Not having my weapon." "Not having my weapon."

"Me too," I said. "And all my dreams are the same. I'm always sleeping out in the field, and I reach over to make sure I have my weapon, and it's not there. And I immediately wake up from looking for my weapon, but I don't have my weapon, because I'm home. So now I can't go back to sleep because I'll just wake up again 30 minutes later looking for my weapon. So I reach over and grab my pistol—but it's just a pistol. Good luck with that in a gunfight. Better not to go back to sleep at all."

"Do you guys all have those dreams?" said the captain.

"Absolutely." "Definitely." "It's my identical dream."

"I'm actually glad," said the captain. "Because I have that same dream every night."

"Okay," said Dragline. "So we're crazy. We just got to ride out the crazy." This was the thought we all clung to. But we were wrong.

That night we went into town and had a pizza and some (okay, many) pitchers of beer at Romas Italian Restaurant. I cannot prove, though I cannot rule out, that this was Dragline's and the captain's plan, but it worked out perfectly.

"So, we're a bunch of nuts," said Dragline. "Jet Set, tell me a funny story about your crazy unleashed on the world."

"Well, team sergeant," I said, "there was one event."

Everybody perked up. "Tell us about it, Jet Set," said Spooky, unable to conceal his prurient interest.

"No," I said, "it's no big deal, it's just that . . . Well, I just don't think we're like these other people anymore. I mean, we're not like them at all."

"Give us the goods," said Dragline.

"You know," I said, "when we first got back, we had about two weeks' leave, so we didn't have to go right back to work. I didn't feel like paying New York City rent, so I stayed with my parents in Maryland."

"Okay," said Jiggy.

"Well," I continued, "I had a lot of free time on my hands, so I started snooping around the basement, looking for some of my old stuff."

"News flash," interrupted Crunk, "porn is online now."

Ignoring Crunk, I said, "I found my old Fuji twelve-speed in the garage. I used to ride a lot in college and in my twenties."

"Wait," said Jiggy, "it took you, like, a decade to graduate, right? So, sayin' 'in college' and 'in my twenties' is sort of redundant isn't it?"

"In any event," I said, "in any event, I pulled the old bike out, pumped up the tires, oiled the chain, and headed out on the road. Of course, I wasn't wearing all that goofiness that cyclists usually wear. I'm not one of those guys who has to dress like a modern art masterpiece just to ride his bike."

"You mean no skintight, fuchsia, orange and electric blue outfit?" said Jiggy.

"You didn't wear the homo-helmet?" said Crunk. "The one that makes you look like the little-boy-who-falls-into-fires?"

"You want to tell this story, or should I?"

"By all means," said Crunk, "continue."

"Anyway, I was riding down the road, watching people watching me, and for the first time I realized why a man with a job, a mortgage and a sense of self worth would dress up like a harlequin just to ride his bike." I stood up, and mimicked myself people watching. "Because when you ride down the road looking so gay you could sneeze glitter, everybody driving by says to themselves, 'Hey, look at that guy getting a work out. . . . Geez, I really need to get back to the gym.' But when you ride down that same road, on that same bike, wearing jeans, tennis shoes and a sweat shirt, everybody says, 'Hey, look at that guy . . . he got a DWI.'"

Dragline laughed, but shook his head. "That ain't the whole story is it, Jet Set? Something set you off. I know something set you off."

"No," I said, hesitantly. "I was riding down the road, and this road has two lanes on both sides, with a hard, concrete curb, so I can't, like, get over on the shoulder and let cars pass me. Anyway, I'm going at a pretty good clip, about 20 miles an hour, but still, the cars are starting to stack up in the right hand lane, but with the left lane moving fine." I walked over in front of the group. "And that's when I started hearing all this crap coming from two cars, both behind me. I did one of those over-the-shoulder looks and I saw that the two cars had a bunch of young twenty-something kids in them, you know, just out joyriding. The first car came up right on my ass—I mean, almost touching my rear tire, and the other car came alongside me in the left lane and threw a bottle at me."

"What the…?" said Jiggy.

"Yeah," I said, "and at that point it was on."

"How many guys are we talkin' about?" asked the captain.

"Well, that's the thing, sir," I said with a smile. "There were seven of them—but they were in two separate cars." I rubbed my hands with delight. "And the dumb-asses didn't know proper patrolling techniques, didn't maintain comms between the two elements, and—worst of all—they lost line-of-sight with each other."

"I like where this is going," said Dragline.

"Anyway, the two cars got ahead of me, but now we are coming up on a light, and the dudes in the first car are like one car ahead of the dudes in the second car. They're also in the right hand lane whereas the dudes in the second car are in the left lane. As the cars come to the light, the driver of the first car pulls all the way over to the curb—you know—to keep me from being able to get past him. And that's when it all came to me, I mean it was like a vision." I paused for a second, remembering it. "I could see it perfectly. I cut over between the lanes, so I'm pedaling between the two rows of cars, and as I come up on the second car, I reach down and grab my bicycle lock, and I wait until I just pass the passenger's door, lean over their windshield and slam that fuckin' lock right onto their windshield—fuckin' BOOM, man! I shattered that son of a bitch!"

"Whoa!" The team lit up laughing. "Jet Set dialed it up on their asses, didn't he?"

"Hell yeah," I said, "and, again, it was like clockwork. I just rode right by 'em as, you know, they bounced all around inside of that car, not knowing whether to sink, swim or scream for help. And what was so beautiful, is that the guys in the first car had no idea what had happened. I pedaled by them and they were absolutely clueless. And, see, the light where we stopped was a light into an office park, so when I got to the light, I took a right into the office park, which had a little island right at the light. I rode around the island, lay my bike down on the grass beside the road, and walked back 30 feet."

"Whatcha do that for?" Spooky said.

"Because I knew that that first car would just drive off, completely unaware of what I did to the second car, and the second car would pull in, turn around that island, and come up alongside my bike."

"So why did you walk away?"

"Because when that second car stopped, that dude in the passenger seat would open his door and step out onto the street, and when he did, I was going to take off running right at him, and I was going to slam into that door so hard it would break his leg right off. And I would take that leg and beat all three of them to death with it."

The captain reached for his notebook, but the team sergeant placed his hand on top of it. "So then what happened?" said Dragline.

"It went exactly as planned," I said. "First car drove off, second car pulled in, turned around the island and came to a stop right even with my bike. The doors opened up, and I charged right at the passenger. It was a thing of beauty."

"So, what'd the guy do?"

"Are you kidding me?" I said. "He jumped his ass right back into that car, slammed the door and mashed down the lock."

"What about the two other guys?"

"The guy in the back, like the guy in the passenger seat, wanted nothing to do with a fight, but the driver jumps out and he's one of those," I stopped myself, not wanting to offend, "white-guys-who-think-they're-black," I said. "He's got his hat on sideways and his pants around his ass and—you know—had it all workin'. And he comes around to me and he's like moving his head from side to side, and he's talkin' with his hands—you know—like he's in some strange "rap-off" competition with me. Like he's gonna diss me, and school me on his flow—it was sort of awkward. Then, after I failed to properly respect what he was representin', he went for his gun."

"What?"

"Well, sort of," I continued, "and this has happened to me a couple times up in Baltimore, too, when I've gotten into some sort of confrontations with black guys on the street. They always go for their waistband. You know, they make that big, dramatic move arching their hand way up over their head, then plunging it down into their waistband, and bringing it up like they got a gun."

"Oh right," said Spooky, "the Emperor's New Gun."

"Yeah," I said, "and I can see why a black guy would do it to a white guy, because black guys think white guys think black guys always have guns on them. So it can be scary for a second when a black guy goes for his waistband. Problem is, when he comes up without a gun, he looks like a fool." I laughed, thinking about some conflicts I'd had years before. "And when they don't come up with a gun, they always do the same thing, they always go for the gun again—as if the pistol pixies miracled a weapon into their underpants while we were standing there."

"So, anyway," Dragline said, wanting to hear the story.

"So anyway, naturally, skinny white wannabe gangsta comes out of his waistband without a gun. And guess what he does . . . he goes for his gun a second time—do these guys all copy their homework from the same kid, or what? And the thing is, it's his lucky-ass day," I continued. "I mean, if he actually did come up with a gun, I would have just taken it from him and killed him with it—a freebie."

"So," asked the captain, "how did this get resolved?"

"Well, sir, that's the thing," I said. "It didn't get resolved. The guy just kept talking shit and going around his car like he left his gun in other places. He even opened his trunk to get his gun out—like who forgets where they put their gun? Meanwhile, the two guys in the car still have no intention of getting out. And they can both see that their homie is about to receive a permanent emotional scar he will never overcome, so they're trying to tell him to get back in the car. Anyway, the guy won't quit, and now it's going on for, like, five minutes." I started pacing around the room, my excitement building as I told the story. "He's throwing his mad rhymes at me like he's Eminem, and it's enough already, you know, it's time for him to go away. But he won't go. So, finally, he comes up to me and says, 'You want some of this?' And I'm so done with the guy I just say, 'Yeah, bitch, I do!' And I wrap my arms around him, and drive my head into his chest—I mean, I just

275

bear-hugged the shit out of him, and he absolutely collapses. He dropped like a prom dress. The first thing that hit the ground was the back of his head."

"UUU! He should have been wearing his bike helmet," said Crunk.

"Nice work," said Spooky.

"Yeah," I continued, "but now I've got a problem. Now the other two bros have to do something—and, of course, skinny white kid knows this, so he's trying to hold me down on the ground. I know I got to get up before those two doofuses get out of the car, so I kinda plant the palms of my hands on his face and use it as a push-off platform to stand up. And he grabs my shoe, and he almost got it off, but I pull away just as those other two dingbats come around the side of the car." I began bobbing my head up and down, like a boxer. "The first guy throws this half-assed punch at me, but I just duck it, and slam him into the side of the car. Now, the skinny kid is up, and he comes at me, and at the same time I see number three getting ready to do something. But the dumbass—and this is how I know he doesn't want to fight—has come out of the car with his can of soda in his hand."

Even the captain laughed at this.

"I'm like 'who shows up for a fight with a can of soda in his hand?' So I grab the skinny kid, and turn him around just as number three decides what to do—he decides to throw his soda at me. But, of course, he hits his buddy instead."

"This is ridiculous," said Jiggy.

"Oh, it gets better," I said. "Just then—I shit you not—this homeless guy comes running out of the wood line to my rescue. He's got his arms up and swinging his fists like a drunken Irishman. It's now three to two, with all of us just sort of standing there circling each other. So, finally—finally—the two passengers convince skinny to go. But he'll be back, he assures me, when he gets 'his boys,' he'll be back."

"So what about the bum?" Cronk asked.

"Well," I said, "so now the 'fight' is over, and, naturally, the bum wants to hit me up for some money, which I don't like, but—you know—we just shared a moment together, and even though he's a bum, he's got his pride. So for a while he doesn't say anything. But finally he says, 'Hey, uh, this is weird, but—'and I'm like, 'Hey, man, don't even think about it, you earned it.' Luckily, I'd just been to the ATM, and I had a bunch of money on me. I handed him a twenty, and he takes it sheepishly, not looking at it, saying, 'Thanks.' About five seconds later he looks at it and says, 'Thanks a lot, man!'"

"Did that shit really happen, or are you just more batshit crazy than the rest of us?" Dragline asked.

"Exactly like that," I said, "right on Park Road, just past East Woodlawn."

"So," said the captain, unimpressed with my rollicking story. "What did you learn from that? What was your take-away?" It was a fair question, and it cut through the bluster of my 'antics-ensued' story telling. And it sort of made me reflect on my own behavior.

"Sir," I said, lowering my eyes, "what I realized was that I shouldn't be around people—that I'm not really fit to be with 'normal' people." I looked at him without any air of triumph. "As I rode back home, I kept looking at everybody around me—you know, men out cutting the grass, moms at the supermarket, kids playing on the swing set—and I realized I had nothing in common with them at all. I don't understand them, and they don't understand me. I realized that I had to be careful around people, that I needed to be with people, but that I had to be very careful around them. I realized I had to find a new order to my life."

Later that night when I got back to Brooklyn, I sent an email to Linda. She had sent me a letter a month before, but it took me a week just to open it. I missed Linda terribly, but to me Linda was Afghanistan, a hot stove I didn't want to touch again. There was just too much there.

GONE FOR A SOLDIER

I was in Criminal Court when I got the call. We were between cases, and I saw that it was Dragline, so I asked the judge for a minute. Dragline wouldn't call me if there wasn't a good reason.

I stepped out into the hallway and answered the phone. "Did you hear about Biker Dave?" he asked.

"No," I said, "why?"

"He bit it."

"Shit," I said. Afraid —but certain—of what I was going to hear next.

"Yeah," said Dragline, a note of despair in his voice. "Went missing two days ago. His wife called up Blue Crab, and they went lookin'. . . . Found him in the wood line just beyond the house this morning, back of his head blown out, his H & K in his hand."

"Shit."

"Funeral's Saturday at Arlington."

"Did he leave a note?" I asked. "Were there any signs?"

"No," said Dragline, "nothing. That's how it usually works." Dragline spoke in a detached manner. "When they want to cry out for help, they get dramatic and—you know—take pills, freak out and do all that crazy stuff." He paused. "But when they just want to end it, they don't say shit."

"And Biker Dave?"

"He didn't say shit."

"What's the unit doing for his wife?"

"We're taking up a collection, of course. And, yeah, drill is this weekend. First formation is at Arlington Cemetery. Class A uniforms with all your medals. We're going to bury Biker Dave."

"The Old Guard going to do it?" I asked. The Old Guard—the 3rd Regiment—is the Army Honor Guard. They pretty much run Arlington National Cemetery.

"Hell, no," Dragline said hotly. "Nobody's gonna touch Biker Dave. We bury our own."

"Who've they got on it?"

"His A Team will do everything—the gun salute, the flag to his bereaved—all of it. You just show up at the right time, in the right place, in the right uniform."

"What's the company commander saying?"

"The Old Man wants Dave's family to see that he wasn't a complete fuck up—that he had friends and stuff."

"Biker Dave wasn't a fuck up."

"Well, he fucked this up."

"Yeah, he fucked this up good."

When we hung up, I didn't really want to go back to court right away. Dave Brewer—Biker Dave—and I had gone through the Q together. We weren't particularly close, but, thinking about it now, we had moments together that rang out. We had been on a jump together back at Bragg that I'd long forgotten. We were flying in a C-130, and the jump was an 'in-flight rig-up,' that is, you go on board carrying your chute and equipment—not wearing it—and the jumpmasters rig you up in flight.

As soon as we got seated in the aircraft, like a good trooper, Biker Dave went to sleep. About 20 minutes after take-off, a fire broke out in the fuselage, and we had to make an emergency landing. Dave, of course, slept through the whole thing, finally waking up when we landed and the doors were thrown open. We all lined up to get out, and Dave was in front of me. When he got to the door, he made a dynamic exit, jumping out the door with both hands covering his midsection, and he hit the ground doing a perfect four-point parachute landing. I got out and looked down at him lying on the ground. "What are you doing, Dave?" I asked.

"I'm jumping!" he replied, looking up at me with confusion.

"The plane is on the ground," I said, "and you don't have a parachute."

That was Biker Dave Brewer, I thought, the guy who jumped without a parachute.

The view from the hills of Arlington Cemetery was at once both uplifting and humbling. The manicured grounds extended out magnificently in every direction, and the row upon row of white tombstones rolled and undulated in perfect keeping with the earth as far as the eye could see. Dave's grave was set among the broad, flat plane behind the hill where the Tomb of the Unknowns sat. The company formed up at close intervals.

"He doesn't deserve this," Jiggy whispered out of the side of his mouth. "He screwed us," he said. "We pulled detail with him, we kicked-in doors with him, and he spit in our faces." Jiggy wasn't the only guy in the company who felt that way. In fact, he was in the majority.

"We guarded him when he slept," Little Spider said to no one in particular, "and we trusted him to watch over us when we went to sleep. And then he goes off and blows his brains out like a total dick."

"We're not doin' this for Biker Dave," I whispered back to Jiggy, "we're doin' this for the unit. We're doing this so everyone can see that we can bury our dead, and the unit goes on living. Everybody needs to see that the unit is at full strength, and this little bullshit maneuver hasn't damaged us at all!" I looked down at the ground and wanted to spit. I adjusted my beret instead. "This has nothing to do with Dave," I continued. "It's got everything to do with the unit."

After the funeral, we milled around a bit until Dragline and the captain signaled for us to rally up. "Crunk," said Captain McMann, "how long ago was it that you were in the Old Guard?"

"About ten years, I guess, sir," said Crunk.

Dragline and the captain smiled at each other. "Well," replied the captain, "once in the Old Guard always in the Old Guard, right? The way I see it, we've got the run of this place. You can give us a VIP tour."

Crunk hesitated.

"Are you kidding?" said Dragline, looking angrily at Crunk, "We're a Green Beret A-Team just back from the war. If we want to go somewhere on this hallowed ground, we'll damn well do it—with or without your help."

Crunk thought about it a minute. "Let's go to the stables," he said, "and I'll show you the pride of the Old Guard."

The Old Guard was stationed at Fort Myer, which backed onto Arlington Cemetery. We walked down the tranquil winding lanes toward Fort Myer, and once on post, walked toward the stables, admiring the beautiful red brick Victorian homes, the well-trimmed grounds and the general orderliness of the small, picturesque post. Coming to the stables, we saw a red brick building with brilliant white framed windows and two enormous wood doors at the end. Crunk turned around. "This, sir," he said to the captain, "is the pride of the Old Guard—the stables of the Caisson Platoon."

"I thought the Tomb Guards were the pride," Spooky said challengingly.

"They think they are," replied Crunk dismissively, "but the Caisson Platoon knows it is."

"Is that what you did in the Old Guard?" the captain asked.

"Yes, sir. Didn't even know how to ride when I first started. They teach you how to care for the horses, how to ride, and how to maintain the tack and the caissons. You get on the Caisson Platoon and you will become an expert horseman."

We entered the stables through one of the large wooden doors, with a sign over the arched doorway reading 'Caisson.' "Wow," Dragline said, almost speechless. "It's immaculate."

"Spick and span," replied Crunk. "That's the way you always have to keep it—everything squared away at all times."

The stables were bustling with busy soldiers, but we looked like we belonged, and Crunk wore the Honor Guard device on his uniform, so no one bothered us. We walked into the section where they keep the caissons.

"Who maintains the horses?" Spooky asked.

"The Old Guard has one military vet, two civilian farriers, and one tack specialist. Everything else is done by the soldiers."

"You guys do your own tack?" the captain said, surprised.

"Yes, sir. Everything but the saddles are made and maintained right here in the stables." We walked down the beautifully-kept stables, passing the stalls one after another. Crunk stopped in front of one of the stalls. "No way!" he exclaimed. "It's Sarge." Crunk put his hands through the bars of the stall and petted the horse fiercely. "Sarge," he said, "you remember PFC Stitch, don't ya?"

"That's a big horse," I said, as Sarge turned in his stall and nuzzled Crunk's hand.

"Draft horse," Crunk said, patting the big beast affectionately, locking eyes with the gaze of the powerful beast. "The two rear horses on the Caisson are draft horses. They do most of the work." Crunk entered Sarge's stall and checked his hooves. He inspected the work of the farrier with grudging approval. We then moved down to the tack room, and as he opened the door, Crunk froze in place, visibly afraid. I peered over his head and saw nothing but an older man bent over a workbench. His white hair was grizzled, he wore a baseball cap and enormous thick eyeglasses. He was overweight and unkempt, and he had a pack of chewing tobacco sitting within reach. "That's Mr. Paul," Crunk whispered with fearful admiration. "I thought he'd be dead by now."

"Who is Mr. Paul?" Jiggy said.

"Mr. Paul is the Caisson Platoon," replied Crunk, in a low voice. "He taught me everything I've ever known about horses, about the Caisson Platoon, and about what it means to be a member of the Old Guard." Crunk stiffened. "I haven't seen him in ten years, and he looks exactly the same."

Crunk cleared his throat. "Mr. Paul," he said meekly, "do you remember me?"

Mr. Paul looked up from his work, his eyes peering over his dropped glasses. He studied Crunk slowly. "I remember a PFC Stitch used to run around my tack room like a duck hit in the head," he replied with a smile. "But it looks like he's moved up in the world." Mr. Paul then pointed over to the table next to us and said, "If it's not too much to ask, Sergeant First Class Stitch, could you hand me that pair of pliers over there?"

The company commander was serious about wanting Biker Dave's family to understand that he wasn't just a suicide: that whatever else he was, he was a Green Beret and a member of Bravo, 3rd of the 20th SFG. So he arranged a dinner at Siné's in Pentagon City. It was nice to eat with the family and to tell them little stories about their son the soldier—who, it can be said, never deserted his post, and never shrank from the fight. After dinner, we retired to the bar, and the family—seeing that things could easily go sideways—said their goodbyes. "It cannot be denied," I pronounced, lifting up my glass, "that Biker Dave was a good soldier."

"Yeah," replied Spooky, staring into his drink, "but you can't hang your life on that. I could pull ten swingin' dicks off the street right now and turn 'em into good soldiers." Spooky looked up. "Let's be honest, it isn't brain surgery. All you have to do is stand your ground and fire your rifle. Anybody can fire a rifle. . . . the only real question is can you stand."

"Dave stood," I said. And we found that a reason to toast him.

Jiggy, Spooky and Crunk found a table, and soon enough Dragline banged his way over toward us. He seemed a little buzzed, but was clearly exaggerating his intoxication level. "How are my boys?" he said. "How are my killers?" He was afraid for us, that was obvious. He didn't want to have to bury anyone from his team. "Tell me a story," he said.

"Tell me a PTSD story."

"Dragline," I said, "we don't have PTSD."

"Denial," Dragline said, "that's a sign." Dragline looked at me. "Tell me a story, Jet Set, and make it funny—otherwise I'll have to tell the captain that you're to be watched."

I hesitated. He was probably right about me—that I had come home crazy—but I didn't think I was that bad. I didn't think I was that pronounced. Even so, I wasn't about to give any intel on myself. He didn't need to know everything about my daily existence. My insanity was my insanity, and I wasn't giving it up to some fake-drunk team sergeant just because he took a weekend seminar entitled 'Dealing with Return.' Besides he was so ham-fisted, it would have been embarrassing to fall for his shtick.

Spooky stepped in to help me out. "What do ya call crazy, Dragline?" he said. "I mean, I did a lot of unusual things before we went over."

"Well, are you doing anything different now that you're back?" Dragline replied.

"Yeah," said Spooky with a grin. And we all turned to look at him, knowing this was going to be interesting. "I screw with people now."

"You did that before," I said.

"Not like this," said Spooky, and he laughed to himself, like there was a joke only he got. "I take a lot of pictures now—at least I let people think I do."

"What do you mean?" questioned Dragline.

"I keep a camera with me in my car," Spooky said. "It doesn't have film, it's just a prop. But I go to various mosques around DC, and I stand out on the street in front of the mosque and pretend to take pictures."

"That's crazy." "It's diabolical." "It's hilarious." "Is it even legal?"

"What, standing on the sidewalk pretending to take pictures?" replied Spooky. "Of course it's legal."

"What do they do?" I asked.

"Mostly they run inside and hide, but one dude came out with a sword and chased me down the street."

"You're psychotic," I said.

"Why?" Spooky replied, looking me dead in the face. "Why is that psychotic? I did nothing wrong. All I did was show up on the sidewalk and pretend to take pictures of a building."

"It just seems wrong," I said.

"So it's wrong to pretend to take pictures, but it's perfectly justifiable to pull out a sword and chase someone down the street with it?"

"But you—"

"The guy came at me with a sword for takin' pictures of a building. How is that not a problem for you?" I didn't have an answer. As crazy as Spooky was, I couldn't see how he was wrong. But it was still troubling. This guy's an accident waiting to happen, I thought.

"What about you, Crunk?" Dragline said. "I know you had to take three days unpaid leave from the Department."

"How'd you hear about that?"

"What?" replied Dragline. "Y'all think I ain't keepin' track of you?"

"So, what happened?" Jiggy asked.

"Just in the wrong place at the wrong time," replied Crunk. "In a way it was the Department's fault for placing me where they did."

"Wait, what?" I said.

"Look," replied Crunk. "I work the hood. Been workin' the hood since I got on the Baltimore Police Force. One day the district commander says, 'Crunk, they're short personnel up in Rawlings Park—it's all rich white people, light duty.'" Crunk shrugged his shoulders. "So I'm workin' Rawlings Park when we get a call. Some guy got his car towed from a supermarket parking lot, and he's getting argumentative. I show up after some other patrol officers are already there, and this white guy is going back and forth with the cops already there. He's pissed off and getting loud—very disrespectful. I don't know nothin' about policing white people, so I just grab the little hipster by the hair, shake him around like a rag doll and say 'Get in the car, bitch, or we gonna gang-rape your ass!'"

We all began to laugh. "I love it when ya get to screw with whitie," Dragline said. "Whitie's always so surprised when you hit him."

"Oh, yeah," continued Crunk. "The other officers were like, 'Whoa, whoa, whoa. This is Rawlings Park, we don't do that to—you know—the people who pay our salaries.'"

The laughter died down, and I thought about it a bit. Jesus, I thought. We're like the walking wounded. There's no way we can continue to live like this. As the other guys laughed and told stories, I walked away. I kept thinking about Biker Dave. I bet that shit made sense to him, I thought. I bet when he pulled that trigger it seemed like a completely reasonable thing to do. I looked over at the guys laughing, glad to at least have each other's comradery. We're like a bunch of broken toys, I thought. We can't go out into that world, and we can't stay in this one either. I don't want to end up like Dave, I kept thinking. But I don't know what to do to change all this.

Later, Dragline came over to me. "What's up with you?" he said. "You play your cards too close to the vest, in my opinion."

"I'm fine," I said, taking a sip of my beer.

"Don't you hole-up on me," Dragline said. "I know all about you up in Brooklyn. I get good intel from the DA's office."

"What do they say?" I replied with surprise.

Dragline drew close, as if he was giving me advice. "They say you're a dick to work with. You do your job, but no one wants to be around you."

"Yeah," I said, a little hurt, but not disagreeing. "I . . . I'm still trying to sort things out."

"Oh, you're 'sorting it out' are you? Don't brush me off, Jet Set. You're up there in Brooklyn all alone—and you isolate yourself. You've always been like that."

"I'm sorting it out, okay! I emailed Linda . . . Captain Paloma, just the other night."

Dragline's eyes widened. "You're talking to Captain Paloma?" he said. "Is that even a good thing?"

"Yeah, I think it is. I need to talk to someone. I . . . I need to . . . sort through some things."

"Well, you don't need to be 'sorting through Captain Paloma' until you get your commission, is that clear?"

"She's got seven more months in The Stan before she comes back, and after that, I don't know what."

"That sounds like some thin soup, Jet Set. What else you got to 'sort yourself out?'"

"I've been going to the gym more."

"That's a good start."

"No," I said. "I mean, I've been boxing again. Gleason's Gym— sort of a famous boxing gym—not too far from my place. I got a trainer and everything, this old black dude, a retired master sergeant. He's been workin' the mitts with me, and training me up."

"Up for what? You're not thinking of getting back into the ring, are you?"

"Nah, I'm too old for that. I just like it, keeps me focused. Besides, I like ole Master Sergeant Rockman. He was in Vietnam. He tells me stuff, and the way he tells me, I know it's true."

"Stuff like what?"

"I don't know, just stuff," I said. "I mean, Master Sergeant Rockman can explain to you how to slip a jab, and it somehow comes out like he's telling you your whole life story." I looked down at the ground, surprised by my own words. "I guess it sounds weird," I said. "But I like to listen to him. It isn't really what he's sayin', it's more the way he says it."

"Well, what do you get from fighting again?"

"The adrenaline rush," I said. "Remember the rush you used to get rolling into some ville?"

Dragline smiled. "Yeah. It was . . . a rush. Just a total rush."

"Even when you were pissing your pants, you were jacked," I said. "It's weird, and I don't ever want to be there again, but I can't stop thinking about driving that up-armor, sitting in Pot Roast's blood. I mean, we did it! We burned those bitches down!"

Dragline laughed, thinking about that day. "We'll never do something like that again," he said.

"It's really all behind us," I said. "The greatest things we ever did are behind us."

"Well," said Dragline, "now we have new challenges."

"Like what?"

"Living with it. With all of it," said Dragline. "What we did, what we will never do again, and what we have to do to continue to live a good and honorable life." I liked that. Dragline said 'honorable.' I liked the fact that both he and I thought about things in terms of honor. But it made me think about Biker Dave. If Biker Dave had only thought about his honor a little more, he'd still be alive today.

THE LAST MUSTER

"One, two!"

BAP! BAP! The leather gloves slapped into the mitts—a left jab, then a straight right.

"One, two, three!"

BAP! BAP! BAP! A left jab, straight right, then left hook.

Master Sergeant Rockman was good with the mitts, working me, moving me around the ring. "Keep that head on a swivel," he said, swinging his hand in a wide arch toward my head, causing me to duck. He walked away from me, and I pursued him, then he swung around, a punching mitt right next to his head. "Double jab!"

BAP! BAP! We knew each other well now. He didn't have to give me orders. He did it for motivation, to keep us both hot; and we were hot, both of us drenched in sweat. He drew his hands up close to his chest, palms down. I stepped in, dropped into a squat, and let off a flurry of uppercuts. "That's it," Master Sergeant Rockman said. "Bend at the knee, not at the waist. Hook to the body, hook to the head," he shouted. "Kill the body and the head will fall!"

When the bell rang, I was smoked, covered in sweat and breathing with my mouth wide open. Master Sergeant Rockman kept at it: "Close that mouth," he said. "Never let the other man know you're tired. Never breathe through your mouth. Dude will break your jaw." The sky beyond the boxing gym was growing dark and I looked at the master sergeant, amazed by his stamina. Well into his 60s, the master sergeant still had the angular features on his face of a young man—the high cheekbones, the sculpted jaw were still intact.

"You gots to do your road work," he said. "Man don't come to the gym to get in shape, man's got to be in shape when he gets to the gym."

"I've been runnin'," I protested.

"What, twice a week?" I didn't answer. He could see it in me. "You want to fight, you gots to be in the gym every day . . . and you gots to be running every day you go to the gym." I knew he was right, but I wasn't sure I wanted to fight anymore. The last thing I wanted to tell him was that I didn't plan on getting back into the ring. If he realized I wasn't serious, he'd lose interest. I needed the master sergeant. I needed our work-outs. It was the only thing keeping me together.

"You shining me?" he asked, probing deeply into our relationship.

"No, sir," I said, "I ain't shining you. I just been busy at work." Of course I was shining him.

"Don't you shine me, boy," he said. "I got stakes in you." I couldn't lose him, I couldn't lose these work-outs. I realized I would have to fight again, I realized I wanted to fight again. I realized I would never stop fighting.

The fact was I had been looking for fights, even as I pretended to 'just be curious.' "There's a four round fight," I said, "up in Binghamton three months from now. The main event's a 10 rounder, but they're still looking for fighters on the undercard. Put me on that card, and we'll see if I still have it in me."

"Oh, it's in you," he said. "The only question is if you can still get it out of you." I leaned over the ropes and looked out of the dirty windows of the gym. Gleason's Gym was something of a New York legend. Champions from Jake LaMotta to Mike Tyson fought out of the gym, but none of that meant anything to me. I have never gotten nostalgic about boxing gyms. No one ever got weepy and nostalgic talking about the auto body shop they took their car too, and that's all a gym is, a place of work.

"Think you'll get called back up?" Rockman asked.

"Oh yeah," I said. "They're getting ready to invade Iraq. They need every gun they can get."

"Yeah," he said. "They sent me back to Nam a second time too."

"Who were you with?"

"173rd Airborne—'Sky Soldier'."

I paused, wondering how I might ask him a question. "Did it . . . change you?" I asked. "Did the war change you?"

Rockman was silent, and looked out over the East River. "I wouldn't say it changed me," he said at last. "War doesn't change you. It accelerates you."

"How do you mean?"

"By the time you get to war, you're already the person you're going to be—maybe you don't know it—but that's you. War concentrates you. It makes you more of what you already are."

"I'm not real crazy about who I am," I said.

"Oh, you'd be surprised by what's inside of you," he said. "I see it. I see a lot of good inside of you."

"I don't know," I said. "I'm a mess."

"Are you really?" asked the master sergeant, looking at me with kindly regard. "What I see is a man who shows up at the right place, at the right time, in the right uniform."

"Yeah," I said, "but what is that?"

"That's everything," said the master sergeant. "You keep doing that and everything else will fall right into place."

Walking home from the gym, I kept thinking about what the master sergeant had said to me. When I reached my apartment on Congress Street, I searched the internet for a phone number, eventually found it, and I made a call I didn't think I would ever make:

"Hello."

"Hello, um . . . is this Mike Sullivan, Little Mike?"

"Who's askin'?"

"Mike, it's me, Tim Redmond—Jet Set. Do you remember me, Mike?"

"Oh, hey, Jet Set, how's it going?"

"Oh, you know, it's going," I said. "It keeps on going."

"Is that right?" replied Mike, getting the drift of the conversation.

"Yeah, I think so. Been back from The Stan for, what, three months. One of our guys capped himself last week."

"That's tough."

"Yeah, it is, but—you know—you got it pretty tough yourself."

"Hey, man, I'm among the living, aren't I? That's a good thing to be."

"Well, I guess that's why I called," I said. "Been feeling a little shaky. Thought it would be a good idea to get your take on things."

"Yeah, I've been hearing about the guys coming home," said Mike. "Those guys at Bragg—murder-suicide—terrible." Mike paused and let out a sigh. "In a way I'm better off than you."

"How's that?"

"I lost my arm and my leg, I know that—there's no way to question it. But it seems like a lot of the guys, what they lost, they have no idea what it is."

"So what do you do?"

"The first thing you have to realize is that 'As you were' isn't going to work here. There is no 'As you were.' You can't un-ring a bell," Mike said, emphatically. "You're not going to go back to the way you used to be. My arm and leg aren't coming back because I forgot that I lost them, and you'll never be that sergeant-with-the-shit-eatin' grin that you once were."

"Okay, but what's next?" I asked.

"You start a new chapter, man," he said. "You don't look back, that's not where the action is. You have to move to the front, to the sound of the guns, that's where the fight is." I could almost hear Mike smiling. "You're different now, different from those people you meet on the street who never saw the battlefield. You have nothing in common with them. You have a different set of challenges—but that just makes it more interesting."

"But you have to live with it day to day," I said. "How do you do it?"

"I do just that. I live with it day to day. Hey, man, we're above ground," he said. "How is that not a good thing?"

"It is great," I said.

"Yeah," Mike replied. "But you have to have your little rituals that you do now. You have to have your daily organizational milestones, just to keep yourself from going sideways. It's a chore, man, being sane. It's a whole to-do."

I hung up with Mike, and emailed Linda:

Dear Linda,

We buried Biker Dave today. You remember him, don't you? He was funny. When we arrived in Kandahar, he was waiting for us wearing a chauffeur's hat.

He killed himself a week ago. Call me when you get this. Please.

Love
Tim

The call came in about 2:00 a.m. Using the call center at Kandahar Air Field, Linda could only speak for 30 minutes, then she would go to the computer center and email me, then back to the phone for 30 minutes, then back to the computer center. It was a big production, but we did that all night until I had to get ready for work.

"Tim, I come home in July. Would—"

"Can I see you?"

"Would you?"

"Yes."

"Tim, I'm tired of this Army life. I want to settle down. I'm sick of the war. I'm so through with pretending to be the cool-JAG-who-used-to-be-a-Jumpmaster. I want us. I want a world where us is a thing.

"So do I. I want to be something more than just me."

"I've been looking around for JAG jobs, and there's one in Charlotte, North Carolina—that's where I grew up, where my family is. There's a reserve unit there and they need an active duty JAG. I want to go home, Tim, and I want you to be there with me. Is that something maybe you'd like?"

"It is. I could take the North Carolina Bar. We could make a real life together." As we spoke it felt like a dream was coming true. Like a castle in the sky was settling down on solid ground.

Getting to work that morning was still the usual episode. I exhausted myself scanning for cover and concealment positions as I walked down Court Street. A truck backfired, and I dove behind a dumpster. That made some school kids laugh at me, and I almost screamed at them. I was sweating by the time I got into my office.

And don't get me started on the office. I'm behind all my peers, because while I was bouncing up and down the wadis of Afghanistan, they were doing actual cases, practicing actual law. I have been persistent, which helps, but I get pissed off by, like, everything. And I don't mean pissed off like The Skipper in "Gilligan's Island," twisting my hat in my hands and shouting "little buddy!"—I mean, I get volatile. Like today: my office is near the water cooler, where all the loafers like to hang out and play grab-ass. And today one of the guys was telling a story and laughing a bit too loudly. I couldn't work with that noise, so I got pissed off, and after repeated attempts to loudly clear my throat— which he did not pick up on—I (of course) went out there and threw it down, *"Callate,* Dude. Shut the hell up, already." Surprisingly, that didn't go over well with him and soon we were going round and round. Naturally I called him a pussy who wouldn't know which end of a rifle to point at the enemy (they totally hate that).

So the guy gets offended (go figure), and said, "Shit, Redmond, I bet you spent the war bringing coffee to the general. Yeah, they're gonna make a movie out of your wartime experience. They'll call it 'Full Dinner Jacket'."

I almost lost it. I went flush with rage, and sprang at the guy. He saw me and realized he'd gone too far. "Hey, look," he started to say, "I didn't—"

I keep a small punch-dagger in my pocket—just, you know, in case—and for a split-second I thought about stabbing him with it. I figured I could punch him a couple times in the chest, they'd pull us

291

apart, I'd make a bunch of noise and wave my arms around like I was all offended, then dramatically storm off to the elevator. I'd be out of the building before the guy even realized he'd been stabbed. Besides, he'd probably live anyway.

It was more than just an idea, it was a plan, and I was shocked by how quickly it came to me. Jesus, I thought. Is this what I've become? I turned around, still shaking with rage, and walked away as quickly as I could, afraid of myself. I raced to my office and closed the door behind me. What have I done wrong? I thought. What great sin have I committed, that I can't even live in the world anymore?

I thought about all the things that had happened: about Little Mike, about the war, and about all the things that had taken place since September 11th. And I realized I'd done nothing wrong. I wasn't irrational, I just had to take care of myself, to live my life as best as I could. And I realized that it was work. I knew right then that I would leave New York. I'd go down South and start a new life in North Carolina.

I looked out of my window across the East River at the hole in the sky where the World Trade Center once stood. And it seemed like a graveyard, like that patch of Manhattan skyline would forever be a graveyard. Looking at it now, I sensed that I needed to make my report, to give an account to the dead. I came to attention and saluted. "We did our duty," I said. "We were called, and we answered." Lowering my hand, I looked away, and then the words came welling up inside of me, "But now our duty is to live, to thrive, and to carry on. You are the dead, and we have a duty to honor you. But we are the living, and it is our duty to go on, ever mindful of you, forever catching you out of the corner of our eyes."

Acknowledgements

The author would like to thank the National Endowment for the Humanities for their support of returning veterans' efforts to articulate their experiences, and the Writer's Center of Bethesda, Maryland, without whose many workshops and dedicated instructors this book could not have been written.

"Sister Clarissa"
Published with permission
Words and music by Michael Peter Smith
© Bird Avenue ASCP

About the Author

Timothy Redmond is a major in the U.S. Army. He is a JAG officer, serving as a prosecutor stationed at the Pentagon. He has one son, and lives in Vienna, Virginia with his beautiful but mean German shepherd, Jetta.

CPSIA information can be obtained
at www.ICGtesting.com
Printed in the USA
LVHW111605250119
605292LV00001B/168/P